# Reuse, Misuse, Abuse

# Reuse, Misuse, Abuse

## The Ethics of Audiovisual Appropriation in the Digital Era

JAIMIE BARON

Rutgers University Press
New Brunswick, Camden, and Newark, New Jersey, and London

Library of Congress Cataloging-in-Publication Data

Names: Baron, Jaimie, author.
Title: Reuse, misuse, abuse: the ethics of audiovisual appropriation in the digital era / Jaimie Baron.
Description: New Brunswick: Rutgers University Press, 2020. | Includes bibliographical references and index.
Identifiers: LCCN 2020007172 | ISBN 9780813599267 (paperback) | ISBN 9780813599274 (cloth) | ISBN 9780813599281 (epub) | ISBN 9780813599298 (mobi) | ISBN 9780813599304 (pdf)
Subjects: LCSH: Stock footage. | Documentary films—Moral and ethical aspects. | Video recordings—Moral and ethical aspects. | Actualities (Motion pictures) | Gaze in motion pictures.
Classification: LCC PN1995.9.S6964 B37 2020 | DDC 070.1/95—dc23
LC record available at https://lccn.loc.gov/2020007172

A British Cataloging-in-Publication record for this book is available from the British Library.



∞ The paper used in this publication meets the requirements of the American National Standard for Information Sciences—Permanence of Paper for Printed Library Materials, ANSI Z39.48-1992.

www.rutgersuniversitypress.org

Manufactured in the United States of America

For my mother, the very ground on which I stand

# Contents

# Reuse, Misuse, Abuse

# Introduction

## Theorizing Misuse

In November 2015, the Montreal International Documentary Film Festival (RIDM) came under fire for including Quebec filmmaker Dominic Gagnon's seventy-four-minute film *of the North* in its program. As with some of Gagnon's previous films, this film's imagery was appropriated entirely from clips posted on YouTube. In this case, all the clips were shot by or featured Inuit people. The soundtrack was composed of music by Inuk throat singer Tanya Tagaq. For his use of neither the images nor the music did Gagnon seek or obtain permission from the YouTube posters or from Tagaq. The latter publicly called the film racist, demanded her music be removed from the soundtrack, and became one of the leaders of a campaign against the film. In response to the film, an Inuk broadcaster named Stephen Puskas began contacting as many of the YouTube subjects as he could locate to let them know that their images appeared in Gagnon's film. As a result, many asked that their images be removed. Gagnon then began screening a version of the film without music and replaced the images he had been asked to exclude with black. Soon after, Gagnon stopped screening the film altogether, and it is now extremely difficult to see in its original form.[1] Nonetheless, Gagnon did not seem to feel he had done anything wrong, claiming in an interview with the Aboriginal People's Television Network (APTN) that he was the target of criticism simply because, as he put it, "I am a man and I am white."[2]

Inevitably, this conflict led to a discussion among filmmakers, programmers, and commentators about freedom of speech versus the long history of white colonial misrepresentation of indigenous peoples.[3] However, it also raises important questions about the artist's rights and responsibilities with regard to appropriating recorded sounds and images of other people, particularly in the digital age when so much is so easily available. One of these questions has to do with consent. As Robert Everett-Green noted,

> The fracas about *Of the North* [sic] isn't just about what's in the film, but about how it was made. Gagnon didn't go to the North, and although he identifies each clip at the end of the film, he never tried to contact those whose footage he used; nor anyone who was pictured in it. He figured that if people had allowed YouTube to show their videos to all comers, no further consent was necessary.[4]

Indeed, one of Gagnon's lines of defense was to argue that the posted footage was already public and, therefore, fair game. Moreover, Gagnon argued that the film was less about Inuit people than about how people record themselves for platforms like YouTube. He said, "To me it's more a story about how Inuit people appropriate social media, how they represent themselves, what they feel like doing."[5] In Gagnon's view, because these videos were posted on YouTube, they became not representations of individuals or a culture but symptoms of a social media phenomenon. A group of Quebec filmmakers came to Gagnon's defense in an open letter, not so much validating the film itself as the need for freedom of expression and the opportunity to discuss the film, writing that the removal of the film from the RIDM program meant that "the public is deprived of the sine qua non condition for a sound democratic debate, the possibility of determining its own opinion."[6]

Despite these defenses, many critics, particularly indigenous viewers, continued to find the film offensive. Inuk documentary filmmaker Alethea Arnaquq-Baril accused the film of representing Inuit people as "violent, wandering drunks that neglect their children and don't care for the lives of animals: that's the image I took away from the film . . . I think it's kind of a cheap move to totally play up a negative stereotype of a marginalized people for your own artistic gain."[7] She noted further that Gagnon clearly selected certain types of clips, choosing to include, for instance, numerous clips of drunken Inuit people. "It's as if he went searching for clips of 'drunk Inuit' or 'drunk Eskimo.' This is a decision he made to portray us this way. He went in with his own perception; it's not a reflection of how Inuit perceive ourselves."[8] At least in Arnaquq-Baril's view, Gagnon's particular choice of videos reflected his preconceived ideas about Inuit people. Arnaquq-Baril also noted that many of the appropriated images were not self-representations but, rather, videos taken without the subjects' permission or perhaps even knowledge. Thus, Gagnon's selection of clips in *of the North* constituted, for many viewers, a harmful misrepresentation of his subjects. Moreover, the sense of skewed representation was not due exclusively to the content of the images but also to how Gagnon fitted them together. As Jonathan Culp wrote,

> In *Of The North* [sic], the ugliness inheres not only in the source material, but in the arrangement of sequences. As Gagnon clearly knows, for all his talk of "how they represent themselves" (the YouTube material was shot by hundreds of amateur Inuit filmmakers), the editor holds the power of meaning and interpretation. And Gagnon's perspective is both alienated and ill-informed, almost proudly so.[9]

Gagnon's perspective, as conveyed through both choice of material and editing, is not innocent but deeply ideological, whether he acknowledges it or not.

Two sequences involving laughter are particularly illustrative of this fact. In one, we see a man in long shot beating a small seal to death as an unseen woman behind the camera laughs. In another, we see images of raw sewage pouring into a pristine landscape followed by images of caribou eating the sewage, again accompanied by laughter. These are upsetting images, no doubt. Yet, what is most egregious in these scenes, like many others in the film, is the total lack of contextual information. The juxtaposition of animal harm and these Inuit people's laughter makes the people seem cruel and heartless. However, we have no idea who these people are, nor do we know anything about the conditions under which they are living, let alone the origins of those conditions. Without such information, the inclusion of these sequences suggests that Inuit people commit and record animal cruelty just for fun—which is, at very least, not the whole story in these videos. By including these sequences and not offering contextual commentary, Gagnon eschews responsibility for their content while nevertheless conveying an extremely negative impression of the people recorded therein.[10]

Thus, the objections to the film are multiple and multifaceted. Not only did Gagnon fail to seek consent to use the images and sounds he appropriated, but he is a white artist who has never even been to "the North" appropriating images of indigenous people. Not only does the content of the appropriated materials reflect negatively on its subjects, but the particular way in which Gagnon selected and then edited the materials together exacerbated the negative misrepresentation of an entire group of people. Not only does he appear to be ignorant of—or at least lacking in critical awareness about—existing stereotypes and racist discourses about indigenous people in Canada (and beyond), but his film reinforces the unequal relations of power inherited from colonialism—wittingly or no. It is in the intersection between these various issues—consent, (mis)representation through selection and editing, and existing power relations—that the ethical question at the heart of this film's production and circulation lies. However, none of these issues can be considered strictly in isolation.

## Beyond Consent

Indeed, if the problem of audiovisual appropriation was reduced solely to consent, certain films by indigenous artists that have not been criticized—and have even been celebrated—might also come under fire. Indigenous filmmaker Kent Monkman's three-minute film *Sisters & Brothers* (2015), for example, was one of four films commissioned by the National Film Board of Canada that "remix archival footage to address Indigenous identity and representation, reframing Canadian history through a contemporary lens."[11] The film begins with written text quoting Native American activist Leonard Peltier saying, "Hope and resiliency. These are your greatest strengths. Sisters and brothers, all of one human family. Your generation and mine." The film then cuts to images of grasslands and a group of white cowboys gazing at bison through a matte that connotes binoculars. The images of bison are intercut with images of indigenous children who—it becomes clear—were forcibly taken away from their families and placed in what were euphemistically called "residential schools," designed to assimilate them into white colonial culture. Throughout Monkman's film, montage is used to create a visual metaphor equating the mass slaughter of the bison with the practices of the residential school system that sought to annihilate native culture. The film ends with another title, "We have recorded the deaths of over 6,000 children [while in residential schools] . . . Many were not returned to their families and most were buried in unmarked graves." This quotation is attributed to Justice Murray Sinclair, writing on behalf of the Canadian Truth and Reconciliation Commission (TRC), completed in 2015.

Regarding consent, Monkman's film is as potentially problematic as Gagnon's. The unidentified residential school children whose images Monkman appropriated did not give their consent either for the original filming—the images were clearly taken by advocates of the residential schools who would have had the power to film regardless of the children's wishes—or for the appropriation. Indeed, it would likely have been impossible for Monkman to locate these people, who are unnamed and many of whom are probably deceased.[12] Nonetheless, if the ethics of audiovisual appropriation were reduced solely to consent, this would be an unethical appropriation. Yet, the fact that Monkman himself is an indigenous filmmaker of Cree ancestry and that his film serves as a critique of the residential school system and a defense of the children who were its victims mitigates the sense that he is violating his subjects' rights. His film is a cry for justice for these children who cannot demand it themselves and, as such, reads as an intensely and actively ethical text. One particularly striking image shows an unidentified (and likely unidentifiable) indigenous girl in a residential school staring back at the colonial camera and, by extension, looking at us across the temporal divide of decades (figure 1). Her returned gaze asserts her identity and presence, which the Canadian colonial government tried so hard to erase. Monkman's inclusion of this image in his film thereby becomes an act of indigenous reclamation.

In the comparison of these two texts, it becomes clear that the ethics of audiovisual appropriation are complex and cannot be reduced to any single variable. Indeed, these are only two examples of a phenomenon that exceeds any attempt to account for all its possible permutations. As different as they are, *of the North* and *Sisters & Brothers* both gesture toward a much broader practice that has become pervasive in contemporary film and video culture. Segments of pre-existing recordings—of which there is now a seemingly endless, accessible supply—have increasingly become the building blocks of new articulations. This "remix" or "Read/Write" culture, in the terms coined in part by Lawrence Lessig, offers opportunities to use recorded sounds and images as a new set of semantic units from which new kinds of previously

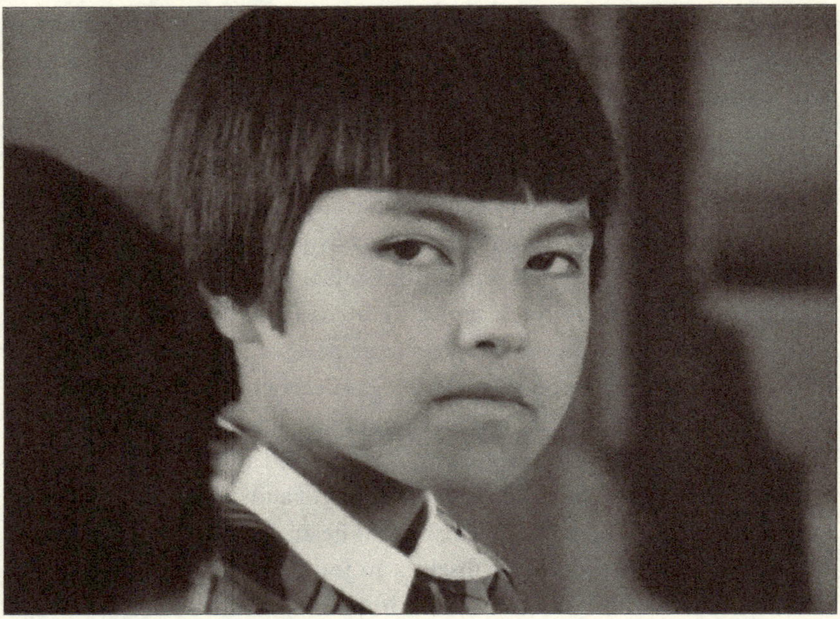

FIGURE 1 Still from *Sisters & Brothers* (Kent Monkman, 2015). I acknowledge my own "misuse" of this image here, which is intended to honor this child. Her gaze as she looks back at us from the pages of this book demands an ethical accounting.

impossible "sentences" may emerge.[13] Drawing parallels between written quotation and audiovisual appropriation, Lessig has written, "Whether text or beyond text, remix is collage; it comes from combining elements of [Read Only] culture; it succeeds by leveraging the meaning created by the reference to build something new."[14] Lev Manovich similarly defines remix as "a composition that consists of previously existing parts assembled, which is edited to create particular aesthetic, semantic, and/or bodily effects."[15] Remix—or what I call "misuse" for reasons that will become clear—enables both the partial retention and simultaneous transformation of the meaning of the original document.

Of course, as numerous theorists have demonstrated, this kind of practice is not a recent development.[16] Quotation of written documents is, obviously, an ancient practice; collage has been a fundamental component of visual art since Picasso; and musical sampling has its roots in 1970s Jamaican DJ culture and African American hip-hop. The reuse of pre-existing film footage goes back to the earliest days of cinema. Even as the first films began to circulate, entrepreneurial exhibitors re-edited and repackaged them as new films. Soviet filmmaker Esfir Shub, however, is credited with producing the first compilation film when she made *The Fall of the Romanov Dynasty* in 1927. By re-editing documentary footage produced by and for former Czar Nicholas II when he was still in power, she transformed footage honoring the Czar and his regime into a celebration of their demise. Meanwhile, Joseph Cornell's 1936 *Rose Hobart*, in which Cornell took the Hollywood melodrama *East of Borneo* (George Melford, 1931) and retained only (with a few exceptions and additions) the footage including the main actress, Rose Hobart, and then set this re-edited footage to music, is generally regarded as the first experimental found footage film. The Situationist practice of détournement also deployed audiovisual appropriation to undermine the power of mass culture. In the 1950s and 1960s, the Situationists made use of elements of popular culture—including photographs, especially advertisements, and film footage—to disrupt its hegemonic discourse through collage techniques of juxtaposition. Guy Debord and Gil Wolman wrote in 1956 that "When two objects are brought together, no matter how far apart their original contexts may be, a relationship is always formed. . . . The mutual interference of two worlds of feeling, or the juxtaposition of two independent expressions, supersedes the original elements and produces a synthetic organization of greater efficacy."[17] In their emphasis on "new combinations" and the "juxtaposition of two independent expressions" to generate novel relationships and syntheses, Debord and Wolman extended the insights of Soviet montage theory to the specific revolutionary potentialities of appropriation of pre-existing visual materials. They theorized the potential of détournement as a weapon of class struggle that could reveal the inner workings of capitalism to further the socialist revolution. And since the times of Shub and Cornell and the heyday of Situationism, the works of numerous experimental film and video makers—along with many musicians and other types of visual artists—have similarly mined pre-existing documents and recordings to produce transformed meanings.

Undeniably, however, digital technologies have made pre-existing recordings significantly easier to acquire, re-edit, and manipulate. Indeed, audiovisual appropriation is now a practice in which almost anyone with access to a computer can participate.[18] As a result, millions—if not billions—of internet videos have emerged from this practice. Moreover, digital media has dramatically increased the speed at which such appropriations occur. The same image or sound clip may reappear as an element of multiple texts days, hours, or even minutes after it was produced and posted online. And this art form includes a huge range of practitioners. Even as amateurs enthusiastically engage in this practice, professional experimental film and video makers continue to create works in this way. Such makers regularly repurpose pre-existing recordings as a means of commenting on the vast archive of images and sounds that are now available to anyone with a computer and an internet connection. Although these experimental works may have different aims from most YouTube appropriation videos, what unites both popular appropriation-based memes and experimental found footage works is a clear sense of the subversion of meaning. We are—for the most part—meant to recognize the appropriation, the repurposing, the change in signification.

In the face of the frequency and rapidity of the circulation, appropriation, and recirculation of these recordings through digital technologies, however, questions arise regarding the *ethics* of such appropriations, particularly when the recordings in question depict actual, as opposed to staged fictional, events—as Gagnon's *of the North* and Monkman's *Sisters & Brothers* both demonstrate. Although there may be ethical issues raised by the appropriation of staged, fictional recordings, the ethics of appropriating actuality recordings is much more fraught. In fictional recordings, we perceive a gap between the self of the performer and the performance; in actuality recordings, we seem to have access to the person's "real" self. Of course, the relationship between actuality recordings and the "real" is complex and involves its own kinds of performance. However, the sense of access to the actual subject is much stronger in actuality recordings, and from this sense of proximity stems the urgency of ethical questions regarding their appropriation.

As indicated by the preceding examples, the ethical implications that arise when the actuality recording's perceived original meaning and affect are subverted are complex and contradictory. The premise of this book is that every reuse of a pre-existing recording is, on some level, a "misuse" in the sense that its new use was not intended or at least not anticipated by its original producer. Indeed, audiovisual appropriations are often compelling precisely *because* the recordings they find and appropriate seem to have been "misused," intended for another purpose. Recordings that we recognize as having been taken from one context of use and placed in another may carry with them a trace of their earlier intended uses even as they are now mobilized for a different intent. This recognition of contrasting intentions generates the often-fascinating experience on the part of the viewer of what I have elsewhere called "intentional disparity."[19] This experience of intentional disparity is based on the perception of a previous intention ascribed to and seemingly inscribed within the appropriated recording that is different from the intention that appears to inform its present use. Of course, we cannot really know the "original intention" behind the appropriated recording. This would be to invoke the intentional fallacy. Nevertheless, we as viewers of a work of audiovisual appropriation often experience some sense that the appropriated recording is in some fundamental way "misused," even if it is only because the original producer of the recording could not have anticipated its use in the present text. Moreover, we often *do* imagine or project an original intention, even if it cannot ultimately be known.

Furthermore, this sense of unintended meanings may offer us an experience of epiphany or even revelation. Sometimes, a significant social or political critique may arise from the play of intended and unintended meanings. And this may make the misuse appear to be worth the ethical "cost" that derives from the appropriation and reuse of actuality recordings. Or not. Indeed, I choose the term "misuse" precisely because it registers the presence—or at least possibility—of ethical dilemmas and negotiations inherent in the form. Whereas the terms "remix" and "reuse" express a neutral value—mixing or using again is neither good nor bad—and theorizations of détournement actively and exclusively celebrate its revolutionary potential, the term "misuse" indicates ambivalence. This does not mean that every misuse is necessarily unethical. In fact, there are many instances of productive misuse of actuality recordings that, although they may generate an ethical disturbance, may nevertheless seem justified. However, as we shall see, there are other instances in which the *mis*use may shade into *ab*use, generating a feeling that the appropriation violates our ethical standards in some way. Watching certain works of audiovisual appropriation, we may feel like we are participating in an act of exploitation, of voyeurism and/or mockery, an experience that forces us to acknowledge the unequal power relations involved in the act of audiovisual appropriation.

While numerous studies and discussions—Lessig's among them—have focused on the legalities of appropriation in terms of the copyright, this study is not interested in the notion of intellectual property or ownership.[20] Rather, it acknowledges that—legally or not—makers are appropriating existing content and it attempts to account for some of the specifically *ethical* ramifications of these appropriations. Moreover, most of the texts examined here fall under the auspices of fair use or fair dealing in that they constitute "transformative" use, which was defined in US courts in 1994 as "altering the original with new expression, meaning, or message."[21] Thus, the ethical responsibility vis-à-vis the legal "owner" of a given image or sound recording in terms of that ownership is not the focus here. Instead, I am concerned with the ethics vis-à-vis those subjects who are inscribed in the recordings and, to some degree, vis-à-vis the audience.

Not all the works engaged in this study can be designated "documentaries." However, many of the ethical concerns raised by the appropriation of actuality recordings are linked to those raised by documentary production. Bill Nichols has written extensively about the question of the ethical responsibilities of the documentary film or video maker in relation to his or her film subjects. Drawing on the concept of axiology, the study of values, he has suggested the neologism "axiographics" which he has argued may "address the question of how values, particularly an ethics of representation, comes to be known and experienced in relation to space."[22] In Nichols's analysis, our sense of ethics is often based on our perception of the *location* of the maker in relation to his or her subject and, by implication, the construction of the viewer's relation to the film subjects who become the objects of our gaze. He has argued that the camera inscribes the ethical stance of the documentary maker vis-à-vis her subject: "An indexical bond exists between the image and the ethics that produced it. The image . . . gives evidence of the politics and ethics of its maker."[23] In other words, as viewers, we read an ethics of the documentary maker in the images he or she has filmed, and we do so through an evaluation of the maker's stance—literal and figurative—toward the film's subjects. Notably, the notion of axiographics rests to some degree on the assumption that the film or video maker was, at some point, in the presence of the film subject, choosing the angle from which to shoot, deciding whether or not to be present onscreen, and so on. The appropriationist, however, operates at an additional spatial—and potentially personal, emotional, and social—remove that further complicates our ethical evaluation.

This spatial remove intensifies several ethical issues already present in documentary production. Whereas the documentary maker often acquires some degree of ethical standing by having "been there" with the film subjects, the appropriationist—in most cases—never comes into direct contact with any of the subjects. This raises the question: what gives the appropriationist the right to take these sounds or images "out of context" (a phrase that has come to harbor immediately negative associations with exploitation and deception)? Beneath this question lies the assumption that appropriationists may feel less responsibility vis-à-vis the original subjects, a literally irresponsible attitude potentially encouraged by the easy access to materials afforded by online digital archives and databases—and their seemingly anonymous origins. In one of the few existing essays devoted to the ethics of audiovisual appropriation, Thomas Elsaesser has described a shift from analog film production to digital postproduction as filmmaking, as follows:

> Whereas analog filmmaking, centered on production . . . seeks to *capture* reality in order to *harness* it into a representation, digital filmmaking, conceived from postproduction, proceeds by way of *extracting* reality in order to *harvest* it. Instead of disclosure and revelation . . . post-production treats the world as data to be processed or mined, as raw materials and resources to be exploited.[24]

The terms Elsaesser chooses to describe audiovisual appropriation—"data to be processed" and "resources to be exploited"—imply an anxiety and perhaps pessimism about the ethical implications of this form of (post) production, suggesting that "the world" and, by implication, the people in it may become simply a series of objects to be manipulated without the appropriationist—or the viewer—having any sense of responsibility to that world or those people.

Moreover, as suggested previously, the question of the subject's consent may quickly arise. Of course, the notion of "informed consent" has long been a standard for regulating documentary filmmaking more generally. As John Stuart Katz and Judith Milstein Katz noted in a pioneering documentary anthology dedicated to "image ethics," "*voluntary* and *informed* consent is required if the film-maker is to be considered as having acted ethically."[25] Katz and Katz detailed many of the problems linked to obtaining truly informed consent, which is far from simple. However, whereas documentarians must generally obtain at least some kind of signed release from their subjects, audiovisual appropriation often involves the use of materials without any form of consent; subjects are rarely even informed of the reuse. If consent of the subjects is taken as constitutive of an ethical reuse of a recording, then the appropriationist gesture appears unethical almost by its very definition. In fact, one common response to the anxiety about people's images and voices being appropriated without limitation is to suggest that these people must give their informed consent for any audiovisual appropriation. Lawyer Lorelle Babwah, writing within the United States legal context about the song and video entitled "The Bed Intruder Song," produced by The Gregory Brothers (whose work I discuss at length in Chapter 2), has argued that Antoine Dodson, the man whose voice and image was appropriated for the song and video, should have the right to sue The Gregory Brothers for violating his "right to publicity."[26] Although he agreed to participate in the original news broadcast that The Gregory Brothers appropriated, Dodson never gave his permission for this broadcast footage to be used in "The Bed Intruder Song." J. Thomas McCarthy defines the right to publicity as "the inherent right of every human being to control the commercial use of his or her identity."[27] Drawing on Dodson's example, Babwah concluded that

> State laws regarding the right of publicity and privacy protections should construe consent as narrowly as possible to protect the rights of an individual private citizen to exert control over his or her personal identity. Specifically, the consent to be filmed should not be interpreted as consent for that content to then be uploaded, manipulated, and broadcasted throughout the Internet.[28]

She further suggested that private individuals (as well as celebrities) should have the legal right to sue anyone who appropriates their image and profits from the appropriation in any way.

Although this legal argument is persuasive on an affective level—given that few of us would like our image or recorded voice reused without our explicit consent—the implication is that audiovisual appropriation as an art form and as social commentary could be drastically curtailed. Moreover, there are numerous problems with requiring explicit consent as the criterion for an ethical audiovisual appropriation. What should a maker do when the film subjects are now dead, are no longer compos mentis, or cannot be found? Is such material then a priori off limits? More importantly perhaps, are there not cases where a subject might, for self-interested reasons, deny permission to use a recording that could be used in the service of attaining justice for someone else? Does the social value of certain potential uses of a given recording ever exceed the recorded subject's right to control it?

Indeed, despite Elsaesser's proposition that audiovisual appropriation cannot disclose or reveal, he simultaneously acknowledges its potential for disclosure and revelation, particularly in cases when the original maker is revealed as ethically suspect in some way. In his analysis of Harun Farocki's *Aufschub* (2007), in which Farocki appropriates and self-reflexively interrogates footage shot at the Westerbork transit camp for Dutch and German Jews bound for Auschwitz, Elsaesser suggests that there are audiovisual appropriations that we may deem actively ethical, attempting to in some small way acknowledge the people in these images, whose rights were so violently disregarded. Likewise, Elsaesser suggests that in Fiona Tan's *Facing Forward* (1999), which appropriates instances of ethnographic footage of "primitive" people in which these people look back at the camera, "the ethnographic film is turned inside out, brushed against the grain where the objects of a particular gaze are allowed to look back and become subjects."[29] Similarly, in *Sisters & Brothers*, the indigenous children who were objectified by the colonial camera can look back and become active subjects in Monkman's film. Elsaesser takes important steps toward theorizing particular instances of audiovisual appropriation he deems ethical. However, the precise process by which we as viewers may evaluate the ethics of a given appropriation remains opaque.

Furthering Nichols's discussion of documentary ethics in her study of French documentary, Sarah Cooper succinctly articulates one of the key bases upon which a documentary's ethics vis-à-vis its subjects may be evaluated. She has written, "It is the difference between an excess of the image that we cannot know, and what we actually perceive, that becomes a space of responsibility which persistently resists any attempt to reduce those we see either to their image, or to an image of ourselves."[30] Drawing on the philosophy of Emmanuel Levinas, Cooper suggests that the fundamental ethical challenge posed by documentary to the viewer is to see those onscreen neither as entirely others—thereby reducing them to their image, to objects rather than subjects akin to ourselves—nor as mimetic reflections of ourselves—thereby disregarding the specificity of their experiences and identities. Cooper further argues that the ethical must actively undercut the certainties of the seeing subject, opening us up to difference but also reminding us that the other can never be fully known through his or her image.[31] (Or, I would also add, voice.) In a later article, Cooper further articulates the tension between proximity and distance that in her view characterizes the ethical in relation to documentary: "An ability to 'let the Other be' suggest[s] the registering of distance from others, yet such distance [does] not correlate with indifference; on the contrary, in Levinasian philosophy . . .

such distance emerge[s] from within relations of extreme proximity, a proximity without which ethics would be impossible."[32] A continuous tension between distance and proximity in relation to the other constitutes a space of responsibility within which viewers may come to see others in a new relation to themselves. Audiovisual appropriation of actuality footage provides a fertile ground for the production of such a tension precisely because it simultaneously suggests both proximity, through the indexical trace of the recorded subject, and distance, through the viewer's awareness of the appropriation. Thus, audiovisual appropriation can offer a particularly productive space for an exploration of the ethics of our relationships with others. Yet, this potential fundamentally depends on how each work of audiovisual appropriation constructs our relationship to the particular sounds and images it appropriates—and, thereby, on the responses it generates for each viewer in the moment of encounter with an other through the text.

Philosopher Martha Nussbaum suggests that the ethical is deeply intertwined with lived experience. Ethics are not a fixed set of rules, and they cannot be divorced from lived encounters. She distinguishes the ethical from the moral by identifying the essential ethical question as "How should one live?" She writes:

> This question does not . . . assume that there is a sphere of "moral" values that can be separated off from all the other practical values that figure into a human life. . . . What they [who seek an ethical life] are asking is not what is the good "out there," but what can we best live by, and live together as social beings.[33]

Although Nussbaum's analyses generally focus on literature, her work is relevant to film as well. In the contemporary world, if we are to "live together as social beings," we must think through how we wish to look at and listen to one another through our recorded images and voices. As viewers, we must constantly assess what we are looking at or listening to and how we are being asked to look at and listen to it by a film or video—and to decide whether that is a position we wish to take up. Moreover, in the deluge of recorded sounds and imagery that circulate and recirculate, repositioning us again and again in relation to others onscreen, this assessment must be constant and vigilant.

Another implication of the Nussbaum quote above, however, is that no external system exists for distinguishing once and for all the ethical from the unethical. Indeed, one of the challenges of discussing the ethics of audiovisual appropriation (like the ethics of any practice) lies in the fact that because ethical evaluations depend to some degree on individual values, orientations, and situations, there is no objective way to determine what counts as ethical and what does not. Cooper suggests, following Levinas, that "an ethics is produced through the encounter, rather than preexisting it."[34] In the end, it falls on the individual viewer, in the moment of encounter with the text, to determine whether he or she deems a given act of appropriation ethical. However, this determination is necessarily based on shared cultural mores. As we shall see, there are certain kinds of appropriations that I will argue most viewers are likely to feel are justified while others are not. Yet, precisely because they derive from shared cultural values, ethics are not rigid and ahistorical but are, rather, socially situated and historically specific. Hence, the rise of digital technologies may be changing what sorts of audiovisual practices we consider ethical. Nichols aptly notes, "Ethics can be said to be an ideological mechanism by which those in power propose to regulate their own conduct."[35] As viewers in the digital era, situated in a position of spectatorial power, we must decide based on shared—but malleable—cultural values what sort of spectatorial acts we wish to participate in.

Writing about narrative fiction cinema, Jane Stadler argues for a key relationship between embodiment and ethics in contrast to theories of ethics grounded wholly in rational assessment to the exclusion of any affective dimension. She has written that "in order to make sense of either a screen text or the ethical dimensions of a given situation we must have an embodied response to the information we are making sense of. We see, hear, feel, and in other ways physically form an impression of the subject matter."[36] Following Stadler, I suggest that it is the moments of embodied response—of whatever kind—that have the greatest potential to provoke an assessment of the ethics of a given audiovisual appropriation. All the works examined in this study provoked in me both an intellectual comprehension and an embodied response—whether laughter, disgust, horror, sadness, or discomfort of some other kind.[37] Although the intellectual aspect allowed me to make sense of my embodied response, it was the embodied response itself that led me to consider the ethics of the appropriation to which I responded so viscerally and affectively.

Close attention to both the cognitive and affective experience of watching works of audiovisual appropriation may offer some clarification regarding their ethics. To further elucidate this experience, we must ask: How do we understand the ethical responsibility of the maker who appropriates (rather than directly records) actuality materials vis-à-vis those represented in the image or sound recordings? What kinds of intellectual, embodied, and affective effects may audiovisual appropriations generate for us as viewers? And what are the structures through which we evaluate the ethics of these effects? Nichols has noted that there is always a "cost" to what he calls "epistephilia, the desire to know."[38] The "misuse" of actuality recordings always involves an additional cost. This study seeks to determine the structures by which we as viewers may decide whether the potential for knowledge—or some other kind of experience—exceeds that cost. As I shall demonstrate in what follows, when it comes to the audiovisual appropriation of actuality recordings, we must determine our ethical evaluation through an interrogation of the complex interplay between three things—our sense of the rights of those recorded, our projection of the intentions of the producer of the original document, and our reading of the intentions embedded in the act(s) of appropriation. Moreover, there is an overarching structure that contributes to our ethical encounter with a work of appropriation, which I refer to as the "layered gaze."

## The Layered Gaze

The gaze in watching an actuality recording is always already layered, the gaze of the maker overlaid by that of the viewer. Often, we do not notice this layering, identifying our gaze unconsciously with that of the maker. Yet, if our affective response to the film subject seems to contradict those of the maker, we may experience a sense of alienation, a feeling that we have been—or else wish to be—expelled by the film and its gaze, which becomes suddenly visible as a figure. When I watch *Mondo Cane* (Gualtiero Jacopetti, Paolo Cavara, Franco Prosperi, 1962), for instance, a film that catalogs "bizarre" practices from around the world with the aim of shocking the (white Western) audience, I am aware of the mocking, objectifying, and often colonialist gaze of the makers. I squirm in my seat. I look away, wishing to distance myself from the filmmakers' demeaning perspective on the people they filmed. However, the potential for these contradictions is literally multiplied in the case of audiovisual appropriation. Indeed, I would argue that appropriation of previously recorded material creates a multilayered structure based on our perceptions: of the film subject, of the ethical stance of the original maker (which may be rooted in his or her historical and social context) toward his or her material, and of the ethical stance of the maker who has appropriated this material, editing and reframing its images and sounds to a new end. It is the relation between these three perceptions that will determine whether we read the reuse as ethical. This constitutes the structure of the layered gaze.

But when this layered gaze is in effect, what precisely determines whether a viewer will read a particular reuse of a particular found image as ethical or not? In her "phenomenology of the ethical gaze," Vivian Sobchack performs a semiotic phenomenology of the filming of actual human death. She notes, "In the indexical representations of documentary the very act of vision which makes the representation of death possible is itself subject to moral scrutiny."[39] She further notes that codes such as camera shake, framing, distance, and duration may serve to justify the filming of real death, constituting our perception of the filmmaker's "gaze" through these codes. She then delineates a series of documentary "gazes" entailed in the filming of an actual death that seem to justify this filming, an act that might otherwise be regarded as unethical. The gazes that she identifies as ethical include the "accidental gaze," the "helpless gaze," the "endangered gaze," the "interventional gaze," and the "humane gaze."[40] In other words, the maker may accidentally record the death, may be helpless to prevent the death, may herself be endangered in the situation, may attempt to intervene to prevent the death, or may record an image of death out of compassion for the dying—all of which seem to justify the filming of indexical, documentary death.

Given that the act of appropriation always occurs at a remove, however, the appropriationist who wishes to *reuse* an image of real death does not share the situation with her filmed subject. Hence, she is not in the same danger. Being in a different space and time, she is helpless in that she cannot intervene, but this does not justify the appropriation because she can choose whether or not to appropriate these images. Her appropriation is deliberate and cannot be excused as accidental. In fact, it is only the humane gaze—or a version of it—that may persist in the act of appropriation. Sobchack writes that "the humane gaze . . . *visibly and significantly encodes in the image its own subjective responsiveness to what it sees.*"[41] She suggests, for instance, that sustained duration is often one of the formal elements that "visibly and significantly encodes" the humane gaze. This sense of encoded "subjective responsiveness" is deeply relevant to the reading of the ethics of audiovisual appropriation. However, in works of appropriation, this subjective responsiveness must be encoded both in the *choice* of existing material and in the *editing*, which includes not only the ordering of images and sounds but also reframing, masking, superimposing, and so on. In other words, whereas in the act of filming, the filmmaker's "gaze" is encoded in the cinematography, in the case of appropriation the appropriationist "gaze" is constituted primarily through the appropriationist's selection and editing of the found recording.

Of course, the demand for subjective responsiveness does not apply only to images of death. Indeed, when it comes to appropriation, there are many kinds of recordings whose "misuse" seems to demand subjective responsiveness on the part of the appropriationist; otherwise, the viewer may experience the appropriation—which is always already a transgression—as an intolerable one. A strong feeling of transgression may arise, for instance, when a found recording we read as having been intended strictly for a private or limited audience (of a romantic or sexual nature, for instance) is used in a public documentary. Even if recordings of these activities exist, if we understand that they were addressed only to a particular audience—the subject's lover, perhaps—it may seem like an ethical violation for a maker to appropriate them for widespread display, raising questions of voyeurism and violation of privacy. However, this sense of transgression may be mitigated, at least in part, by our sense of the subjective responsiveness of the appropriationist, how she or he chooses to edit and thereby reframe these private recordings—and to what end.

By the same token, there are works of appropriation that actively undermine any sense of subjective responsiveness, and this sometimes constitutes an ethical gesture in that it serves the function of critique. For instance, when the image or recorded voice of a powerful political figure is appropriated in the service of political critique, this may appear to belong to the tradition of political satire, which we generally understand as an integral aspect of freedom of expression within a democratic setting. When the critique serves to disrupt hegemonic media forms that—for instance—exclude minority identities and experiences, this also serves the function of social criticism. Yet, the ethics of such a critical gaze depends on how we perceive the target of the mockery and the power relations between the appropriationist and the appropriated subject. When this mocking gaze is aimed at a different kind of subject, it can serve reactionary functions, its humor disguising discrimination based on race, gender, sexuality, class, ability, and so on. In such instances, we may perceive the absence of subjective responsiveness as an ethical failure.

Thus, the concept of the layered gaze may help us to articulate these complex relationships that ultimately inform our ethical evaluation of the appropriation. Significantly, however, while Sobchack's articulation of the gaze in relation to ethics is extremely useful, its focus on the visual elides the importance of audial experience. In English, there is no audial term that is parallel to "gaze," a fact that has been a source of great frustration for me. Because I prefer not to generate an awkward neologism, I will occasionally use the term "ear" as the closest audial parallel to "gaze." Nevertheless, I want to emphasize that the layered gaze is often a layered act of listening as well.

The layering of the gaze also gives rise to a secondary structure involved in the experience of audiovisual appropriation: a reorientation of the viewer's attention in relation to the found recording. Writing about the appropriation of Civil War photographs in the PBS documentary *The Civil War* (Ken Burns, 1990), Judith Lancioni points to the ways in which reframing as a cinematographic technique—the famous "Ken Burns effect"—can redirect our attention to elements of a photograph that were less noticeable. For instance, she notes how this technique is used in *The Civil War* to foreground African American experience. Moreover, in redirecting our attention, she suggests that the film may lead us to notice the fundamental polysemy of each image.

> The effect of reframing is analogous to the operation of a very elemental perceptual gestalt, namely the figure/ground relationship. Figure and ground are relative, but exclusive, terms; in other words, what is conceived as background cannot be reconstituted as figure without a certain amount of conscious adjustment. When viewers see in close-up (i.e., as figure) an individual whom they have just seen as part of a group shot (i.e., as background), they must make perceptual readjustments that may make them more conscious of the epistemology of seeing.[42]

While the reframing Lancioni describes is one important way of generating this "perceptual readjustment," there are numerous other ways in which appropriationists transform the relationship between figure and ground, bringing latent visible—and audible—elements of the recording to consciousness. In addition, the act of appropriation may also constitute the gaze (or ear) of the original producer itself as a figure to be interrogated. Hence, in bringing to light something suppressed and important in a recording that had been overlooked or actively ignored, certain works of audiovisual appropriation may justify their acts of "misuse." By the same token, however, the appropriationist's own gaze—as conveyed through his or her editing—may also become the object of scrutiny, particularly when misuse begins to feel like abuse. Thus, the "perceptual adjustments" that occur in the viewing of a work of audiovisual appropriation often involve a shift in attention between the layers that constitute the layered gaze. Because the sense of what constitutes an ethical appropriation ultimately depends on the individual viewer, she must perform a complex (if not explicitly thought out) evaluation of multiple ethical layers and figure/ground relationships. Through this layered act of viewing, she must decide for herself if the strategies and ends justify the misuse of the pre-existing recordings. The remainder of this book will attempt to illuminate further the structures that may guide this decision.

Chapter 1, "(Re)exposing Intimate Traces," examines some of the ways recorded sounds and images that we understand as "intimate"—considering all the various meanings of the word—have been repurposed. Through an examination of films that appropriate banal home movies, explicit medical photographs, audio love letters, and surreptitiously taken audio recordings, I pose the question of whether and in what ways such recordings can be ethically reused. I suggest that certain films have variously solicited an attentive gaze, an occluded gaze, or a disclosing gaze that may—at least for some viewers—mitigate the sense of ethical trespass that these films necessarily produce to some degree.

Chapter 2, "Speaking through Others," examines instances of audiovisual appropriation that may be understood as a form of what I call "archival ventriloquism." By manipulating a subject's recorded body and voice, an appropriationist may "speak through" that other's body and voice in a manner not entirely unlike that of a ventriloquist. I suggest that this act of "speaking through" can have a variety of ethical implications, depending on the obviousness of the act of ventriloquism to the audience and on the power dynamics established between appropriated subject and appropriationist (and, by extension, the viewer). These factors help determine whether we read the gaze of the appropriationist as "playful," "satirical," or "denigrating." Moreover, I suggest that when audiovisual appropriation overlaps with cultural appropriation, the ethically suspect specter of racial ventriloquism may emerge. Nonetheless, I argue that archival ventriloquism retains its potential as a tool for meaningful social critique.

Chapter 3, "Dislocating the Hegemonic Gaze," examines a range of texts that disrupt their appropriated materials through a practice of what I call "embodied interruption" and the production of a "dislocating gaze," which may engender an essential critique of hegemonic media tendencies. I argue that by inserting minority bodies or voices into texts aligned with dominant identities and ideologies, these films make visible the erasure or distortion of minority identities and experiences in mainstream media. In producing moments of both temporal and spatial incoherence, these films refuse to allow the texts they appropriate to cohere, both literally and figuratively. Moreover, by placing the minority body where it does not "belong," these interruptions offer a critique that does not deny or disguise its situated, embodied origin.

Chapter 4, "Reframing the Perpetrator's Gaze," examines several films that attempt to use audiovisual appropriation as a form of ethical intervention by "repairing" an injustice that lurks within the appropriated materials. Such films appear to consciously misuse their materials in order to attempt to right a wrong. Whether they appropriate recordings originally produced by Nazis, in the service of a flawed judicial process, or in the name of "national security" within the context of the "war on terror," such works attempt to reverse the relation between figure and ground, drawing our attention to the corrupt, unethical gaze of those who produced these recordings in the first place. Although there may be an ethical "cost" involved in these appropriations, I suggest that these films allow—or force—us to see something that we might otherwise disregard and that not looking, in these cases, is far worse than looking.

My fifth and final chapter, "Abusing Images," examines a series of texts that arguably, at least for some viewers, fail to adhere to a certain ethical standard in relation to their imaged subjects and/or their audiences. In particular, I examine two sets of texts that appropriate the image of a murdered child and may produce—though only in certain viewers—a sense of actual endangerment. In some cases, this sense of endangerment is inadvertently elicited; in other cases, it is intentionally solicited. In either case, however, albeit to varying degrees, the texts that elicit this gaze constitute an unethical form of audiovisual appropriation.

The appropriated other, though seemingly distanced from us in space and time, is nevertheless our responsibility. As viewers who look and listen (and like and share), we can hide behind neither the screen on which we watch the image nor the excuse that the recording was "already out there." In looking, in listening, we are complicit. This book attempts to, at very least, help us become aware of this complicity so that we may actively decide to what degree we are willing to be party to a given misuse. Although legal means are too blunt a tool for regulating audiovisual appropriation, which is a complex, rich, and generative form, we must nonetheless continually pose the question of, as Nussbaum puts it, what values "can we best live by" so as to "live together as social beings." Or, in other words, in a digitized media landscape in which all our images and voices are potentially up for grabs, we must ask: how can we best live with ourselves?

# 1

# (Re)exposing Intimate Traces

One of the specters haunting the contemporary practice of audiovisual appropriation is the widespread and justifiable fear that one's own most intimate documents may—without one's permission or even without one's knowledge—be made public. Instances of celebrities whose supposedly secure digital documents have been hacked and whose nude photos have been distributed against their will across the Internet—revenge porn, a practice in which someone posts nude photos of, for instance, an estranged lover next to his or her name—and other forms of "outing" of intimate recordings give many of us the sense that we should not even take such pictures because—no matter how careful we are—they could become public and their use spiral out of our control. Even nonsexual but still intimate recordings have the potential to be exploited. Though perhaps not as upsetting as the circulation of nude or sexually explicit images, the idea that even our most banal family photographs and videos could be taken out of our hands and reused by a stranger suggests a violation of our intimate space.

Yet, depending on the specific content of the images, might there be a range of ways in which intimate images can be appropriated and repurposed, as well as different ends to which they might be put? Is this kind of violation inherently wrong, or might there be degrees of violation and justification? This chapter examines a number of texts that appropriate images and/or sounds that we might describe as "intimate" but that use their appropriated documents for different ends and produce a range of effects and affects, in order to argue that there may be an ethical spectrum when it comes to the appropriation and misuse of even the most intimate documents.

## Public Intimacy

The word *intimate* has a strangely contradictory etymology. On the one hand, the adjective comes from the Latin word *intimus,* which means "inmost, innermost, deepest," which suggests a private, protected space.[1] On the other hand, the verb *to intimate* comes from the related Latin word *intimare*, which means "to make known."[2] Thus, the word itself suggests both that which is kept private and the betrayal of that privacy. Various subjects may be described as "intimate." Events or experiences that are personal and private, in the sense that one does not expect them to be displayed for public view, may be considered intimate. Close family interactions and romantic relationships, for instance, particularly those that give rise to emotionally vulnerable states, often seem to belong to such a personal, private, intimate realm. Secret activities, those intentionally concealed because outsiders might view them as shameful, also connote intimacy. Domestic space is generally considered an intimate domain where one can do and say what one likes (at least within the limits of the law) without the expectation of public exposure. Finally, the body itself and particularly sexual organs are often referred to in terms of the intimate. Regardless of the type of intimacy, however, what is intimate is likely precious to the subjects involved. Hence, we may wish to preserve such experiences in order to remember them more clearly, and this may be one of the main reasons that recordings of intimate moments and encounters are made.

Yet these recordings—like all other recordings—have the potential to move beyond the control of those who produced them. They may even outlive us, traces of our voices and bodies circulating long after we are gone. When the subjects of intimate audiovisual recordings are dead or impossible to find, one might argue that the most ethically sound act would be to erase these recordings so that they cannot be exploited. And yet, from another vantage point, erasure also seems ethically suspect, a potential loss to society of knowledge and history. To leave them lying unused in the archives might be another solution, but this simply postpones the question of whether these recordings can ethically be reused in any way.[3] In this chapter, I want to argue that when intimate recordings are appropriated, the editing strategies of the appropriationist have the potential to generate an experience of what Vivian Sobchack refers to as "subjective responsiveness" to the film subjects even as the act of appropriation does violate their intimate space.[4] I suggest that our reading of the gaze of the appropriation filmmaker in relation to the intimate gaze of the original producer may mitigate (without necessarily eliminating) our feeling of voyeurism by simultaneously establishing both proximity and distance from the found film subjects. At the same time, however, there are works—due to the recordings' content and/or the appropriationist's editing—that may fail to produce this sense of subjective responsiveness and end up evoking an exploitative gaze. In these instances, we become complicit in the unjustified violation of the subjects' privacy, a position that an ethically conscious viewer will likely find untenable.

## The Attentive Gaze

One of the consequences of our contemporary media overload is a tendency toward distraction, an inability, unwillingness, or simply a deficit of time to pay close attention to the images we see and sounds we hear. As Frances Guerin notes in her introduction to her anthology *On Not Looking*, "while images have never been so readily available, we increasingly don't look at them."[5] We glance, we skim, or we click away to another channel or site. Often, there is nothing particularly unethical about such distraction. At other times, however, it seems like an affront. Once I was screening Alain Resnais's Holocaust documentary *Night and Fog* (1955) for my undergraduate university class and noticed a student texting while images of emaciated concentration camp prisoners flashed across the screen. Had he been texting during most films, I would have been annoyed because he was not participating fully in the class and possibly irritating other students. In this case, I was horrified simply that he would look away from this particular film and its (appropriated) actuality images of atrocity against fellow human beings. His lack of concentration seemed to me a violent disregard for the people whose suffering and deaths are commemorated and mourned by the film. Although he may have had reasons beyond simply wanting to answer a text, in his texting this viewer appeared to reject the subjective responsiveness solicited by Resnais's film by failing to attend to the images at all. Conversely, depending on the film and circumstance, the very act of attending closely can become a gesture of respect, an ethical stance vis-à-vis the represented other and—beyond our own particular spectatorial activities—such attentiveness may be structured through the filmmaker's aesthetic choices. These include not only the sustained duration of the "humane gaze" that Sobchack articulated in relation to images of death but also other strategies that focus or reorient our gaze.[6] Indeed, through a variety of formal strategies, films that appropriate intimate audiovisual documents may sometimes prompt (though certainly not guarantee) a kind of attentiveness that diminishes the sense of voyeuristic exploitation that almost inevitably inheres in this type of appropriation.

Home movies (whether made on film or video) constitute one familiar type of intimate document, and they hold a particular allure: that of contact with their subjects' personal lives.[7] This is, at least in part, because the recordings' subjects seem to expect them to remain private, in other words, that the subjects will retain control of who sees or uses the recordings. The notion of the "private" and its value is, of course, contested. Although in common discourse, we may assume "privacy" to be an inherent good, political scientist Colin J. Bennett points to its ideological roots in liberal individualism. As Bennett suggests, the right to privacy often stands at odds with other more communal and collective rights.[8] However, this fact does not stop us from valuing our privacy, especially in certain situations. Within United States law, the right to privacy is built on the Fourth Amendment's prohibition against "unreasonable searches and seizures." It was further codified in *Katz v. United States* according to "a twofold requirement, first that a person has exhibited an actual (subjective) expectation of privacy and, second, that the expectation be one that society is prepared to recognize as reasonable."[9] The notion of a "reasonable expectation of privacy" is subjective because there is no objective measure for what is "reasonable." However, this definition has become one of the cornerstones upon which legal decisions about privacy in the United States (as well as numerous other countries) are made, and it has become deeply ingrained in societal ideas about privacy.

Although any recording can theoretically be made public, certain recordings exhibit an *expectation* of privacy, in their subject matter and/or in their perceived address. Indeed, this quality is part of what makes home movies feel like home movies. In other words, the sense of privacy that seems to inhere in home movies is in part a function of their seeming unselfconsciousness due to their lack of expectation of a broad public viewing. This is in contrast to amateur films, made with a public audience in mind. As documentary theorist Efrén Cuevas notes, unlike amateur filmmakers, "home moviemakers mainly shoot their daily activities or events happening in their surroundings, to be shown just in family gatherings."[10] Although this is perhaps an overly limited vision of home movies' intended sites of exhibition, home movies often do seem to offer a reflection of daily life without an eye to a public viewing, shot through what I call a "secluded gaze." The term "secluded" literally means to be "set apart" and was used in the 1600s to mean "guarded from public view."[11] A secluded space, then, allows for relatively unguarded behavior. Thus, even if they contain nothing that seems specifically meant to be kept hidden, home movies may still give us a sense of being in proximity to an individual's unguarded and therefore private experience. At least partly for this reason, they have often been appropriated by both experimental and documentary filmmakers seeking to offer viewers an intimate encounter with their subjects' private lives. Steve Anderson notes how this appropriation constructs a new, public gaze. "Removed from the closed circuit of intrafamilial production and reception, appropriated home movies images become 'declassified,' that is, opened to a different kind of public scrutiny."[12] And, for this reason, the reuse of home movies is always also a misuse whose ethics must be interrogated.

In some cases, home movies taken by or of public figures become a source of an alternative and more personal view of those figures than what official recordings convey. For instance, in her 2013 film *Our Nixon*, Penny Lane appropriates Super 8 footage shot by Nixon aides H. R. "Bob" Haldeman, John Ehrlichman, and Dwight Chapin before the Watergate scandal, in which all three were convicted. This footage was then seized by the FBI and shut away in the National Archives for forty years. Lane's appropriation of this home movie footage offers a renewed vision of Nixon, whose memory had become sedimented along the lines of the official representations that constantly recirculate. Much of what we see in the home movie footage is quite banal: the aides standing around airstrips or lounging in lawn chairs, Nixon sitting alone rubbing his nose, birds and squirrels eating seeds outside the White House, and so on. The interest in the images lies in trying to better understand a group of individuals—Nixon and his aides—as more than caricatures of government corruption. Lane's film contrasts these seemingly "innocent" images with the damning audio recordings made in the Oval Office as well as official interviews conducted before and after the Watergate scandal. As Rachel Stevens writes in her review of *Our Nixon,* "What becomes legible through this replaying of the Nixon archive is a psychological take on the interpersonal dynamics of Nixon's inner circle. Nixon, Haldeman, Ehrlichman and Chapin are seen more as people than villains."[13] The appropriation serves to "humanize" people who have been codified as corrupt crooks, offering a more nuanced portrait of these figures rather than further demonizing them. In other words, the gaze laid over the secluded gaze of the original is not entirely unsympathetic. And even as the misuse of the home movies of Nixon aides does constitute a transgression of a private sphere, this particular private sphere directly intersects with public events. The Watergate scandal is an episode whose ramifications continue to reverberate beyond the private lives of the individuals involved. Hence, these particular documents have a public historical interest that seems to justify the trespass. (In addition, if one regards Nixon and his aides as crooks, then their right to privacy may seem moot.)

In other cases, makers reuse home movie footage from their own lives or families as a form of autobiography. For instance, in *Sink or Swim* (1990), Su Friedrich uses home movie images of her father's and her own childhoods in order to reflect on her complex relationship with her father. Only a few home movie images appear in the film: of Friedrich as a baby being tossed in their air by her father, of Friedrich's father carrying her on his shoulders, of Friedrich as a young girl performing a pirouette for her father, and a series of images of her father and his sister (who died tragically) as children. The use of slow motion, freeze frame, repetition, and voiceover narration in combination with these images serves to undermine the idealistic and nostalgic qualities of the images, pointing to Friedrich's family's troubled dynamics. Anderson has written of the film:

> Implicit in this "confessional" mode of home movie appropriation is the possibility that the film/videomaker will be forced to occupy a position of vulnerability in relation to his or her audience. Unlike the traditional ethnographic subject, this individual is in control of the images included in the final work. However, a standard trope of the confessional essay . . . seems to require the maker to allow for a degree of authorial vulnerability through self-exposure.[14]

As Anderson indicates, even though the subject is the filmmaker and "is in control of the images," this act of self-exposure and the attendant "vulnerability" of the maker/subject still raise ethical questions: Can one violate one's own past self's privacy? Is one's past self an "other" in relation to the present self? Moreover, the presence of other family members within home movies reused in this way raises concerns about the violation of their privacy. Cuevas has also noted that there are many different strategies appropriationists have used when reusing their own family's home movies in autobiographical documentaries.[15] Thus, I do not want to overgeneralize regarding the ethics of this form. However, I would argue that usually the reuse of one's own family's home movies does not seem unethical precisely because the gaze of the original is aligned—though not entirely coincident—with that of the appropriationist. There is still a layered gaze, but the different gazes seem to originate with the same—or else a closely related—eye, so ethical issues regarding the other are, at very least, repressed or diminished.

But what of the appropriation of seemingly innocuous home movies of unknown strangers, of those images (and sometimes sounds) these private individuals found precious enough to preserve? In other words, what are the ethics of appropriating someone else's home movies, of violating their presumed seclusion, when there is no obvious public historiographic justification?

In Tony Gault's *Ghost of Yesterday* (2012), we see a variety of anonymous figures engaged in recognizable home movie activities, dated to the mid-twentieth century by the quality of the images and the clothing styles of the subjects. We see a mother handing her child to a priest for baptism, a woman holding a small child's hands helping him walk, a family eating dinner together and sharing drinks, a bride walking down the aisle with her veil flowing behind her, and a toddler sitting on a beach, among other images. What is most striking about these images, however, is that—in Gault's film—much of each one has been eliminated. Only certain parts of these figures are visible, floating against a black background before they fade back into the black. In the very first image, we see two gloved hands carrying a blue ladies' handbag, but the rest of the figure is missing. In place of the rest of the woman's body and the space around her, there is only the blackness of the screen. In the scene of the baptism, we see candlesticks and their flames, a baby tightly swaddled in white, a mother's wide-brimmed Sunday hat, and

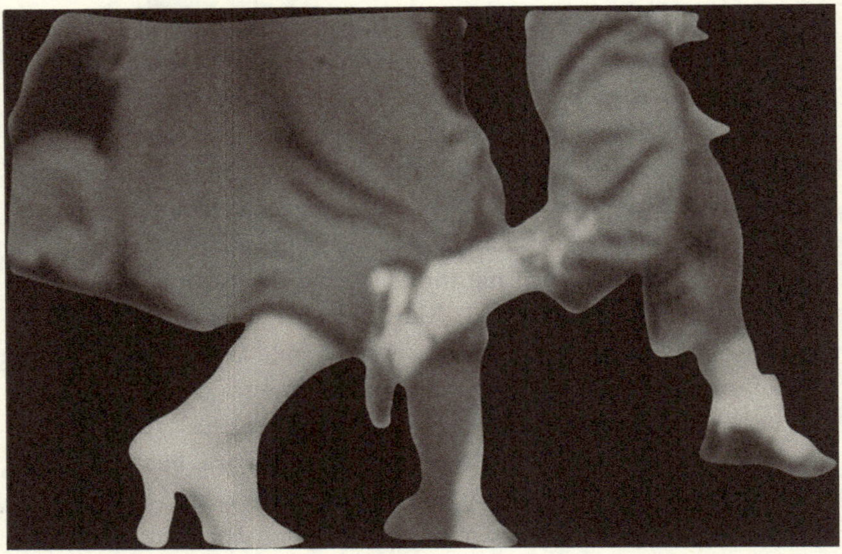

FIGURE 2 Still from *Ghost of Yesterday* (Tony Gault, 2012). Courtesy of the artist.

the priest's hands as she passes her baby to him. But everything else is black. Beyond her white hat and dress, even the mother is visible only as a wavering black silhouette. The toddler sitting on the beach is lit by the bright sun, but he is surrounded by darkness, which is interrupted only by two pairs of bare legs that walk by, accompanied by the outline of their shadows quivering on folds of sand that become visible as they pass. The soundtrack of these first scenes consists of foleys—the echo of high-heeled footsteps and the rustle of paper, an organ and the clink of a spoon, the sound of waves and birdsong. As the toddler, the disembodied legs, and the beach disappear, we hear Billie Holiday begin to sing "Ghost of Yesterday" (1940), the song from which the film takes its name. These partial images are, indeed, ghostly, a series of unexplained but suggestive fragments that haunt the black screen (figure 2).

These are intimate images in the sense of being private; they read as personal and precious, intensely meaningful to those pictured and those who loved them but not to anyone else, at least not in the same way. There is nothing in these images to shock or titillate, and yet, watching such images once they have been appropriated is an incursion, like attending someone else's family gathering to which we were not invited. In other words, they evoke the secluded gaze. While the appropriation and reuse of such "innocent" home movie footage is common—usually to illustrate a film subject's childhood or some aspect of his or her past—and rarely remarked upon from an ethical standpoint, this does not negate the ethical dilemma of using someone else's home movies for one's own ends. What, if anything, mitigates or justifies Gault's misuse of these images in his film?

First of all, there is a preservationist impulse involved in Gault's appropriation. These home movies had already been discarded, put on sale online, although it is unclear precisely who decided to sell them. Gault says, "I am . . . sad to see people sell their family heirlooms on eBay for 10 or 15 bucks. I think it's mostly film transfer houses doing this after they've convinced families that their flimsy little DVDs are the best way to archive their home movies. What a scam. Another example of how swaths of human culture are being lost to the digital age."[16] In this sense, Gault has rescued and (partially) preserved traces that would otherwise likely have disappeared for good. Yet this does not automatically excuse the violation of the subjects' privacy at work in inserting these images into a new film for public exhibition.

The particular form of Gault's film, however, serves to direct the viewer's attention in a particular way. A colleague of mine who studies home movies was once asked if she had any home movie footage that could be used as a backdrop in an installation. My colleague refused, noting that this request assumed that someone else's possibly precious private moments were essentially available as wallpaper. And, indeed, home movie imagery is often used as a generic trope indicating "pastness," a use that denies the particularity of the actual subjects' personal, private experiences. Gault's film, however, does not treat these private images as wallpaper but, rather, quite literally *attends* to every frame. To "attend" may mean "to be present," or "to give one's attention to," but it may also mean "to take care of." Martha Nussbaum has written, "Obtuseness and refusal of vision are our besetting vices. . . . Responsible lucidity can be wrested from the darkness only by painful, vigilant effort, the intense scrutiny of particulars."[17] Gault's film embodies this "vigilant effort" and "intense scrutiny of particulars," producing a "responsible lucidity" that may be felt by the viewer even if at a subconscious level. To make this film, Gault searched for Super 8 home movie footage on eBay, purchasing images that he found "compelling," meaning, he says, that they included "good camera movement (especially smooth pans), relatively long takes, shot on Kodachrome stock . . . magic hour light if exteriors, lyrical moments in family life and not so lyrical moments where family dysfunction is revealed (often through drinking or anger/discomfort toward the camera)." He then blew up selected images to 16mm using an optical printer because he wanted to "emphasize and retain the grain from the Super 8," which is something he believes he would not have been able to achieve if he had skipped this step and transferred them immediately to digital files. After he was satisfied with the 16mm blow-ups, however, he had them transferred to digital files so that he could work with the shots in After Effects, a program he had never used before. He realized that he could use After Effects in the same way that he might use an optical printer—manipulating images frame by frame. He discovered he could "mask" out all of the elements of a frame he wanted to discard. He says, "I was basically copying the old analog method of painting each frame with fingernail polish and then bleaching off what isn't under the fingernail polish. In [After Effects], they call it 'rotoscoping,' but their instructions about how to rotoscope in [After Effects] are very different than the way I went about it." Instead of tracing every few frames and allowing the program to approximate what he wanted between those frames, he created a unique mask for each frame. Other After Effects users told him that he was "crazy" because he could have achieved a very similar effect in a fraction of the time, but Gault says he "can always sense repetition and time-saving shortcuts in digital approaches to filmmaking" and that he believes "humans have a very sensitive (if sometimes unconscious) awareness of the difference between nature/randomness and digital order." Although one might not be fully aware of Gault's painstaking process simply looking at the film, I believe that his incredibly careful attention to each frame is nonetheless conveyed—and transferred—to the viewer.

Marcel Merleau-Ponty writes in *The Phenomenology of Perception,* "To pay attention is not merely to elucidate pre-existing data, it is to bring about a new articulation of them by taking them as *figures*."[18] Gault's method incites us to actively take the people and objects we see in these images as "figures," whereas they might otherwise have been—as in the proposed installation mentioned above—background, wallpaper. Had Gault simply copied the complete images and edited them together, our attentiveness might be weak, the figures only slightly standing out from their backgrounds. The images might just have read as "old home movie footage," intimate, beautiful, nostalgic, and yet banal. We might dismiss them without really looking at them and, in doing so, dishonor these anonymous people through our "refusal of vision." Paradoxically, we would be invading their private lives and (literally) disregarding these lives in the same moment. However, Gault's careful excision of each figure from its ground produces an intense attentiveness.

Moreover, Gault's film does not offer the whole figures to our vision but, rather, only fragments of them—an arm, a handbag, a worn teddy bear, an occasional face. Part of the experience of watching the film is one of wishing to "look past," to see what is behind the black, to that which has been masked. Our attention has been limited to the fragments of figures framed against the darkness, but this only heightens our sense of the missing ground. And because of Gault's method of tracing the figures frame by frame, the edges of these partial figures also constantly waver, as if we might catch a glimpse of what lies behind the black. As a result, while the black space sometimes feels like a background against which the figures emerge, at other times, it feels like a tangible object in the foreground coming between viewer and figure. It is at the line of encounter between figure and ground—which continually switch places in our perception—that the sense that it might be possible to see more—to see beyond—comes into being. Yet, even as it is evoked, this desire is thwarted. Although there is still voyeurism involved in watching fragments of these strangers' most treasured moments, we are prevented from seeing the whole; we will never be able to get a "good look." Gault's film both focuses our attention and obstructs our gaze, suggesting that a full picture of these people's lives is precisely not for us to see. In addition, there is no original sound, so the particular voices as well as details that might emerge from spoken comments are absent. Although the foleys offer a sense of immediacy, they are also clearly added, and they fade away when Holiday begins to sing. Merleau-Ponty has written, "If a phenomenon—for example, a reflection or a light gust of wind—strikes only one of my senses, it is a mere phantom, and it will come near to real existence only if, by some chance, it becomes capable of speaking to my other senses."[19] We may expect muteness from old home movies, but the lack of original sound also emphasizes the temporal distance between the subjects and us. We see glimpses of their lives, but we are prevented from eavesdropping on their conversations. Although the sounds and music we hear may "speak to our other senses"—in this case, hearing—they come from a different origin, thereby underscoring the silence of the images. As a result, the subjects remain inaccessible "phantoms"—the ghosts of yesterday.

The way in which Gault's film encourages us to really attend—while also refusing to let us see the whole—mitigates our sense of trespass. Thus, over the intimate, secluded gaze of the original producers of these images, Gault's film solicits an intensely "attentive gaze" and we might call the ethics of the film one of attention. And yet, what is gained through this appropriation, this trespass? I would suggest that *the film's* greatest value and power rests in its approximation of the synaesthetic experience of remembering—and of remembering as a shared human experience. While all films can be considered synaesthetic in their engagement of multiple senses, *Ghost of Yesterday* functions as a "hinge" that opens up space for a synaesthetic experience. Jennifer Barker draws on Brian Massumi's definition of synaesthesia as "as a visible, tangible 'hinge' between two systems of sensual perception: one visual and cognitive, the other proprioceptive," to theorize how cinema can generate a synaesthetic experience.[20] Working in tandem with our visual and cognitive perceptions, the proprioceptive system is that which, through our muscles, inner ear, and other organs, allows us to judge our body's position relative to the surrounding space. Barker argues that "the surface reality ascertained by vision is only one layer; the big picture is more complex, and its perception and depiction are necessarily synaesthetic."[21] The elimination of most of the image in *Ghost of Yesterday* conveys a powerful sense that "the surface reality ascertained by vision is only one layer." The combination of foleys and music with the fragmentary appearance of objects suggests other layers, a space we cannot see but of which we are intensely aware. Moreover, this suggestion of other layers that may lie "beyond" what I can see leaves space for my own multisensory memories to emerge: the sound of my mother's high-heeled shoes as she carefully made her way down the wooden stairs of our house each morning, the sight of my infant son sitting up and looking around for the first time, the smell of sunscreen and hot sand, the textured fur of a shabby teddy bear I once loved too well. On the one hand, the home movies are specific to the particular people who made and appeared in them; the secluded space into which we peer belongs exclusively to them. On the other, the gaps opened by Gault's appropriation and excisions offer a space for each viewer to "fill in" with what he or she can "sense" behind and beyond what is visible. This is not a reduction of other to self, but rather the lure of embodied passage and contact across a temporal gap, even if the gap can never actually be bridged.

This sense of attentive, embodied contact may be extended to appropriations of a very different kind of "intimate" audiovisual material. While home movies are intimate in the sense that they were intended by their subjects to be seen only by a select few, there are also intimate recordings that were always intended for public view whose subjects might, nevertheless, be exploited if these recordings are repurposed. The term "explicit" derives from the

French *explicite*, which means to "open to the understanding," and from the Latin *explicare* "to unfold, unravel, explain."[22] More recently, the "explicit" has also come to refer to the pornographic, particularly in relation to media representations. The found source material in Scott Stark's *Speechless* (2008) combines these two meanings of the explicit, and the film itself "opens to understanding" something that might easily read as pornographic.

In this film, the appropriated imagery is intimate in that it depicts a private part of the body. In 1976, two medical professionals published a textbook called *The Clitoris* as part of the Marital Therapists Training Project for the California Department of Health. This book was accompanied by a set of Viewmaster 3D reels displaying twenty-eight extreme close-ups of human vulvae considered "within the range of normal." In Stark's thirteen-minute film, some of these stereoscopic photographs are rapidly edited together with images of surfaces and textures such as rusted metal, grass, stones, and earth. The quick editing, along with the swift alternation of each pair of stereoscopic images, generates a flicker effect that appears to animate these intimate body parts. The whirring hum of the mesmerizing soundtrack further enhances this sense of vibration. When the film is projected, the images are also magnified so that all the details of each vulva become intensely visible.

The awareness of the source of these images is important to evaluating the ethics of *Speechless*. The credits note that the stereo images derive from *The Clitoris,* edited by Thomas P. Lowry M.D. and Thea Snyder Lowry M.A. in 1976, but only the program notes specify their distribution as 3D Viewmaster reels accompanying the textbook. The fact that these images come from a textbook for marital therapists rather than a pornographic source is crucial to our understanding of Stark's transformation of their meaning. The subjects whose bodies are displayed with the textbook presumably gave their consent, and the textbook was intended to inform therapists about the human clitoris in order to help couples improve their sexual relationships. Moreover, the people whose bodies are shown are anonymous; all identifying details are occluded. Thus, the intentions of the original images do not seem unethical; they read as justified by the "clinical gaze" associated with the medical profession. In this sense, these images are explicit because they seek to explain and educate about a part of the body that many people are embarrassed to examine. At the same time, however, there are elements of the original that suggest the other meaning of "explicit." For instance, the fact that these images were intended to be viewed through a Viewmaster suggests not a clinical gaze but rather, the viewing structure of the peephole, which is closely aligned with voyeurism. In addition, the presence of someone's fingers and measurement devices in some of the images, as well as the designation of "within the range of normal" imply the objectifying nature of the clinical gaze. Explicit in both senses of the word, these images solicit an "objectifying gaze" that transforms the human subject into an object of pleasure or analysis.

Although these images were always intended for public use, Stark's appropriation does constitute an ethical trespass to a degree. We can only assume—or hope—that the women whose vulvae are pictured gave their permission to be included in the textbook. Moreover, in the original images, the women's identities were already hidden and protected. The women in these images did not, however, give their consent for their intimate body parts to be appropriated and projected onscreen in Stark's experimental film. (Precisely because of their anonymity, Stark could not identify let alone track down these women to obtain their permission.) Yet, the solicitation of the simultaneously clinical and voyeuristic qualities in the original makes Stark's appropriation read less as exploitation than an investigation and deconstruction of these pre-existing ways of looking at the female anatomy. The "objectifying gaze" of the original becomes as much a figure as the vulvae themselves as Stark's strategies act to expose our habitual ways of looking at the female body.

David Finkelstein suggests that the very nature of the images in *Speechless* could be "controversial," because "explicit images of female genitals are guaranteed to affect viewers powerfully and personally."[23] Indeed, images of such an intimate part of the body may produce a range of embodied responses: sexual arousal, disgust, or fascination. They might also be assumed to solicit the "male gaze" theorized by Laura Mulvey. Much of psychoanalytic film theory rests on the notion of identification, which emerges through an imaginary relationship with the onscreen figure grounded in the mirror phase. Mulvey famously pointed out how Classical Hollywood films tend to be structured so that the viewer is led to identify with a male character, who is the possessor of the gaze. Through point-of-view shots, the viewer is often aligned with the male character as he looks at women's bodies, which become the object of his gaze; the camera and viewer are thus identified with the "male gaze." Moreover, Mulvey also theorized the way in which the woman's body onscreen may be transformed into a fetish object. The psychoanalytic notion of fetishism is based on the trauma of the recognition of sexual difference, based in the possibly mythical moment when the small boy sees that his mother does not have a penis. In compensation for this trauma, the woman's body (or some related object) becomes an object of voyeuristic fascination. This fetishization accounts for the repeated appeal of the female striptease, wherein the shocking "lack" is gradually revealed, or of certain heterosexual pornography.[24] Images of vulvae then, at least from a psychoanalytic perspective, are likely to trigger a voyeuristic or fetishistic form of spectatorship, a version of the male gaze.

By virtue of its subject matter, one might read *Speechless* as soliciting this male gaze. Yet Mulvey was writing about Hollywood fiction films, which construct a distance between the viewer and the body onscreen. A clinical gaze—that of the doctor looking at a patient's body—also constructs distance. *Speechless*, by contrast, actively undermines this distance. Finkelstein notes that "the extreme close-up of the clitoris images, probably a bit closer than one would experience even in the most intimate of acts, acted effectively to de-emphasize their sexually arousing effect and make the images more poetic and evocative, at the same time that they are even more powerful in their sheer physicality."[25] Unlike the Viewmaster slides, which were designed to be viewed individually through a peephole, from which the vulvar images derive, *Speechless* is designed to be seen projected onto a large screen in a public space. Thus, Stark's magnification of these images creates a sense of unfamiliar scale. Moreover, although interspersed with other images, Stark's film asks us to look at close-ups of vulvae for an extended period, generating a prolonged—though heavily fragmented—stare through which every detail becomes intensely visible. In addition, the rapid editing does not allow the vulvae to become inanimate objects; they are constantly in (slight) motion suggesting bodies full of vitality. Anything shocking or potentially pornographic about the images seems to recede over time so that we are confronted only with an intense vision of something most of us rarely, if ever, look at with such close attention.

Of course, *Speechless* is hardly the first experimental film to take vulvae as its subject. Anne Severson's *Near the Big Chakra* (1971), for instance, is also constituted of close-ups of vulvae. However, *Speechless* differs from Severson's film in that Severson filmed these vulvae herself while Stark reused existing images. *Speechless* is not only a look at the vulva but also an interrogation of an existing gaze previously directed at the vulva. In other words, Stark's film's gaze is layered over the one we perceive as already at work in the images.

Through its strategies of magnification, extended duration, and frame-by-frame "animation," *Speechless* solicits a version of the "attentive gaze" I described in relation to *Ghost of Yesterday*. In addition, it evokes a mimetic relation to the body of the other onscreen. Jennifer Bean has written:

> Mimesis stresses the reflexive, rather than reflection; it brings the subject into intimate contact with the object, or other, in a tactile, performative, and sensuous form of perception, the result of which is an experience that transcends the traditional subject-object dichotomy.[26]

Watching *Speechless*, we are engaged in a visceral perception of flesh from which we are not entirely able to distance ourselves. Instead of being given space for reflection, we are reflexively returned to our own bodies. Whether male or female, the viewer is placed in extremely "intimate contact" with an other's flesh. We are offered a "tactile" and "sensuous" relation to a body that seems to quiver with life, like our own bodies breathing and shifting in the theater. Moreover, the flicker effect works directly on our own nervous systems. Instead of producing a unified 3D experience like the Viewmaster originals, the flicker agitates our own scopic nerves, potentially inducing a sense of vertigo. Within this space of intimate contact, the sense of bodily presence—that of the bodies onscreen and our own—is contagious, disorienting. In its mimetic address, the film asks us to "transcend the traditional subject-object dichotomy," which persisted in the original medical imagery. As a result, in *Speechless,* the female vulvae onscreen can no longer be fully objectified. Moreover, as we look at these flickering vulvae for an extended time, they become complex, dynamic figures, unique and individuated—rather than sexualized spectacles or medical evidence. Although the women to whom they belong are not fully visible, their bodies nonetheless appear as sites of vital being.

Hence, as the attentive, mimetic gaze is layered over the clinical, voyeuristic, and objectifying gazes of the original, two sets of figures emerge, that of the vulvae themselves and that of the way we are normally positioned to look at them. Because the vulva is something that we are generally not "supposed" to look at, it has become an object of fascination, revulsion, or obsession. When I first saw *Speechless,* my first impulse was to stop watching. I felt I should not be looking. Without knowing precisely why, I felt ashamed. In his analysis of several of Bill Viola's video works, media theorist Mark Hansen refers to Levinas's definition of shame as "being consigned to something from which we cannot take any distance."[27] He argues that Viola's works "bring home exactly how our own vitality, that which is most intimate in us, can become the agent of the shame that supports our contemporary experience of subjectivity."[28] The feeling of shame that watching *Speechless* has at least the potential to generate may stem from a similar recognition of our own embodied vitality, our own intimate selves, how our physical bodies, over which we have only limited control, constitute a fundamental aspect of our subjectivities. This recognition transcends gender or sexual identity, but it is often obscured in the fetishization of the vulva. By not allowing us to distance ourselves and establish a voyeuristic or clinical relation to female genitalia, *Speechless* encourages us to consider the origins and meaning of this shame. In this sense, *Speechless* makes us look until we see—and feel—differently in regard to both the bodies of others and our own. Through its aesthetics and ethics of close attention, Stark's film denies us the distance from these images and bodies that we may desperately seek to regain. By letting us—or making us—see "too much," *Speechless* thrusts us into an embodied engagement with the other that exposes not just the bodies onscreen but also the vitality and vulnerability of our own.

## The Occluded Gaze

There are times, however, when the attentive gaze is not enough to justify the misuse of certain intimate documents, particularly those that read as secret. The home movies appropriated in *Our Nixon, Sink or Swim,* and *Ghost of Yesterday* are personal and private; the footage in *Speechless* is explicit in its hyperbolic exposure of a part of the body we generally hide away. Yet, none of these recordings appears to have been secret. In her book on the ethics of secrecy, philosopher Sissela Bok distinguishes between the private and the secret. She defines privacy "as the condition of being protected from unwanted access by others—either physical access, personal information, or attention. Claims to privacy are claims to control access to what one takes . . . to be one's personal domain."[29] Secrecy, by contrast, connotes intentional concealment and separation. Bok writes, "The separation between insider and outsider is inherent in secrecy; and to think of something secret is already to envisage potential conflict between what insiders conceal and what outsiders want to inspect or lay bare."[30] As Bok demonstrates, exposing something secret is not necessarily unethical—for instance, revealing secret government corruption is often regarded as an ethical act. In *Our Nixon*, segments of the secret Oval Office tapes are appropriated along with the home movies and television footage. The appropriation of these tapes, which Nixon explicitly states on tape are for his ears only, does not read as unethical because they are evidence of presidential misconduct about which the public had every right to know.[31] Yet, when the personal and the secret coincide, when the secret belongs to the personal domain, the desire to "inspect or lay bare" the secret becomes more ethically fraught.

Indeed, to expose someone else's intimate personal secret runs the risk of becoming gossip, which Bok defines as "informal personal communication about other people who are absent or treated as absent."[32] According to this definition, gossip is not inherently bad. It serves an important function as a channel of public information and interpersonal understanding. However, gossip can become "reprehensible," for instance, when it is "unduly invasive." Bok argues that such unduly invasive gossip occurs when it concerns "matters legitimately considered private."[33] Moreover, she suggests that gossip can be harmful when it serves to "trivialize and demean."[34] Thus, when secret, personal, private recordings are appropriated, in order to evaluate the ethics of this misuse, we must ask whether it is unduly invasive and whether it trivializes or demeans its subjects. In other words, is watching such a misuse a genuine attempt to understand others through their intimate traces or does it constitute a form of reprehensible gossip?

An analysis of Jane Gillooly's 2013 film *Suitcase of Love and Shame* may offer some insight into this complex question. The soundtrack of this film comprises selections from sixty reels of audiotape recorded over three years in the 1960s and found in a suitcase Gillooly purchased on eBay in 2009. These audiotapes were recordings of the love "letters" of two people, Tom and Jeannie, who were having an affair. Most of the time, each recorded the audiotapes alone and then sent them to the other. At other times, they made tapes together. As a whole, these recordings—along with other documents and souvenirs—constituted what Jeannie refers to on one tape as their "memory library." In *Suitcase*, the sounds of Tom and Jeannie speaking to each other on these recordings are accompanied by partially visible found images of Tom and Jeannie, images of the suitcase and the reels themselves, Gillooly's own evocative images, and sometimes a black screen.

The appropriated recordings in *Suitcase* are much more intimate than those in *Ghost of Yesterday*. They are not simply private, personal, and domestic but also romantic, sexual, and secret. Gillooly used these recordings without the permission of either Tom, who had died by the time she began making the film, or Jeannie, who Gillooly did track down only to find that she had dementia and, although she would have signed any form given to her, would not have understood what she was consenting to.[35] Given that neither party could give real consent, perhaps the only truly ethical thing to do would have been to destroy the recordings.[36] However, in doing so, something of value to other people might have been lost. In an essay about ethics and autobiographical filmmaking, John and Judith Katz argue that

> The privilege of entering the homes of others, on an intimate basis, should not be undervalued as an educative and humanizing experience. What we have a 'right' to know about particular families is debatable. But the value of knowing, in more realistic fashion, about other people's interior lives is unquestionable.[37]

Whether *Suitcase* constitutes such an "educative and humanizing experience" that offers us valuable knowledge of "other people's interior lives" or whether it just allows us to "snoop" constitutes the ethical question at the heart of Gillooly's film. Undeniably, one of the primary attractions of Tom and Jeannie's recordings is their intimacy, their sense of being both private and secret. Gillooly has noted,

> the recordings were made in a uniquely unselfconscious state with the goal of reaching out to another human being—the lover—so much so that we listeners, a half-century later, can feel as though they are speaking directly to us, that we are in the room with them. Yet we know that Tom and Jeannie never expected these tapes to be heard by anyone [else].[38]

The couple's lack of self-consciousness is precisely what makes these recordings seem so "authentic." In the digital era, most of us are aware that private or secret recordings can be made public with a single click, but this was not the case in the 1960s. Tom and Jeannie seem completely unaware that anyone other than themselves might ever listen to their recordings, so there is almost no sense of inhibition. Indeed, if we are to read a gaze (or ear) associated with these recordings, it might be termed a "hermetic gaze," enclosed within an intimate, secret realm.[39]

Gillooly's appropriation of these recordings places us in the ethically compromised position of the eavesdropper. Watching the film generates a powerful sense that we should not be listening to the details of these strangers' intimate lives. Sometimes, these details are sexual. At one point we can hear Tom and Jeannie having sex, breathing hard and moaning. Later, during one of the more humorous parts of the film, Tom describes the process of casting his penis in wax to send Jeannie for Valentine's Day. On a later tape, we then hear Jeannie talking about and then masturbating with the wax dildo. Although this may seem rather funny, after Jeannie climaxes, she begins to cry saying, "I'm sorry darling but I cry when it's not you there and I just have to make out. Oh darling, oh how I love, how I miss you." Arguably, while the sexual moments seem intensely private, the emotional displays seem perhaps even more so. On another tape Jeannie recorded, we hear her crying and talking about her longing for Tom and her sense of worthlessness without him. She says:

> I love you. I just worship you, Tom. I think you know that I love you so much. It-it's terribly hard being away from you so long at a time. You have so many, many things to fill your days, and your mind overflows with the preparations that you make for your classes and your article. And sometimes I feel as though I—I'm not contributing anything anywhere to anybody. With the exception of my deep love that I have for you, try to express to you, that's about really all I accomplish in the way of relations with other humans, Tom.

During this poignant confession—clearly meant only for Tom's ears—Jeannie's vulnerability heightens the sense that we were not meant to hear these recordings. The intimate, hermetic space that Tom and Jeannie created and inhabited together is violently torn asunder by our presence.

*Suitcase* reflexively foregrounds questions of its own ethical status, inviting us to actively reflect on the filmmaker's—and by extension our own—act of documentary eavesdropping. On her website, Gillooly describes the effects she attempted to achieve:

> the listener/viewer is variously located within and outside of the events—complicit and voyeuristic. The "eavesdropping viewer" [is] compelled despite feeling embarrassed and uncomfortable with the knowledge and access they [sic] have been given and the transgressions they imagine they see.[40]

The film confronts viewers with our own experience of listening in on a conversation not meant for our ears. By presenting us with audio but not images of what we are hearing about, the film opens a space within which we cannot help but picture what we are hearing. We are, then, actively and ethically complicit in constructing the image of the relationship between Tom and Jeannie, visualizing in our minds the intimate moments of which they speak. When we hear Tom describing his penis in Jeannie's mouth, it is quite difficult not to imagine the scene even though we are not presented with an image of it. This act of imagination emphasizes not only the filmmaker's but also the viewer's role in the violation of Tom and Jeannie's private space.

"No one has ever told me I shouldn't have used the recordings," Gillooly says of the response to her film, but she notes that a few audience members have reacted negatively—an older man angrily shouting "we don't need this" during a screening, a woman leaving the screening room during a Q&A with the filmmaker after belatedly realizing that Tom and Jeannie were not actors.[41] These reactions suggest that some viewers may see Gillooly's appropriation as encouraging a prurient gaze, which we generally understand as unethical. However, the generally positive response to the film suggests that most viewers perceive the gaze of the film as sympathetic—in other words, subjectively responsive—to Tom and Jeannie, telling their story not to exploit them but rather to try to understand their experience. In other words, for most viewers, it does not appear to constitute the kind of "reprehensible gossip" that Bok places outside the bounds of ethical discourse.

Moreover, while the film does often feel "unduly invasive," I would argue that it does not "trivialize or demean" its subjects. *Suitcase* uses several formal strategies to mitigate the sense of ethical transgression and to give viewers the sense that Gillooly's is at least a respectful gaze. First, except for their first names, Tom and Jeannie remain anonymous; from the soundtrack, we never learn any details that would allow us to identify them. As Gillooly has stated,

> I don't use their names and . . . I avoided certain narrative threads that would more closely reveal who they were. I edited passages to deliberately mislead the audience to think something happened in a different geographic location. As much as possible I try to discourage the audience's impulse to figure out who they are.[42]

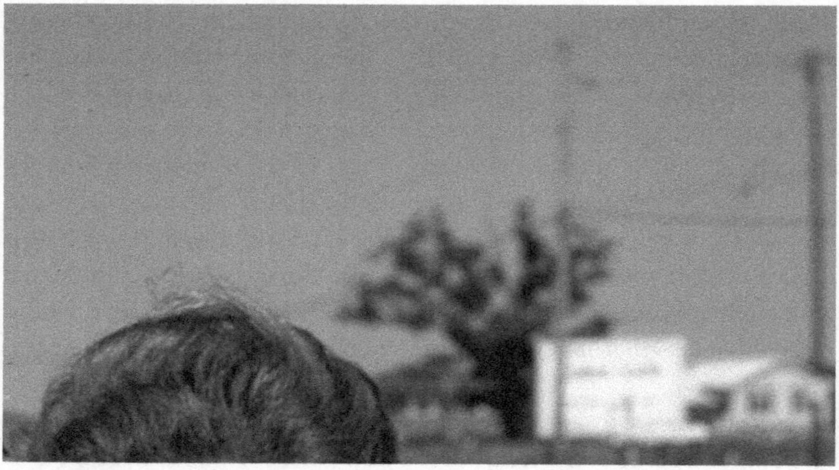

FIGURE 3 Still from *Suitcase of Love and Shame* (Jane Gillooly, 2013). Courtesy of the artist.

Yet, anonymity alone is not necessarily enough to constitute an ethical misuse. Someone—a family member or friend—might recognize their voices; and even if Tom and Jeannie remain unrecognized, we are still invading their secret, intimate space. However, Gillooly's strategies go beyond excluding information that might identify her subjects. She also refuses to share with us any visual representation of Tom and Jeannie. Gillooly did have access to some images of Tom or Jeannie, mainly in the form of photographic slides that were also found in the suitcase. Yet, the film includes only fragments of these images so that we never actually see what Tom and Jeannie look like. Instead, we see a shoulder, an ankle, the top of a head revealing a swath of red hair, a hand holding a glass (figure 3). Although we hear a great deal, our voyeuristic desire to see—or at least to see clearly—is thwarted.

Michel Chion, following Pierre Schaeffer, defines "acousmatic listening" as "a situation wherein one hears the sound without seeing its cause."[43] In *Suitcase*, we find ourselves in this situation, listening to Tom and Jeannie but unable to see them. This is partially a function of the recordings themselves—for which there is no synchronous visual counterpart—and partly a function of Gillooly's refusal to show the entirety of the photographs in her possession. Instead, our look is often diverted to the playback apparatus itself. In these images, the image is "de-acousmatized," as Chion puts it, but the source revealed is the reel-to-reel tapes, not the speaking bodies we imagine as the source, the bodies that we—simply by virtue of hearing their voices—

desire to see. Whereas in *Ghost of Yesterday* we are given partial figures that evoke a desire to see more, the figures of the speaking subjects in *Suitcase* are "visible" only in our imaginations. Chion refers to Merleau-Ponty's definition of the "phantom" in defining his concept of the *acousmêtre,* the acousmatic character who functions as "phantom" character.[44] Although Chion focused primarily on characters in fiction film, Tom and Jeannie in *Suitcase* also function as acousmêtres, figures we long to see but who remain immaterial, invisible phantoms. Like the subjects in *Ghost of Yesterday*, they hover just beyond our full perceptual reach. Gillooly's film, then, activates an "occluded gaze" and performs an ethics of occlusion.

Moreover, the justification for the trespass in *Suitcase* lies also in the transformation of its appropriated recordings into metonyms for the wider historical and cultural moments in which they were produced. Krista Ratcliffe suggests that eavesdropping

> may offer an effective rhetorical tactic: standing outside, in an uncomfortable spot, on the border of knowing and not knowing, granting others the inside position, listening to learn. Through such a composite definition, eavesdropping becomes not a gendered busybodiness but a rhetorical tactic of purposely positioning oneself on the edge of one's own knowing so as to overhear and learn from others.[45]

*Suitcase* positions us at this border of knowing and not knowing, offering us the possibility of learning not just about others but also from others. Gillooly has suggested that Tom and Jeannie's story is not unique but represents many other liaisons that occurred behind closed doors during the 1960s. She notes: "I want to protect their anonymity, but I also don't feel that knowing the details of where they were from is important. I believe the film is much stronger for your not knowing—*Suitcase* represents a way of life that was hardly exclusive to Tom and Jeannie or to any particular American location."[46] Tom and Jeannie become metonymic representatives of similar hidden experiences during a particular era of American history. Moreover, beyond their voices, the ambient sound on their recordings also generates a sense of the particular space and time in which Tom and Jeannie lived. We hear the sound of the Miss America Pageant on television, which Jeannie included on one of her tapes. We catch the snippets of dogs barking and secretaries querying in the background of a few of Tom's tapes, some of which were recorded at his veterinary practice. Often, we can hear someone speaking on the radio or a record playing music. The larger historical space beyond Tom and Jeannie's hermetic relationship emerges through the ambient sounds captured incidentally or intentionally.

Furthermore, Gillooly does not reenact Tom and Jeannie's story in any literal sort of way on the image track. Instead—in addition to the occluded images of Tom and Jeannie, and of the suitcase, the audio cases, and the turning audio reels themselves—Gillooly inserts evocative images of the façades of typical middle-class American homes, a lighted window on a dark night, an empty street corner from above, a dark room with light coming through a door that is open just a crack, the lights of a passing car. These images produce an affective substitution that further suggests that Tom and Jeannie's situation was not exceptional. What we are seeing is the evocation of a context. The façades of multiple homes suggest the complex private relationships that continue to occur behind those walls, the unrecorded secrets of which we will never know. Thus, the film's metonymic representation of an otherwise undocumented aspect of a particular kind of experience at a particular moment in American life acts as at least partial justification for the ethical transgression.

Because of the secret, romantic, and sexual nature of its appropriated recordings, *Suitcase* treads an ethical line. However, Gillooly's editing strategies are, at least, not entirely complicit with the voyeuristic exploitation that may make a work of audiovisual appropriation become demeaning, ethically intolerable gossip. The film's ethics of occlusion denies our most prurient desires, allowing us only to eavesdrop, never to see clearly. Yet, even if eavesdropping generates less of a sense of ethical transgression than peeping, it is still treacherous territory. In other words, visual occlusion does not automatically entail an ethical stance.

## The Disclosing Gaze

In the preceding examples, the appropriated recordings were produced either by the subjects themselves or by people with whom they were intimately acquainted. In every case, the subjects knew they were being recorded. Hence, there was nothing unethical in the *production* of the original recordings vis-à-vis the recorded subjects; questions of ethics arise only in the act of appropriation. A related but distinct set of ethical questions arises when intimate recordings produced *without* the subjects' knowledge or consent are appropriated.

The "Shut Up, Little Man!" phenomenon originated as a series of "audio vérité" recordings of two argumentative elderly alcoholics, Peter J. Haskett and Raymond Huffman, who lived in the Lower Haight district of San Francisco along with a man named Tony Newton. The recordings were made by two young men in their early twenties, "Eddie Lee Sausage" and "Mitchell D," who moved into an apartment in 1987 and discovered that their next-door neighbors, Haskett and Huffman, argued nearly constantly and—according to Eddie and Mitch—threatened their neighbors when asked to quiet down. Eddie and Mitch began tape recording the arguments and, soon after, distributing copies among their friends. These tapes were copied and further circulated. Then, in 1992, Seymour Glass at *Bananafish* magazine arranged for a commercial release of the tapes, which developed a cult following. Audiophiles collected and memorized these recordings.[47] Numerous artists began using the recordings either as inspiration or as actual material in their works.[48]

The recordings of Haskett and Huffman are not "intimate" in the same way as those in *Suitcase of Love and Shame* in that there is no overt sexual content, and there is nothing that seems specifically secret in the recordings. Nor do they seem to embody someone's precious family memories like the home movies used in *Ghost of Yesterday*. Instead, these recordings feel "intimate" mainly because the subjects were inside their home and were mostly unaware of being overheard or recorded. Huffman and Haskett usually seem to be drunk, barely in control of themselves, clearly not presenting themselves in the best light. They are entirely immersed in their violent and vitriolic relationship with one another. For instance, on one tape we hear the following, which is typical of how Haskett and Huffman speak to one another:

HASKETT Where are the checks I wrote you for the rent? I want them.
HUFFMAN None of your fuckin' business.
HASKETT Uh, they are no good. There is no rent paid.
HUFFMAN I catch you touchin' my fuckin' shit and so help me . . .
HASKETT Uh, there is no rent paid!
HUFFMAN I'll stick a fuckin' . . .
HASKETT Goodnight, sweet prince!
HUFFMAN I'll stick a fuckin' . . .
HASKETT Oh, shut up! You said you'd be quiet then do it! You wanna stick me with that fork? You get back in there.

This is typical of all of the tapes. There is no private or secret information conveyed. Haskett and Huffman argue about food or the rent or other domestic issues, but the topics themselves are banal; only the tone and (sometimes) the originality of the insults and threats are remarkable. So, it is not the specific content of these recordings that makes them intimate but rather the domestic location and psychically unguarded state of the subjects at the moment of surreptitious recording. (There is one tape that indicates that Huffman did know that the neighbors were recording them at that moment, and he does not seem to care. However, he was likely drunk and, regardless, this does not constitute consent.) They therefore solicit what I will call an "illicit gaze" (or ear).

The "illicit" suggests the illegal, but it also connotes the unlicensed, that for which permission has not been given.[49] Whether or not the production of the "Shut Up, Little Man!" recordings was illegal is unclear, given that the voices did carry beyond the confines of Haskett and Huffman's domestic space. But even if it was legal, it was still illicit in that permission was never granted. Eddie and Mitch have stated that they made the recordings because they feared for their own safety after they complained of the noise and Huffman purportedly threatened to kill them. However, once the threat was gone and they decided to circulate the tapes, this justification became irrelevant. Haskett, Huffman, and Newton at this point became objects of amusement, and even more so once these recordings were repurposed in other texts. While being amused is not necessarily unethical, being amused by someone else's abjection may be. Thus, the "Shut Up, Little Man!" recordings and their appropriation raise the question of whether surreptitiously produced recordings can be ethically reused and, if so, for what ends. One can argue that certain illicit, intimate recordings have historical or social value. William E. Jones's *Tearoom,* for instance, which appropriates police surveillance footage taken surreptitiously of gay men having sex in a men's public bathroom in Mansfield, Ohio in 1962 has been criticized for re-exploiting these men but also celebrated as a reclamation of queer history.[50] However, in contrast to the silent and serious *Tearoom,* the main purpose to which the illicit "Shut Up, Little Man!" recordings have been put appears to be comedic enjoyment.

Even if, as they claim, Eddie and Mitch first made the recordings because they were afraid of their neighbors and wanted evidence of their dangerous nature, when they began to entertain their friends with them, their supposedly "defensive gaze" immediately transformed into a "tourist gaze." Writing about IMAX films, Charles Acland notes that "the tourist gaze marks an access point to the formation of knowledge about otherness."[51] He further argues that this tourist gaze—whether implemented through actual or virtual travel—constitutes a "reinvestment of the forces of orientalism and colonization," emphasizing how many IMAX films recreate global structures of domination.[52] Although the "Shut Up, Little Man!" recordings could not be any more different from IMAX films in their lack of visual spectacle of any kind, they are perhaps their audio equivalent. In listening to the "Shut Up, Little Man" recordings, we are primed to anticipate "knowledge" about the subjects who are positioned as "others." Moreover, without their consent or even awareness, these others have been made sonically available to us for our auditory domination. Worse, this tourist gaze is that of the "poverty tourist" who uses "their privilege to indulge their curiosity about other people's misfortunes."[53] No matter how unsavory one may find these two men, taking pleasure in their verbal abuse of one another reveals the listener's relative privilege.

Mike Mitchell's appropriation of the recordings does nothing to undermine this tourist gaze; in fact, it exacerbates it. Mitchell produced a series of short films entitled "Shut Up Lil' Man!" featuring puppets whose actions were edited to match brief segments of the "Shut Up, Little Man!" recordings. The shorts are, visually and sonically, quite compelling. As with Tom and Jeannie's audio recordings, no recorded image exists to match the voices. Mitchell's film, however, acts to fill in this gap, allowing us to imagine Huffman, Haskett, and Newton as grumpy felt puppets, giving form and weight to the disembodied voices. In a video entitled "fork," for instance, we first see a puppet of a frowning old man sitting on a couch framed by a window. Another old man puppet appears as the handheld camera moves closer to the window. The puppets' mouth movements are then synched to the dialogue of the "Shut Up, Little Man!" recording quoted above. As the Huffman and Haskett puppets "speak" these lines, the camera cuts into the house where we see a series of shots of the puppets arguing, a close up of Huffman's plate, a shot of him lifting his fork as the Haskett puppet yells, "You wanna stick me with that fork?" We also see a puppet meant to be Newton in the background holding a liquor bottle, looking dazed as he watches the other puppets scream at one another.

Puppetry has been used in combination with appropriated actuality voice recordings in other instances. For instance, *It's Like That* (Southern Ladies Animation Group, 2003), a short film about children detained under the

Australian Migration Act of Mandatory Detention of Asylum Seekers combines puppetry with the recorded interviews of three children detained under this act. We hear the three unnamed children's accented English voices speaking but—in addition to hand-drawn animation illustrating their words—we see hand-knit puppets in the form of colorful birds, moving as if they were speaking the words we hear. They talk about the foods they like or do not like, their feelings of being trapped behind locked doors, their harrowing tales of leaving their countries, and their fears that they may never see certain family members again. As Annabelle Honess Roe has written of the film, "The innocence of the children is further expressed by the design of the soft, knitted puppets . . . [T]he absence of the body of the documentary subject can be seen as representative of their lack of power or control over their world."[54] In the case of *It's Like That,* puppets serve as a metaphoric substitute, emphasizing the vulnerability of the speaking subjects we cannot see. In contrast to the "Shut Up, Little Man!" tapes, these are not surreptitious recordings. They are appropriated from an ABC interview conducted over the phone by journalist Jacqueline Arias in 2002; the children knew they were being recorded. These recordings are personal but not private. Moreover, the gaze of the appropriationists reads as "humane" and "subjectively responsive," pointing to the injustice of keeping young children imprisoned for years simply because they did not have permission to enter a country. The somber music and the written dedication to the children and their families at the end of the film further emphasize the fact that this misuse of these children's voices was done with the intention of bringing public attention to their situation and thereby—hopefully—helping them.

Alongside their ethically suspect use of surreptitiously taken recordings, this sense of sympathy and advocacy is absent in Mitchell's "Shut Up Lil' Man!" shorts. Huffman, Haskett, and Newton serve primarily as objects of ridicule. The puppets look like Jim Henson's Muppets, which are generally associated with comedy. Moreover, the music and title framed by a curtain that opens each short is reminiscent of the opening to a *Looney Tunes* cartoon, further inviting a comic attitude toward these figures. The films do acknowledge the voyeuristic element of the recordings by sometimes shooting the puppets from outside a window so that we feel we are peeping in on them. However, in contrast to *Suitcase of Love and Shame,* the film does not seem so much critical of its own voyeurism as much as reveling in it. The shorts are undeniably funny. The clever combination of puppets, often linked to the innocence of childhood, with the foul language we hear on the soundtrack provides a surprising and hilarious juxtaposition. And if Mitchell had not used Haskett and Huffman's own voices, it probably would not be so funny since vocal reenactments would lack the unselfconscious spontaneity of the originals. The humor, however, is based on exploitation. The fact that Mitchell does not have access to Haskett and Huffman's images does allow them to remain—like Tom and Jeannie in *Suitcase of Love and Shame*—acousmatic phantoms. By necessity, their actual visages are occluded, the puppets substituting for their actual bodies, but this does not make Mitchell's appropriation ethical. First, the fact that the recordings were surreptitiously produced makes them already ethically suspect materials. Second, Mitchell, unlike Gillooly, did not choose to protect his subjects' privacy by hiding their faces; he simply did not have access to them. Finally, using intimate recordings for humorous ends does not justify the violation of Haskett and Huffman's intimate space. For these reasons, these shorts constitute a form of unethical gossip, by invading the subjects' privacy, trivializing their experiences, and demeaning them by disregarding their identities as actual human beings.

The degree of exploitation in both the circulation and appropriation of the "Shut Up Little Man!" recordings becomes increasingly apparent the more one learns about Haskett, Huffman, and Newton as well as Eddie and Mitch. Matthew Bate's 2011 documentary, *Shut Up Little Man!: An Audio Misadventure* provides the contextual information that is missing from appropriations such as the "Shut Up Lil' Man" shorts. Huffman, who died in 1992, and Haskett, who died in 1996, were alcoholics who lived in poverty and squalor for most of their lives. Eddie Lee Sausage and Mitchell D were privileged recent college graduates, who were hoping to "make it" in the entertainment industry when they moved in next door to Huffman and Haskett. While Eddie and Mitch essentially made a career out of the recordings, Huffman and Haskett continued to live—and died—in poverty. As documented in Bate's film, when several different groups were vying for the rights to make a movie based on the "Shut Up Little Man" tapes, Haskett was still living in near destitution. There is one existing videotape of Haskett, made by movie producer Henry Rosenthal, one of the people who wanted to make a film based on the "Shut Up Little Man!" recordings; the video was made as proof of the validity of Rosenthal's claim. Bate included this video in his documentary. In it, we see Haskett—astonished to find out that he has a cult following—sign away his rights to his own experiences for \$100. He does ask, "When do I sue?", suggesting that he understands that others have already made money off of him without his consent, but then says he is "too old" to care anymore. Later in Bate's film, which was filmed after both Haskett and Huffman died, we see Eddie and Mitch track down Newton (who spent three years in prison for assaulting Haskett after Huffman's death) and—with great effort—convince him to be interviewed by offering him money and beer. Newton is living in a single occupancy room, clearly one step away from homelessness.[55]

In contrast to Mike Mitchell's "Shut Up Lil' Man" shorts, Bate's documentary attempts to interrogate the ethics both of making the recordings and of listening to and appropriating them. In other words, the film examines not only the act of surreptitious recording and its illicit gaze but also the tourist gaze associated with the fans and appropriationists. In one scene, Bate asks Eddie and Mitch if they felt bad about making and circulating the recordings. The two defend themselves by saying that they never intended to make a career out of the recordings; it just "happened" to them. They refer to tracking down Haskett, trying to explain the tapes to him, offering him $200, and then feeling disappointed that Haskett would not accept it. Although Bate never explicitly condemns Eddie and Mitch, a montage at the end of the film clearly suggests a critique; images of homeless people on the streets of San Francisco—not far from where Haskett, Huffman, and Newton lived—are intercut with images of Eddie and Mitch with their respective families in their comfortable middle-class homes. Although it remains unspoken, the film clearly suggests that their middle-class lifestyle rests to a great extent on the fame Eddie and Mitch garnered from the "Shut Up, Little Man!" recordings.

Bate does not, however, rest the blame entirely on Eddie and Mitch. He also traces the fandom associated with "Shut Up, Little Man!" In the tapes, the gratuitously hateful phrases with which Huffman and Haskett address one another are exceedingly original. Yet, the almost orgasmic pleasure that audiophiles in Bate's documentary display as they listen to the recordings is frankly revolting when juxtaposed with accounts of the miserable lives these men actually lived. Their misery is precisely the source of the audiophiles' pleasure. Bate also asks various fans and appropriationists about whether they feel unethical about their "misuse" of Haskett and Huffman. Although they each admit to feeling a little bad, this did not stop them. Rosenthal, one of the people who tried to make a movie based on the tapes and videotaped Haskett in the process, argues that the unethical gesture lay in the recording itself, not the appropriations. He thereby lets himself off the hook.

Other artists take refuge in the notion that Haskett and Huffman's conversations reveal something essential about the "human condition." None of these justifications is wholly endorsed by Bate's film. Rather, by confronting the recordists, fans, and appropriationists with the reality of Haskett, Huffman, and Newton as actual people, Bate's film solicits a "responsible gaze" from both his interviewees and from the viewer. Like Gillooly, Bate asks us to take responsibility for our own acts of listening and looking.

Nevertheless, even as Bate raises these questions, his documentary participates in the further exploitation of the subjects, appropriating these recordings once again. In fact, in putting the actual faces to the voices of Haskett and Newton, his film potentially exacerbates the ethical violations it seeks to critique. The one thing that protected the "Shut Up, Little Man!" subjects to some small degree was the fact that, while we could hear them, we could not see them. This was probably due not to any ethical compunction on the part of Eddie and Mitch but rather to the limits of what the two could obtain without alerting their nonconsenting subjects. (As Bate's documentary shows, they did follow and photograph Huffman once at a liquor store while wearing disguises.) Yet, this limitation did serve to occlude their faces in the same way that Gillooly (albeit intentionally) occluded Tom and Jeannie's faces. Bate's inclusion of Rosenthal's video of Haskett as well as his participation when Eddie and Mitch track down Newton serves to expose these two people—whose voices had already been widely exploited—to the visual gaze of the camera. When we see and hear Haskett say "Shut up, little man!" in the same way we have heard it many times on the surreptitious recordings, there is an uncanny sense that he himself has become a puppet, his body inhabited by others' agendas. Haskett, Huffman, and Newton remained phantom acousmêtres—until Bate's documentary made them visible.

And yet, it is possible to instead read this "de-acousmatization" as an ethical gesture. When obsessive fan Doug Levy watches the video of Haskett saying "shut up little man," he first giggles with glee at seeing voice and body united at last. However, a moment later, his glee fades as he admits that he feels sorry for Haskett. In *Suitcase of Love and Shame*, it is Gillooly's occlusion of Tom and Jeannie that makes her appropriation seem respectful by allowing them to remain "phantoms." In the case of *An Audio Misadventure*, perhaps it is in no longer allowing Haskett and Newton to remain phantoms—by uniting voice and body to demonstrate that these were real people—that constitutes the ethical gesture of this film. Whereas *Suitcase of Love and Shame* performs an ethics of occlusion, *An Audio Misadventure* might be said to enact an ethics of disclosure, making us look at the actual human subjects whose disembodied voices had become a site of touristic exploitation.

The ethics of appropriating intimate recordings depends on a variety of factors, including the specific content of the recordings, the particular strategies the appropriationist uses in editing these recordings, and the actual effects produced for the viewer of the appropriation. I have here attempted to describe a range of different intimate recordings: private recordings seemingly intended for only a limited audience but not specifically concealed; explicit recordings of the body that show us something often considered literally obscene—not meant to be seen; secret recordings apparently meant to be kept from the eyes or ears of anyone outside a certain circle; and surreptitious recordings that exhibit a lack of awareness on the part of their subjects, who do not know they are being recorded. Regardless of their differences, the appropriation of such intimate recordings always involves an act of audiovisual trespass, but this does not necessarily mean that the appropriation is unethical. Over and above these original gazes, we also perceive (or project) a second gaze that is solicited from the viewer through the appropriationist's formal strategies of editing the appropriated recordings, and this—in its relation to the original—will largely determine the ethics of the appropriation.

Yet, while strategies of attentiveness, occlusion, and disclosure may mitigate the sense of ethical trespass, these strategies alone are not enough. Whenever intimate recordings of whatever sort are reused, we much ask ourselves what—if anything—justifies the trespass, what authorizes the appropriationist to reuse and the viewer to look. Our oft assumed "right to know" and the gratification of our curiosity or epistephilia are not enough unless, perhaps, a major public issue is at stake. Only if a sense of a shared humanity emerges—rather than simply the satisfaction of our curiosity about what happens in other people's homes, bedrooms, and medical labs—may the benefit of misusing intimate recordings outweigh the ethical cost.

# 2

# Speaking through Others

"You Won't Believe What Obama Says in This Video!" opens with an image of Barack Obama in suit and tie sitting next to a flag, looking and speaking into the camera.[1] Immediately, there is something about his voice that is slightly uncanny and disconcerting, but at first this feeling could easily be dismissed. However, the uncanny feeling grows as the content of Obama's speech becomes increasingly absurd. Obama begins:

> We're entering an era in which our enemies can make anyone say anything at any point in time, even if they would never say those things. So, for instance, they could have me say things like, I don't know: "Killmonger was right," or "Ben Carson is in the sunken place," or—how about this—simply "President Trump is a total and complete dipshit." Now see, I would never say these things, at least not in a public address, but someone else would. Someone like Jordan Peele.

At this point, the video switches to split screen and, as Obama continues to "speak" in the right-hand frame, comedian Jordan Peele appears in the left-hand frame speaking in synch with the image of Obama beside him. We realize that the voice we have been hearing and to which Obama's image has been synched is Peele's impersonation of Obama, not Obama's actual voice.

However, Obama's image has been digitally manipulated so that his lip movements appear to match Peele's words. "They" continue: "This is a dangerous time. Moving forward, we need to be more vigilant with what we trust from the internet. It's a time when we need to rely on trusted news sources." Here, by revealing the constructed nature of this voice/body combination—first through absurdity and then through visible demonstration—Peele offers a warning about the possibilities of contemporary technologies to allow one person to "speak through" another in perceptually convincing ways.[2]

Technologies that allow for this kind of audiovisual manipulation may be the most frightening form of such "speaking through." However, even without this level of digital manipulation, the widespread practice of sound and image appropriation in the digital era raises fears about the potential for misrepresentation. Even recordings that were made for public consumption can easily be recontextualized so that, for instance, previously dignified subjects suddenly appear ridiculous. This form of audiovisual appropriation may sometimes be "all in good fun," perhaps undermining dignity for the sake of comedy but not to the point of insult. In other instances, it may function in the tradition of satire, critiquing those in positions of power and revealing their flaws and hypocrisies in the service of desired social change. At other times, though, it may denigrate recorded subjects in misleading and exploitative ways, raising serious ethical questions about whose images and voices should be appropriated, how their images and voices may be ethically manipulated, and for what ends. Through the metaphor of ventriloquism, this chapter explores a range of video works that emphasize the manipulation of voice—in relation to imaged body—to articulate both the powerful critical potential of this form of misuse and its possible abuses.

## Appropriation as Ventriloquism

Ventriloquism, of course, is the art of "throwing one's voice" or making "voices appear to issue from elsewhere than their source."[3] Originally a religious practice, it later became a form of entertainment, often utilizing dolls or dummies that appeared to speak and eventually becoming a primarily comedic form. Sometimes—like the Peele video described above—works of audiovisual appropriation almost literally ventriloquize, actually substituting another voice for the voice of the recorded subject we see. The popular online series of Bad Lip Reading videos, in which a voice speaking nonsense is convincingly dubbed over an unaltered image to match the subject's lip movements, is another example of this type of ventriloquism. Other instances of audiovisual appropriation ventriloquize in a more clearly figurative fashion, the appropriationist's "voice" coming through the re-editing or manipulation of—rather than the replacement of—the subject's own voice. This type of ventriloquism is exemplified, for instance, by videos in which a politician's actual words are rearranged to make him or her say something other than what he or she originally said. However, ventriloquism is still an apt metaphor for this type of audiovisual appropriation, which does allow the appropriationist to "speak through" another's voice and body.

In his study of ventriloquism, Steven Connor theorizes what he calls the "vocalic body," an illusory body that is brought into being through voice.[4] A simple example of this is a sock puppet that is made to "speak" and suddenly seems like an animate being. A more elaborate case is, of course, the ventriloquist's dummy. Connor writes:

> So strong is the embodying power of the voice, that this process occurs not only in the case of voices that seem separated from their obvious or natural sources, but also in voices, or patterned vocal inflections, or postures, that have a clearly identifiable source, but seem in various ways excessive to that source. This voice then conjures for itself a different kind of body; an imaginary body which may contradict, compete with, replace, or even reshape the actual visible body of the speaker.[5]

Certain works of audiovisual appropriation bring into being such vocalic bodies that contradict, compete with, replace, or reshape the visible bodies of the speakers, and this bringing into being may have a variety of ethical consequences. I refer to these as works of "archival ventriloquism," because they draw from an archive of recorded images and voices to perform their ventriloquial acts.[6]

Indeed, the production of vocalic bodies from recorded voices and images of actual subjects (who are rarely asked for their consent) is significantly more ethically fraught than the animation of a sock puppet or a wooden dummy. In works of archival ventriloquism, the actual people—in the form of their recorded bodies—become dummies in the hands of the appropriationist/ventriloquist. As Connor notes, "Ventriloquism has an active and a passive form, depending on whether it is thought of as the power to speak through others or as the experience of being spoken through by others."[7] This tension between the active and passive positions within the ventriloquist structure points to the ethical questions that come with "speaking through" another person's recorded image and/or voice. When recorded subjects become—to a degree—ventriloquist dummies, they are placed in the passive role Connor mentions; they lose control over their own voices as they are "spoken through." In some works of audiovisual appropriation, this is primarily a loss of control over signification through one's voice. In these cases, the subject is made to "say" something he or she never said, or—more precisely—to signify something he or she never signified. In other cases, the subject's voice is replaced or distorted; he or she loses control not simply of signification but of vocalization itself. In both cases, the subject also loses control over his or her image, but the primary focus is on the appropriationist's ability to control another person's speech and its meaning. And in both cases, new vocalic bodies are constituted—imaginary bodies that are nonetheless indexically related to the real bodies of the recorded subjects.

## The Playful Gaze, the Satirical Gaze, and the Denigrating Gaze

One of the main ends to which archival ventriloquism has been put is comedy. Henri Bergson's classic theory of laughter is useful in elucidating why archival ventriloquism is often so funny. His theory is dependent on a particular conception of life and living human beings as "elastic" or adaptable to new circumstances. He suggests that repetition is anathema to our notions about human beings as they are "supposed" to be. Because no situation is ever exactly like those that preceded it, human beings are required to be in a state of constant flux, never repeating themselves. However, Bergson notes, although they "should" be continually adapting to ceaseless new circumstances, human beings frequently do not adjust fully to each novel situation but, rather, respond habitually. For Bergson, this occasional inability to adapt to circumstance is the root of the comic. One of his primary examples is that of a person slipping and falling. It is the mismatch between the heterogeneous flow of life and the rigidity of human habit that frequently generates a comic effect. Bergson argues more specifically that the comic is often generated when a human being behaves in some way like a machine. By behaving in a habitual and therefore seemingly *mechanical* manner, a person may come to appear ridiculous because he or she does not adapt to a new situation. Bergson writes, "The attitudes, gestures and movements of the human body are laughable in exact proportion as that body reminds us of a mere machine."[8] He continues, "The truth is that a really living life should never repeat itself. Wherever there is repetition or complete similarity, we always suspect some mechanism at work behind the living . . . This deflection of life towards the mechanical is here the real cause of laughter."[9] When human behavior appears to be automatic, people appear to be like puppets or marionettes—or dummies. Because this undermines our sense of human beings as nonrepetitive and constantly adapting, such an appearance must be "corrected" by the socius, and Bergson sees laughter as the means of that corrective.

Although Bergson was writing about the comic in life, theater, and literature, his observations are particularly relevant to a discussion of any form of recorded media, which by definition is repeatable and precisely not-live. It is even more relevant when discussing works of audiovisual appropriation, which always entail at least two forms of repetition: the reproduction of the profilmic event on the recording and the reuse of the pre-existing recording in a new text.[10] Many such works are funny because the recorded subjects (precisely because they are recorded) cannot "adapt" to the new situation imposed upon them by the appropriationists' editing. Their recorded behavior remains the same despite the transformation of context engendered by the appropriationist. In this sense, they are transformed into mechanical figures—made to, for instance, speak nonsense, as in the case of Bad Lip Reading (subsequently discussed further).

In addition, comedy often involves incongruity—the juxtaposition of two things that conventionally do not belong together; however, as some theorists have noted, there must always also be a point of congruity between the two things for the juxtaposition to be funny. Neil Schaeffer suggests, "With incongruity we see two things which do not belong together, yet which we accept at least in this case as going together in some way. That is, when we notice something as incongruous, we also simultaneously understand it to be in some minor way congruous."[11] Meanwhile, as Paul Arthur has noted, "Found footage collage is . . . by definition a dialogical operation, piecing two (or more) enunciative agents against each other."[12] Because of the dialogical nature not only of found footage collage but of all forms of audiovisual appropriation, the combination of multiple enunciative agents holds the potential for producing the unexpected congruities within incongruity that may produce humor. As we shall see, the pleasure of archival ventriloquism, in particular, often turns on this tension between the congruous and incongruous.

Many comedic appropriations solicit what I refer to as a "playful gaze." I draw on Johan Huizinga's foundational definition of "play," which he suggests is a "free activity standing quite consciously outside 'ordinary' life as being 'not serious' . . . an activity connected with no material interest, and no profit can be gained by it."[13] As a mode that is "not serious" and uninterested in material interest or profit, the "playful" audiovisual appropriation suggests a delight in manipulating sound, image, and/or meaning but does not entail an argument nor aim to influence the viewer's perspective in any particular way. Such appropriations pursue comedy as an end in itself. This does not mean that they cannot raise ethical issues; however, the intent is rarely to make a specific point, so their politics—if there is any—generally reads as unintended or unconscious.

In addition to comedy, archival ventriloquism has also—and often simultaneously—been used in the service of satire. Dating back to Greek and Roman times, satire is a form that uses ridicule to critique human wickedness or folly. Although often humorous, it is not the same as comedy. According to M. H. Abrams, satire "differs from the comic in that comedy evokes laughter mainly as an end in itself, while satire 'derides;' that is, it uses laughter as a weapon."[14] Archival ventriloquism has frequently been used as such a weapon, often producing a critique of the very subjects whose voices and images it appropriates. This may be the appeal of audiovisual appropriation for satire: the subjects appear to "hang themselves." This is not unique to the digital era. Emile de Antonio is a crucial precursor to contemporary practices of satirical appropriation, in particular in his use of footage of Richard Nixon in *Millhouse: A White Comedy* (1971). In this film, Nixon's speeches are viciously undermined by de Antonio's editing, which reveals the falsity of Nixon's assertions through juxtaposition with other footage that contradicts his words. Thus, because *Millhouse* uses footage of Nixon speaking to satirize Nixon, it could be considered an instance of archival satire. However, because it does not change Nixon's voice or alter what he said but, rather, juxtaposes his words with other materials to reveal the deceptiveness of what he is saying, it does not precisely coincide with my definition of archival ventriloquism. Nonetheless, certain examples of archival ventriloquism perform—or at least aspire to perform—a similar form of satirical political critique.

Some exuberant theorists have wholeheartedly endorsed audiovisual appropriation (or "remix") as a progressive, critical form because it comments on existing media. Byron Russell, for instance, writes "the power and purpose of remix can be seen in greatest relief embodied by the activist artist, waging a war of ideas against an overwhelming opponent, using the power of media to redress injustice, intolerance, and the hegemony of discourse."[15] Although this utopian view of audiovisual appropriation has merit in many instances, Russell implies that all "critical remixes" serve the cause of social justice—which suggests the ethical stance often associated with satire. However, "critical" is a slippery concept. Lisa Colletta distinguishes between postmodern irony, which self-referentially winks at the viewer but suggests that the notion of effecting any real change is naïve, and satire, which she notes is a more optimistic mode. She writes, "Not only does satire depend upon a stable set of values from which to judge behavior, it also rests upon engagement, the satirist and the viewer need to feel that something could possibly change."[16] While most audiovisual appropriations depend to some degree on irony—the awareness of a double meaning that inheres in the experience of "misuse"—not all share the progressive aim of satire. Hence, this difference between a complacent irony that mocks without seeking to enact change and an activist satire may help distinguish some of the ethical valences of different acts of audiovisual appropriation. Moreover, beyond the evidence of a productive critique, another important factor in the ethical evaluation of a work of audiovisual appropriation has to do with the target of critique. When a public and powerful figure like a United States President is ventriloquized, this act can often be read as "speaking truth to power" in some way. When the "dummy" is a private individual without any particular economic or political power, however, the ethical justification for the ventriloquist gesture is less clear.

Indeed, some instances of archival ventriloquism are quite difficult to read as either innocent play or as satire. When the target—of laughter and/or critique—is someone who holds less social or political power than the appropriationist (and perhaps the viewer), the act of appropriation can feel like an exploitation of the subject, who may actually suffer material consequences as a result of his or her image or voice being appropriated. This exploitation is further exacerbated when the appropriationist also willfully misrepresents the appropriated subject, distorting facts and misleading the viewer.

Problematically, ethical questions may be obscured by the very fact that many works of archival ventriloquism are experienced—at least by a large number of viewers—as funny. When we find ourselves laughing, it is easy to dismiss questions of ethics. Yet our laughter does not guarantee that the work at hand is ethical. On the contrary, laughter generally offers the viewer a position of superiority or distance vis-à-vis the appropriated subject, which lends itself to the deprecation of others. Bergson notes that comedy may occur only inside a social group within which certain norms have been established. He writes, "Our laughter is always the laughter of a group. . . . However spontaneous it seems, laughter always implies a kind of secret freemasonry, or even complicity, with other laughers, real or imaginary."[17] While such laughter at and with a given work of audiovisual appropriation may sometimes constitute a benign joke or a productive satire, this very much depends on the power dynamics established between film subject, appropriationist, and audience. And this is true even when the work in question is not funny. Such appropriations, then, potentially solicit a "denigrating gaze" vis-à-vis the appropriated other that may be experienced as ethically intolerable. And the "denigrating gaze," with its etymological implications of "blackening," often involves a racial politics.[18]

## The Ethics of Archival Ventriloquism

When archival ventriloquism involves only the manipulation of signification, it alters not the subject's voice per se but the meaning of his or her recorded words in some way. In these cases, the subject's original words are made to signify something other than what he or she originally said. The voice still belongs to the subject, but the message belongs to the appropriationist. One of the major ways in which this may be accomplished is through what I call "verbal collage," which includes the subcategory of the "supercut." The "verbal collage" entails using fragments of synchronized image and speech but rearranging the words in some way in order to change their meaning. In the case of the "supercut," this is generally done by excising everything except one particular word, phrase, or type of phrase from one source or else collating multiple iterations of a word or phrase from multiple sources.

In more complex instances of verbal collage, words or phrases are rearranged to generate a message distinct from the original message.

Verbal collage has often been used to solicit a satirical gaze. "States of the Union—Bill Clinton" (1997) by Aaron Valdez is an early (and still analog) example of a "supercut,"[19] which was defined by technology writer Andy Baio as "obsessive-compulsive montages of video clips, meticulously isolating every instance of a single item, usually clichés, phrases, and other tropes."[20] This is not an entirely new practice; Tom McCormack traces it back to Joseph Cornell's *Rose Hobart* (1936), Bruce Conner's *A Movie* (1958), Dara Birnbaum's *Technology/Transformation: Wonder Woman* (1978–79), Mathias Muller's *Home Stories* (1990), and Christian Marclay's *Telephones* (1995).[21] However, it has become a staple of digital culture. Often, supercuts are relatively apolitical, made up of, say, every expletive uttered during a Quentin Tarantino film. Yet, when actuality footage is used, the supercut can become a political intervention and/or raise ethical questions about its "misuse." For instance, for "States of the Union—Bill Clinton," Valdez took a single State of the Union speech by Bill Clinton and cut out everything except the numbers.[22] We hear Clinton say,

> For two-hundred-nine years, fourteen million, twenty-four, thirty, five, twenty-seven, seven hundred, twenty, twenty-first, five, third, thirty-five, twenty-first, three-hundred-fifty-seven billion, ten, three, six, eleven, six, zero, four, four, two, three, twenty, ten, three-thousand, two-hundred-twenty thousand, fifteen hundred, one-hundred thousand, first, second and third, eighteen, two-hundred-and-forty, one-third, double, triple, single, hundreds, millions, millions, millions, first, first, first, first, first and foremost, second, two million, two, one, a thirteen, seventy, ninety, one hundred, twenty-two, thirty, two, four, three, five, thirty, five, ten, two, three, two, one, simply [long pause] zero.

This litany of numbers is followed by almost a minute of the audience clapping. The video is quite funny because we keep expecting these numbers to come with the nouns they modify. Instead, we get a list of numbers without objects so that it becomes a nonsensical list, ultimately signifying nothing.

This supercut predates the digital era by a few years, but another, more complex form of verbal collage goes back at least as far as Cliff Roth's 1988 video "The Reagans Speak Out on Drugs."[23] In this video, footage from

Ronald Reagan's "Speech to the Nation on the Campaign Against Drug Abuse," made on September 14, 1986, is re-edited so that the phrases are reordered and, together, form a message precisely opposite to that of the original. Ronald and Nancy Reagan seem to be endorsing the value of drugs. We hear Ronald say,

> From the early days of our administration, Nancy has been using marijuana on a daily basis and her personal observations and efforts have given us such dramatic insights that I wanted her to share them with you this evening.

Nancy then adds,

> For five years I've been traveling across the country, learning and listening, and one of the most hopeful signs I've seen is this new drug: crack. Every time I meet someone new I yearn to share the message that drugs open your eyes to life, to see it in the vivid colors that God gave us, as a precious gift to his children, to enjoy life to the fullest and to make it count.

When two of Ronald's phrases that were not originally contiguous are spliced together, the image track cuts to Nancy, and vice versa when Nancy is speaking, so that there are no visible jump cuts. The video ventriloquizes the Reagans, putting words in their mouths that they did say, but not in the order we hear them in Roth's video.

The humor in these two videos derives in part from the subjects' unexpected and apparent lack of control over their own signification. Following Bergson, there is a blurring between the flexible, fully agentic behavior we see as the human ideal and the way in which Clinton and the Reagans are manipulated by an outside force. They are transformed into dummies, who must speak the lines they have been given. In "States of the Union," the incongruity between the conviction with which Clinton delivers each number and the absence of actual content in his (imposed) speech adds to the hilarity. In the case of "The Reagans Speak Out on Drugs," at least for the viewer who has some knowledge of the Reagans and their campaign against drugs, the hilarity comes from the reversal of their message—and the absurd, incongruous description of the prim and conservative Nancy Reagan smoking marijuana and enjoying crack.

Yet, beyond the humor, there is a point to each of these videos. Valdez's editing emphasizes Clinton's focus on quantities. Clinton's own voice is made to reveal something latent about his politics. In other words, this video ventriloquizes the President in order to indicate how numbers function as a rhetorical device in political speech. Although it does not suggest any particular solution, "States of the Union—Bill Clinton" exposes something about political discourse, suggesting the need for a change of some kind, however unclear this suggestion may be. By its very form, the supercut is limited in its ability to generate critique, but its value lies in revealing latent tendencies. The critique in "The Reagans Speak Out" is more focused. The Reagans' War on Drugs has been criticized for incarcerating massive numbers of people and particularly targeting minorities while failing to reduce drug trafficking. In this video, the Reagans' words are turned against themselves and become, implicitly, a critique of the Reagan Administration's drug policies.

Hence, these two videos—which both provide a predigital model for many of the digital supercuts and verbal collages that have followed—constitute a form of archival ventriloquism that most viewers will likely find ethical. These are appropriations of public, political speech in the service of satirical critique. Clinton's State of the Union address and the Reagans' "Speech to the Nation" were both staged for the camera, and it is partly this staging that is also the target of (and fodder for) critique. The critique is also aimed at the subjects as political figures, not as individuals. Moreover, the editing is not deceptive. The jump cuts that occur throughout Clinton's litany of numbers make it impossible to think that he actually stood at a podium reciting a list of quantities. Likewise, for any viewer who knows who the Reagans were, it would be very difficult to believe that the Reagans actually spoke these lines as we hear them spoken in "The Reagans Speak Out on Drugs." Although the editing creates believable speech patterns, the video does not (nor does it strive to) convince us that Nancy Reagan really supported the widespread use of crack cocaine. The point of the video is to create a gap between what we hear the Reagans saying and what we know they actually said in the original. Thus, I would argue that, while one might disagree with the politics of these videos, at the level of rhetoric, target, and effects, they are ethically irreproachable.

Digital media, of course, has made producing this kind of verbal collage much easier. Footage of public figures is readily accessible, and home-computing software makes it simple to re-edit words and phrases into new orders. The sort of critique pioneered by Roth and Valdez continues, for instance, in Edo Wilkins's 2002 remix, "State of Union . . . Not Good." Here, we see then-President George W. Bush saying,

> During these last few months, I've been trained by Al-Qaeda. I am weak and materialistic. I've told Al-Qaeda and I've told the world, 'If it feels good, do it.' I hope you'll join me in expressing fear and selfishness. We will embrace tyranny and death as a cause and a creed. We can be summed up in one word: evil.[24]

Of course, any viewer who knows even the most basic facts about Bush will know that the footage of an actual speech has been edited to rearrange the order of Bush's words and put sentences in his mouth that he never spoke. As in "The Reagans Speak Out," to smooth over the temporal jumps, the image cuts away from Bush whenever two separate phrases are sutured together. Nevertheless, the editing is obvious and—combined with the comic absurdity of what Bush appears to be saying—it would be difficult to think he actually spoke the sentences we hear. Clearly, the target of critique is Bush, the "war on terror," and the effects of this war on America's vaunted "moral standing" in the world. And this is just one example of many politically oriented verbal collages made since digital media became widely accessible. In the past two decades, there has been an endless supply of this kind of video appearing on YouTube, which has become—among many other things—a venue for witty political satire. And as satire, the ethics of such verbal collages that visibly re-edit politicians' words generally appear unproblematic.

A somewhat more complex set of ethical problems is presented by "Palin's Breath" (2011), a short piece by Wreck and Salvage, a video art trio made up of Adam Quirk, Aaron Valdez (who made "States of the Union"), and Erik Nelson.[25] In this video, we see former Alaska Governor and former U.S. Vice-Presidential candidate Sarah Palin giving a speech responding to the 8 January 2011 shooting in Tucson, Arizona, in which Jared Lee Loughner shot U.S. Representative Gabrielle Giffords and eighteen others. Six people died, including nine-year-old Christina-Taylor Green. Palin received criticism in the wake of the attack for having earlier placed Giffords, among nineteen other Democrats, on her "targeted list," using images of crosshairs over their districts on her website. In an MSNBC interview that took place after Giffords's offices were vandalized (but before the Tucson shooting), Giffords herself implied that Palin's imagery had the potential to incite violence.[26] In the original version of the speech, Palin expresses sympathy for the victims of the shooting but also invokes the anti-Semitic term "blood libel" to describe the media's criticism of her target list and use of crosshair imagery.

In Wreck and Salvage's version of Palin's speech, however, all of Palin's actual words have been removed. What remains is a series of breaths and the sound of her lips smacking together. Instead of the content of her speech, our attention is rerouted to her body—her eyes, her lips, her teeth, her eyebrows—and her microexpressions. The video ends with Palin finally speaking, saying "Yes, may God—beep!—America!" with a brief image of color bars covering her mouth as the "beep" obscures the verb. Setting aside the brief line at the end, this video might be best characterized as a "nonverbal collage."

McCormack reads "Palin's Breath" as "a brief musical composition out of all the awkward pauses in Palin's crazed video response to the 2011 Arizona shootings."[27] Although there is something strangely musical in this video, I wish to read it in terms, rather, of ventriloquism. Like "States of the Union—Bill Clinton" and "The Reagans Speak Out on Drugs," this video is funny, but as several reviewers noted, it is also creepy.[28] Here, the tension between the indexical imagery of a living human body and the unnatural, mechanical motions imposed upon her by Wreck and Salvage's editing blurs the line between human and machine. Palin seems almost robotic. Returning to Bergson, one of the things being subverted here is precisely the "non-repetitive flow of life" as each of Palin's microexpressions is repeated without the interruption of words. Also relevant to "Palin's Breath" is Bergson's distinction between "gesture" and "action." Bergson has written,

> Instead of concentrating our attention on actions, comedy directs it rather to gestures. By gestures we here mean the attitudes, the movements and even the language by which a mental state expresses itself outwardly without any aim or profit, from no other cause than a kind of inner itching. Gesture, thus defined, is profoundly different from action. Action is intentional or, at any rate, conscious; gesture slips out unawares, it is automatic.[29]

Through Wreck and Salvage's editing, "Palin's Breath" emphasizes the involuntary aspects of Palin's facial movements, her gestures rather than her actions, thereby revealing the automatic tendencies that underlie all human behavior. Miriama Young suggests that "the piece demonstrates the power of the breath and other non-logos vocalisations to convey meaning and intent."[30] Indeed, through their isolation via Wreck and Salvage's editing, Palin's "breath and other non-logos vocalisations" reveal more than the conscious, intended message that Palin attempted to convey with her words.

Through Wreck and Salvage's misuse, a vocalic body is generated that is both nonverbal and intensely affective. Without the presence of her words, the affect that she is attempting to convey is foregrounded but also made to feel rehearsed and artificial. Given some knowledge of Palin's politics and her opposition to any restrictions whatsoever on gun ownership, audiences predisposed to dislike Palin may read this video as evidence of her hypocrisy. In contrast to *The Daily Show*, on which original host Jon Stewart pioneered the montage of multiple clips of politicians making completely contradictory political statements at different moments to reveal their insincerity, "Palin's Breath" achieves this exposure without words. Palin's bodily performance of "sadness" is implicitly contrasted with her unqualified support for gun culture and her active participation in the polarized politics that contributed to the Tucson shooting. Moreover, the video points not only to Palin's particular performance of politicized "grief" but also to the staged nature of all political speeches in which sentiment is used in the service of particular political agendas, even—or especially—after a horrible tragedy or crime. The vocalic body produced by Wreck and Salvage's editing exposes the inauthenticity of the original body and voice, as if Palin were already a ventriloquist's dummy even before the footage was appropriated.

In terms of its ethics, "Palin's Breath" is perhaps unfair to Palin. Editing the words out of anyone's speech will reveal the automatic tendencies of the body that underlie any spoken discourse. We all breathe and make mouth noises when we speak; we all express our emotions, however genuine, through a limited range of repeated gestures. Palin's own body is used as a weapon to undermine her dignity. One may also wonder whether her identity as a female politician made her easier to mock in this way, whether the same editing of a male politician would be so affectively loaded and, therefore, such excellent fodder for ridicule. Of course, Palin was and is a public figure who made this recorded appearance to further her political agenda. Before Wreck and Salvage made this video, she had already been widely criticized for her anti-Semitic (and nonsensical) reference to "blood libel" during this speech. Moreover, the target of this satire is, arguably, not just Palin but mediated politics more generally. The widespread use of real tragedy to further political agendas is revealed here through Palin's bodily performance. At the same time, because the verbal content of her original speech is absent in Wreck and Salvage's video, it is easy to simply watch it and laugh at Palin and her "stupid" expressions without actually engaging with the politics. Thus, "Palin's Breath" indicates the fine line between political satire and personal mockery.

Despite this fine line, all the verbal collages discussed thus far can be regarded as political satire, soliciting a "satirical gaze." Yet, there are other forms of verbal collage that do not so clearly fall into the category of political satire, for instance, the "musical verbal collage" that tends to solicit a purely "playful gaze." For instance, for "Barack Obama Singing 'Call Me Maybe' by Carly Jepsen" by YouTube artist baracksdubs, individual words were culled from many different actuality recordings of then-U.S. President Obama's speeches. They were chosen and then edited to match a pre-existing set of lyrics, and instrumentation was added, so that Obama appears to "sing" the lyrics of the pop song "Call Me Maybe." We see and hear Obama saying (or singing) "Hey, I just met you / And this is crazy / But here's my number / So call me maybe."[31] The editing is obvious because Obama's clothing and environment change from word to word. Yet, through this editing, the appropriationist makes Obama's words collectively signify something other than their original contextualized meanings.

"Obama Singing 'Call Me Maybe'" is funny, but it does not solicit a satirical gaze because there seems to be no critique. It feels more like an homage, suggesting that Obama is not only a powerful politician but also that he has the "aura" and "cool" of a pop star. There is no ethical issue because Obama is not being mocked or insulted, nor could anyone think that he actually sang "Call Me Maybe"—though it would hardly be a problem if he did. He is simply being made to "sing" a pre-existing song. The pleasure in the video is mainly in the incongruity between the hallowed office of the Presidency and the triviality of Jepsen's lyrics. I would therefore argue that it is the "playful gaze" that is at work. A very similar effect is achieved by many of baracksdubs other videos, which include, "Barack Obama Singing 'Hotline Bling' by Drake," "Barack Obama Singing 'Sexy and I Know It' by LMFAO," and "Barack Obama Singing 'Get Lucky' by Daft Punk (ft. Pharrell)." Although Obama was the first African American President of the United States, there does not seem to be a particular racial politics—conscious or unconscious—to any of these videos. Although there is something particularly incongruous about Obama singing a Carly Rae Jepsen song—as opposed to some of the other songs listed above—because he is an African American male and she is a Caucasian female, this racial and gender blurring seems to attest to Obama's ability to partially transcend such categories.

Yet the playful gaze is not always so ethically innocent, as we can see in the "Brian Williams Raps . . ." videos produced by Jimmy Fallon and the Tonight Show. Williams has been edited to rap Snoop Dogg's "Gin and Juice," Warren G's "Regulate," and Sir Mix-a-Lot's "Baby Got Back," among others, but my personal favorite is "Brian Williams Raps 'Rapper's Delight,'" the 1979 hit by the Sugarhill Gang. Like Obama in "Barack Obama Singing 'Call Me Maybe,'" we see Brian Williams in a variety of outfits and against a range of backgrounds speak one or two words per shot as he raps: "I said a hip hop / The hippie, the hippie / To the hip, hip hop, and you don't stop, a rock it / To the bang bang boogie, say, up jump the boogie / To the rhythm of the boogie, the beat . . ." Later on, African American newscaster Lester Holt joins the song, rapping: "Check it out / I'm the C-A-S-A, the N-O-V-A / And the rest is F-L-Y / You see I go by the code of the doctor of the mix / And these reasons I'll tell you why . . ." In the finale, the two rap together, speaking the same words simultaneously, ending with the lines "Everybody go Ho-tel, Mo-tel, Holiday Inn / Say if your girl starts actin' up / Then you take her friend."[32] As the video ends, they both look into the camera for several seconds in a seemingly seductive manner.

There is clearly a playful gaze at work here; however, this playfulness does not excuse the video from ethical interrogation. Beyond the Bergsonian subversion of the nonrepetitive flow of life (which is fundamental to all verbal collages), the humor of this video—and most of the other "Brian Williams Raps . . ." videos—derives from the fact that a very wealthy white man like Williams would be quite unlikely to ever write or sing such a song of his own inspiration or volition, rap having its origins among working-class African Americans. (And while Lester Holt is African American, he likewise performs a certain class status through his three-piece suits and expensive Robert Marc glasses.) As in the baracksdubs video, the mockery seems largely benign. Yet it does point to Williams's race and class privilege—which makes his singing of "Rapper's Delight" appear slightly ridiculous but also bestows on him a certain aura of "cool." In other words, like the baracksdubs videos, "Brian Williams Raps 'Rapper's Delight'" celebrates its subjects. However, in contrast to the baracksdubs videos, I would argue that a form of racial ventriloquism is at work. Rachel Hall defines racial ventriloquism as a practice in which "a particular black person appears in white imagery or is interpolated into white discourse to serve the communicative and representational needs of . . . white cultures."[33] This term, of course, brings to mind traditions of minstrelsy and blackface performance in which whites dressed up as African Americans. Moreover, the lyrics and music of the African American group The Sugarhill Gang are being appropriated into white discourse to serve the "communicative and representational needs of white cultures." Hence, although I do not find "Brian Williams Raps 'Rapper's Delight'" particularly offensive or unethical given that it uses publicly broadcasted footage of a powerful, public figure exclusively for humor, it does nonetheless invoke traditions of both minstrelsy and cultural appropriation.[34]

In all these examples, archival ventriloquism involves rearranging subjects' words in order to change their meanings. However, as noted, archival ventriloquism may also involve a different form of "speaking through," not simply transforming the signification and meaning of a subject's words but rather replacing the subject's voice entirely. I will refer to this form of ventriloquism as "mismatch," a term that registers both the synchrony and incongruity involved in the form. Mismatch is not always—or even usually—political. For instance, the previously mentioned Bad Lip Reading (BLR) is a series of online videos in which actual video footage from music videos, movies, news broadcasts, and other public media are dubbed with an alternate set of words that exactly match the speaker's lip movements, producing hilarious nonsense speech. In BLR videos, the appropriated subject becomes the dummy who is made to convincingly appear (at least perceptually) to say something other than what he or she actually said. For instance, in "Inauguration 2013: A Bad Lip Reading of Barack Obama's Inauguration," we see actuality footage of Obama giving his Oath of Office. However, instead of hearing Obama's actual Oath of Office, we hear nearly convincing imitations of an unseen Chief Justice John Roberts saying and a visible President Obama repeating: "I'm proud to say your mama took a Cosby sweater. Elvis Presley had sex appeal. Spaceman boogie. I'll brush on my sassy face. There's two different Einsteins. I enjoy makeup."[35] The image has not been manipulated or re-edited at all, but the voice has been replaced so that Roberts and Obama become conduits for another person's—utterly silly—words. Yet the nonsensical dialogue genuinely appears to match Obama's lip movements, and this implausible synchrony is what makes this video hilarious.

Along with Obama, BLR has also done readings of Michelle Bachman, Rick Perry, Donald Trump, and Ted Cruz—as well as many fiction films and NFL Broadcasts. The humor lies in the convincing production of a new vocalic body without editing the image. Indeed, mismatch is often funny precisely because of the production of a new, perceptually convincing but still unbelievable vocalic body. Mats Carlsson reads a politics into BLR, stating that

> while our ears are being filled with a stream of rantings from somewhere beyond the actual footage, we get to focus on the field of the visual; the isolated body, not the body endowed with the full symbolic authority of a president but a castrated rendition; the nullity of man exposed, the gap between symbolic power and its pathetic human occupant laid bare in front of us.[36]

Mismatch does often have the effect of undermining symbolic power by emphasizing the speaker's bodily movements, drawing our attention back to the materiality, vulnerability, and absurdity of the human body. However, aside from a sense of the farcical nature of political discourse generally, there is usually no particular critique in BLR videos. Moreover, ethical issues in BLR are offset by the exclusive use of public, political, or fictional materials. BLR videos can therefore be considered examples of mismatch whose effects are more playful and comedic than satirical, and they do not tend to denigrate even as they make fun of their subjects. Yet, depending on the sets of materials being matched, mismatch can raise more pressing questions of ethics.

Produced by a YouTube user known as FuntToob, "Hitler Sings The Jeffersons Theme" combines re-edited footage from one of Adolph Hitler's speeches taken from *The Triumph of the Will* (Leni Riefenstahl, 1935) with the theme song of *The Jeffersons*, a U.S. television show about an upwardly mobile African American family which aired on CBS between 1975 and 1985.[37] The video begins with an image of the Nazi flag hanging before a packed audience, followed by a man who solemnly introduces "Die Fuhrer." Next, Hitler comes to the podium, but just at the moment we expect him to begin a nationalistic tirade, we hear a few notes on the piano. Instead of starting an anti-Semitic rant, Hitler instead begins to sing the song "Movin' on Up" in the voice of African American singer/actress Ja'net DuBois, accompanied by a gospel choir—a combination of body and voice that is clearly constructed and, yet, perceptually convincing.[38]

There have been many Internet videos that re-edit footage of Hitler and add a variety of soundtracks, many of which are quite funny.[39] The hilarity of this one, however, stands out for several reasons. First of all, *The Triumph of the Will* and the Nuremberg rally Riefenstahl's film documents were carefully choreographed texts, designed to emphasize Hitler's power through elaborate ceremony. Bergson notes, "Any image . . . suggestive of the notion of society disguising itself, or a social masquerade, so to speak, will be laughable . . . the ceremonial side of life must, therefore, always include a latent comic element, which is only waiting for an opportunity to burst into full view."[40] Once Hitler's words are replaced with music, the "social masquerade" of the Nazi rally is exposed. Second, Hitler is well known for his dramatic physical mannerisms during his speeches. When they are divorced from his actual words, they appear particularly ridiculous, already making him look more like a spastic puppet than an "elastic" human being fully in control of his own actions. The emphasis on his involuntary gestures, separated from his intentional speech acts, reveals his automatic bodily tendencies. Third, for those viewers familiar with *The Jeffersons*, the incongruity between Hitler, a notorious racist, singing a song celebrating the upward mobility of an African American family has a great potential for humor. Finally, what ultimately makes this video so brilliant is its points of perfect visual and thematic congruity. The filmmaker matches Hitler's most flamboyant gestures with the most dramatic moments of the song, so that his gestures seem to perfectly match the music and lyrics, recasting Hitler as a performative Black woman. Without these inspired matches, the video would still mock Hitler, but the matches generate the sense that—despite our knowledge to the contrary—he is really performing this song. In addition, the viewer who knows roughly what Hitler was saying will recognize that, in fact, the lyrics do reflect the overall content of his speech. The song begins, " Well we're movin' on up / To the east side / To a deluxe apartment in the sky / Movin' on up / To the east side / We finally got a piece of the pie." The "we" in Hitler's speech, of course, is not upwardly mobile African Americans in the 1970s but the German "Volk" in the 1930s, to whom he is promising a better life through his leadership. This play on the pronoun "we," which could refer to either group, further emphasizes both the congruity and incongruity of the combination of the images of Hitler with this particular song.

On the one hand, the ethics of this video vis-à-vis Hitler can be read as entirely unproblematic. Hitler was a public figure who held a great deal of power, and he is widely viewed as a mass murderer whose image and voice do not, therefore, deserve ethical treatment. As Calvin Pryluck notes, "If subjects by their own actions have abrogated a claim to humane consideration, then filmmakers have little ethical responsibility toward them."[41] Hitler clearly belongs among those who have abrogated their claim to ethical treatment. Moreover, his original Nuremberg speech—which was public, political speech—is widely regarded as propaganda. In other words, the original footage solicits a complicit gaze, intended to persuade the viewer to support Hitler's particular political agenda. To resynch this speech, then, reads as speaking back to power, soliciting a revelatory gaze that shatters the persuasive power of the propaganda (if it still has any), undermining any dignity that Hitler might once have had, as well as the validity of anything he had to say. It reads as a satirical send-up of Hitler for his racist ideology. Moreover, there is nothing misleading about this video. Throughout the video, most viewers will be aware that the synch is a false, imposed synch, a clear instance of mismatch.

On the other hand, "Hitler Sings" once again raises the issue of racial ventriloquism. While Hitler is the target of critique here, the use of Ja'net DuBois's voice has some troubling implications. Mismatch of this sort—using two pre-existing recordings and matching them, rather than adding an entirely new voice as in the case of Bad Lip Reading—involves a certain reversibility. Even if the dominant critique is aimed at Hitler, there is also an implicit—though possibly unintended—critique of *The Jeffersons* and perhaps of African American upward mobility more generally in the video. However unintentionally, African American middle class aspirations are equated with the aspirations of Germans under Nazism. Moreover, in synchronizing Hitler with an African American woman's voice, there is the suggestion that being aligned with an African American and female identity is inherently denigrating. While this video is hardly racist (or misogynist), like "Brian Williams Raps 'Rapper's Delight'" it makes use of an African American performance to illuminate whiteness. Of course, "Movin' on Up" is the theme song of a television show, a public performance that has become part of popular culture, and "Hitler Sings the Jeffersons Theme" is clearly a satire aimed at Hitler. I doubt many would find this video unethical (though someone did flag it on YouTube). And yet, the convergence of archival ventriloquism with racial ventriloquism is worth acknowledging as a troubling trend.

The problem of racial ventriloquism becomes significantly more pronounced in The Gregory Brothers' video "Dead Giveaway" (2013), which exemplifies a form of archival ventriloquism for which I use the term The Gregory Brothers themselves coined: "songification." The Gregory Brothers have produced numerous viral videos by digitally "AutoTuning" speakers—

in other words, turning their spoken words into sung words through computer manipulation. In "Dead Giveaway," we see the beginning of the original television news interview with Charles Ramsey—the man who discovered and freed a woman who had been held hostage by Ariel Castro in Cleveland, Ohio, for many years. Looking at Ramsey, we hear an off-screen newscaster say, "I'm talking with Charles Ramsey. He's a neighbor. Walk me through again what happened this afternoon." In response, Ramsey suddenly begins to sing—through AutoTuning—with background musical accompaniment:

> I knew something was wrong when a little pretty white girl ran into a Black man's arms / Dead giveaway, dead giveaway / My neighbor got big testicles cause we see this dude every day / We eat ribs with this dude, but we didn't have a clue / That that girl was in that house / She said: please help me get out! / Dead giveaway, dead giveaway . . .

The image track cuts between several different interviews with Ramsey and loops several times as the chorus repeats. "Dead Giveaway" ends with Ramsey giving a thumbs up to the camera.

Some of the humor of this video—and all of The Gregory Brothers' videos—lies in the obvious disparity between what we perceive as the original purpose of the interview—a spoken report on events that just occurred—and a highly processed and edited song complete with chorus repetitions. This transformation of news into catchy tune is funny in part because we understand that Ramsey is what The Gregory Brothers refer to as an "unintentional singer." In fact, Williams in "Brian Williams Raps . . ." and Hitler in FuntToob's video can also be referred to as "unintentional singers." And like verbal collage, "Dead Giveaway" appropriates the original subject's actual spoken words and voice. However, the ethics of this video are much more disturbing than any of the above. In all the previous examples, people who hold or held positions of power are made to speak, stutter, or sing. In "Dead Giveaway," we have a working-class African American man being made to sing by a group of successful white artists from Brooklyn. Beyond his "automation," an additional level of humor derives from Ramsey's vernacular speech and his disheveled appearance, particularly his unkempt hair. Donald Bogle notes the frequent deployment in Hollywood of the "Uncle Remus" stereotype. Bogle writes, "Harmless and congenial, he is a first cousin to the tom, yet he distinguishes himself by his quaint, naive, and comic philosophizing."[42] In this brief clip, Ramsay is neatly slotted into this pre-established stereotype, which certain audiences may be predisposed to find funny.

Of course, The Gregory Brothers usually take something that has already gone viral and simply add to the meme. They also generally share their profits with their subjects, whom they describe as their "lyricists" and "collaborators," which is certainly to their credit. Nevertheless, in this video, a working-class Black man's image and voice are "interpolated into white discourse" and, moreover, into a genre that serves exclusively to entertain. Although this was a public recording—a television interview—Ramsey was a private individual who happened to get caught up in a public event. One could argue that this video does generate a satirical effect: the line "I knew something was wrong when a pretty little white girl ran into a Black man's arms," repeated in each chorus, does point to the continued racism and segregation that makes this an unusual scenario. Despite his scruffy appearance and nonstandard grammar, Ramsey is offering an extremely telling diagnosis of the persistent racial divide within contemporary American culture. In this sense, one could read this video as taking a critical, satirical stance vis-à-vis a racist society in which a Black man is shocked that a white woman would run to him for help. However, such a satirical reading is subsumed by the way the speaker is coded as "poor" and "uneducated," the transformation of his speech into song, and especially the catchiness of the tune, which transforms this man into a comic and ridiculous figure. We are hardly encouraged to listen and think about the meaning of his words even as we cannot help but sing along. The sense of remove from the actual content of what Ramsey was saying created through songification suggests the distanciation Colletta associates with postmodern irony that places both ironist and viewer somehow "above it all," thereby devaluing the actual content of what is said.[43] As a result, Ramsey becomes an unwitting performer in a song and video that uses his image, voice, and speech to generate responses of "LOL" rather than a serious engagement with his experience or opinions. Like the "Shut Up Little Man!" recordings (discussed in Chapter 1), "Dead Giveaway" solicits a gaze aligned with that of the "poverty tourist." The viewer revels not simply in watching a speaker suddenly sing but—in this case—specifically in watching a poor, Black man sing.

This stands in contrast to many of The Gregory Brothers other videos in which powerful, public figures are songified. In "Obama Mixtape 1999," for instance, we see Obama speaking at a podium, but instead of giving a somber speech, he begins to "sing" through The Gregory Brothers' AutoTuning.

We hear him sing, "Our economy is growing like 1999 / The crime rate came down for the first time / For the first time / For the first time." Then we see Republican Senator Joni Ernst, who gave the Republican response to Obama's State of the Union Speech, also AutoTuned, singing, "I worked the morning biscuit line at Hardees / That's why you elected the Republican Party / The Republican Party / The Republican Party." Later, Obama sings, "I have no more campaigns because I won both / My agenda is the same since the day I swore oath / Since the day I swore oath / Since the day I swore oath."[44] Although the tune is not related to Prince's canonical song "1999," Obama's lyrics follow Prince's exhortation to "party like it's 1999." Like "Barack Obama Sings 'Call Me Maybe,'" this reads as an homage to Obama. The President is presented as the cool, singing President once again. After many of Obama's lines, we see various members of Congress nodding and clapping, edited to move with the music. In contrast, Joni Ernst is not only AutoTuned and edited to make illogical statements, but her movements are also looped to make her appear mechanical. Like Palin in "Palin's Breath," Ernst is made to look ridiculous. Obviously, this video favors Democrats over Republicans, but the salient point here is that these are public figures making political speeches. Regardless of whether they appear cool or absurd, this kind of public speech is fair game. Joni Ernst may look like a fool, but she is a U.S. Senator, who should expect this sort of thing. Charles Ramsey, in contrast, could have had no idea that he was going to become the center of a social media frenzy. Whereas we may laugh at Ernst (or even Obama) for being powerless dummies in the hands of The Gregory Brothers, outside of the text they are far from powerless. Ramsey, however, was only fleetingly famous for rescuing three women from captivity, and his identity is now preserved online primarily as a singing Uncle Remus.

These specters of racial ventriloquism and minstrelsy emerge even more sinisterly in another form of archival ventriloquism that transforms signification: conservative white commentator Andrew Breitbart's video of Shirley Sherrod, a former official at the U.S. Department of Agriculture (USDA) who is African American. This video takes the form of what I call "framing." Originally posted on the website BigGovernment.com, Breitbart's video appropriated an excerpt of a speech Sherrod made on March 27, 2010, to a Douglas, Georgia, chapter for the National Association for the Advancement of Colored People (NAACP). On the website, the video was titled *Video Proof: The NAACP Awards Racism—2010*. An opening series of titles reads, "On July 25, 2009, Agriculture Secretary Tom Vilsack appointed

Shirley Sherrod as Georgia Director of Rural Development . . . Ms. Sherrod admits that in her federally appointed position, overseeing over a billion dollars. . . . She discriminates against people due to their race." Next, we hear Sherrod describe a white farmer in economic trouble who came to her for help. She admits that she only helped him to a limited degree, in part because of her own family's history of racial violence at the hands of white people; whites lynched her father in 1965. At one point she says, "I was struggling with the fact that so many Black people have lost their farmland, and here I was faced with having to help a white person save their land. So, I didn't give him the full force of what I could do." Breitbart then juxtaposed this excerpted footage with footage of Geraldo interviewing NAACP Senior Vice President Hilary Shelton stating that he opposes racism within the ranks of the NAACP, following by a repetition of Sherrod saying she did not give the white farmer the "full force" of what she could do.

Breitbart's video was intended to "reveal" Black-against-white racism within the government, and the outrage directed at Sherrod in response to the video confirmed that this was how it was read. Even President of the NAACP, Ben Jealous, denounced her speech, and she was asked to resign from her USDA post.[45] However, the complete speech was soon released online, revealing that the excerpt was only the first part of Sherrod's story. As Shayla C. Nunnally has put it,

> As the news story developed, the actual travesty lay in the fact that the video snippet did not capture Sherrod's *full* speech. In fact, in the unedited, full video of Sherrod's speech, she actually challenged the NAACP audience to think about supporting justice for all, despite their personal discrimination experiences and misgivings about historical racial discrimination and mistreatment of peoples (by whites, in particular).[46]

In the full speech, Sherrod explains that she overcame her initial bias and ended up doing everything she could for the white farmer. Moreover, while the Breitbart video presented this story as if Sherrod was talking about something that happened while she was a USDA official, she was actually talking about an event that happened in 1986 when she worked for a non-profit organization.

All audiovisual appropriation involves decontextualization, so the act of taking an excerpt of a video clip "out of context" is not inherently unethical. Even a celebrated satirical film such as the aforementioned *Millhouse* by

Emile de Antonio could be construed as a form of "framing" because it takes Nixon's words "out of context" and juxtaposes them with other statements that make Nixon's statements appear mendacious. However, the difference lies in, first, the conspicuousness of the editing, and second, the intent to misrepresent meaning—which can be demonstrated by reference to the original, complete statement. Verbal collage involves excerption, but the excision from context is foregrounded and obvious. In contrast, the strategy of "framing"—with its associations both of placing a frame around an object and of blaming an innocent person—attempts to conceal its excerptions, thereby misrepresenting its subject and misleading its audience. Moreover, these excerptions are *significant* in the literal sense of altering signification, transforming *meaning*, not just our attitude toward a given statement. As the Sherrod case demonstrates, framing can make a subject appear to say almost the exact opposite of what she meant—without viewers being aware of this fact. While the reversal of meaning in the case of the verbal collages like "The Reagans Speak Out on Drugs" is obvious in both its editing and its absurdity, the reversal in Breitbart's video is achieved instead by omission and is therefore obscured. Like "Hitler Sings" and "Brian Williams Raps," this video can also be construed as a form of racial ventriloquism, but of a different order. Sherrod's body and voice were actively and disingenuously "interpolated into white discourse to serve the communicative and representational needs of white cultures." In this case, this "representational need" is evidence that racism against whites is just as much a problem as racism against Blacks, which would justify the obliteration of any policies intended to help Blacks in the continued struggle against structural racism. Moreover, Breitbart's video solicits a "denigrating gaze" in multiple senses of the word. It impugns Sherrod's character, and it makes her blackness (the root of the word "denigrate") the salient figure within the video in order construe her as an antiwhite racist.

Eventually, after seeing the complete video, the NAACP apologized to Sherrod, Secretary of Agriculture Tom Vilsack also apologized and offered Sherrod a new job, and even President Obama called to apologize and encourage her to return to the USDA. (Sherrod respectfully declined.) Despite Sherrod's vindication, the Breitbart video reveals the problematic ethics of certain forms of archival ventriloquism. First of all, this video cannot be justified as satire. Even if it pretends to call for a corrective (of Black government officials discriminating against whites), Breitbart knowingly constructed a false problem. Although the juxtaposition between Sherrod's excerpted speech and the NAACP condemnation of racism generates a most basic form of irony in the form of contradiction, this irony is also (deliberately) false. Instead of offering insight into a real issue, this work of audiovisual appropriation is designed to mislead without revealing its misrepresentation. Only after the fact in a separate text was the misrepresentation discovered and disseminated. Rather than satire aimed at correcting a problem, this is an instance—however well disguised—of racial ventriloquism, of a white man (mis)using a Black woman's body and voice to articulate his own views.

Another factor that makes this an unethical use of audiovisual appropriation is the fact that Sherrod, a minor figure on the Department of Agriculture, did not have the cultural capital to withstand this attack. Obama has frequently been a victim of a similar form of framing. For instance, in a campaign speech he gave on July 13, 2012 in Roanoke, Virginia, Obama said,

> Look, if you've been successful, you didn't get there on your own. You didn't get there on your own. I'm always struck by people who think, well, it must be because I was just so smart. There are a lot of smart people out there. It must be because I worked harder than everybody else. Let me tell you something—there are a whole bunch of hardworking people out there. If you were successful, somebody along the line gave you some help. There was a great teacher somewhere in your life. Somebody helped to create this unbelievable American system that we have that allowed you to thrive. Somebody invested in roads and bridges. If you've got a business—you didn't build that. Somebody else made that happen. The Internet didn't get invented on its own. Government research created the Internet so that all the companies could make money off the Internet. The point is, is that when we succeed, we succeed because of our individual initiative, but also because we do things together.[47]

This, too, is an excerpt from his longer speech, of course; however, specific phrases, including "If you've got a business—you didn't build that," were excerpted and replayed endlessly by conservative media to disingenuously suggest that Obama did not believe that people built their own businesses, rather than that government services and infrastructure helped support the building of those businesses. In his presidential campaign against Obama, Mitt Romney made particular use of framing strategies.

For instance, a television advertisement entitled "These Hands," paid for by the Romney Campaign, begins with a series of split screen images of a pickup truck, a middle-class home, a middle-aged white man identified in a title as "Jack Gilchrist, Owner," and a workshop identified as "Gilchrist Metal Working Company," over which we hear mellow guitar music and Obama saying,

> If you've been successful, you didn't get there on your own. You didn't get there on your own. I'm always struck by people who think well it must be cause I was just so smart. There are a lot of smart people out there. It must be because I worked harder than everybody else. Let me tell you something [. . .] If you've got a business, you didn't build that. Somebody else made that happen.

Then the video cuts to Gilchrist saying:

> My father's hands didn't build this company? My hands didn't build this company? My son's hands aren't building this company? Did someone else take out the loan on my father's house to finance the equipment? Did someone else make payroll every week and figure out where it's coming from? President Obama, you're killing us out here. Through hard work and a little luck, we built this business. Why are you demonizing us for it?

The advertisement continues in this vein, ending with a clip of a speech in which Romney denounces Obama's "attack" on entrepreneurs.[48]

This is another instance of framing because Obama's words are carefully and convincingly re-edited to alter their meaning. The ellipses in the Obama excerpt within the Romney ad are, of course, both invisible and inaudible. Indeed, if there is a punctuation mark most clearly associated with framing it is the (concealed) ellipsis. By excising—without indication—the sections in which Obama describes the ways teachers, roads, bridges, and government investment in the Internet contribute to the development of businesses, Romney's ad significantly transforms Obama's message into a debasement of hard work rather than an acknowledgment of social and governmental support for this work. Gilchrist's "response" is then based on this active misrepresentation of Obama's meaning. Like the Breitbart video, this appropriation is not satire, because it is based on an intentional misrepresentation of meaning—the critique has no actual target, only a concocted one.[49] In the end, this framing was perhaps damaging to Obama's campaign (although, of course, he did ultimately defeat Mitt Romney), but as sitting President, Obama could endure such maligning. Sherrod, however, could not and lost her reputation and her job (even if she was later offered a new position). While framing is fundamentally unethical in its intentional misrepresentation and deception, it becomes increasingly so the less power the target holds. At the same time, in the era of "fake news" and "alternative facts," this kind of framing even of public, political figures can have serious ramifications, allowing people to be elected under false premises. Thus, Mitt Romney's advertisement should also be regarded not only as unethical in its misleading editing but also as dangerous.

These examples illustrate how strategies of verbal collage, mismatch, songification, and framing can serve as forms of archival ventriloquism. When the target is a powerful figure and the change in meaning is obvious, this kind of audiovisual appropriation has the potential to constitute an innocuous amusement or a valuable political satire. However, when the target lacks power and/or the appropriation is designed to misrepresent and mislead, it may become ethically untenable. Worse, when these works of archival ventriloquism also take the form of racial ventriloquism, unequal relations of power become even more problematic. The Breitbart video of Shirley Sherrod is perhaps the worst-case scenario: it solicits a denigrating (racist) gaze against an individual with very limited power in the service of a lie. Whether or not one agrees with Breitbart's political views in general, his ethics in this case are indefensible.

## Ventriloquizing the Social "Unconscience": Natalie Bookchin's *Now he's out in public and everyone can see*

The limited length of the preceding examples—which is common to online videos—also limits the complexity of their rhetorical strategies. I now turn to a longer piece made for exhibition within an art gallery whose form allows for much more nuance and therefore deserves a more extensive unpacking in terms of both its effects and its ethics. Natalie Bookchin's video installation *Now he's out in public and everyone can see* (2012) can be considered a form of verbal collage and a work of archival ventriloquism. In this case, however, the ventriloquized subject is not a single, named individual but, rather, a group of anonymous individuals. Rather than an instance of racial ventriloquism, Bookchin's piece is ventriloquism about race—specifically about African American masculinity—and attests to the potential for archival ventriloquism to reveal discursive and ideological trends within contemporary culture.

*Now he's out in public and everyone can see* is a sixteen-minute, eighteen-channel loop designed to be displayed on monitors dispersed around a dark room. Clips of various men and women of different ages and ethnicities—all appropriated from YouTube video blogs, or vlogs—appear periodically on different monitors, speaking about various news stories involving prominent African American men. Yet, the specific names of the men are never mentioned, so it is up to the viewer to sort out the various stories as they are filtered through many perspectives. Through this chorus of voices, a complex kaleidoscope of contemporary views on African American masculinity emerges. Collectively, these videos attest to the continued discursive struggle taking place around blackness and masculinity. In drawing on YouTube video blogs, Bookchin's work also raises many questions about this relatively recent format through which anyone can send a virtual missive to an unknown and unspecified audience. Furthermore, it traces the limits of what different people understand as allowable speech about Black masculinity in contemporary culture as they are renegotiated and realigned by digital technology. By "speaking through" a variety of voices and bodies, Bookchin's work of archival ventriloquism constitutes a "cartographic gaze" that maps not the (endlessly mapped) Black male body but, rather, the discourses about that body.

Mark Anthony Neal has argued that what he refers to as "the 'legible' Black male body" is "continually recycled to serve the historical fictions of American culture."[50] He further notes that "the most 'legible' Black male body is often thought to be a criminal body and/or a body in need of policing and containment."[51] The trope of the Black "thug" circulates constantly in popular culture, becoming familiar and hence immediately legible through its repetition. What is striking about the four men we ultimately discover to be the topics of the YouTube vloggers' discourse—Barack Obama, Henry Louis Gates, Jr., Michael Jackson, and Tiger Woods—is the fact that they do not fit this model of legibility. Within Neal's framework, these four men possess "illegible" Black bodies that thwart our expectations, that refuse to be clearly Black. In the case of Obama, Gates, and Woods, this is partly rooted in their genetic heritage. Obama is the son of a white American mother and a Kenyan father. Although he explicitly identifies as African American, both his blackness and his Americanness have been challenged. Gates, although he also identifies as African American and has devoted his academic career to studying African and African American lives, revealed after he had his genome sequenced that he has more European ancestry than African. Meanwhile, Woods, who is often celebrated as the first African American golf champion, does not identify as African American but rather as a person of mixed race. And finally, Michael Jackson, although of African American heritage, bleached his skin so that he appeared increasingly white. Moreover, beyond their complex genetic and physical relationship to blackness, all of these men are (or were, in the case of the late Jackson) extremely affluent and successful. Although they all appear or once appeared physically Black, their achievements radically disrupt the widespread societal expectation that Black men are "thugs" in need of surveillance and containment. In fact, their illegibility seems to be one of the reasons that the YouTube vloggers feel compelled to speak about these men, whether to condemn them, defend them, or both. Even those who are sympathetic to these men are involved in a process of attempting to increase their legibility, thereby participating in the surveillance and disciplining of these Black male bodies. These men's involvement in public "scandals" opened the door to these attempts to reinscribe them as legible Black bodies—in other words, as criminals.

One common frustration the vloggers express is that their subjects cannot be easily and immediately known. Towards the beginning of the loop, one girl complains, "I don't know what race you are." "No one knows the first thing about him," adds a young man. "Even his name's a mystery," says another young woman. This short series of statements about an unidentified "he" and "him" all point to "his" illegibility. No one knows the first thing about him. Even his name is a mystery. And most disturbingly of all, his race is uncertain. Such articulations of "his" illegibility are then countered by a variety of attempts to make "him" legible.

In one section, legibility is explicitly tied to a faith in government documentation. Several men join together saying in unison, saying, "You gotta show your ID." A young white woman then commands, "State your full name and place of birth." "Why can't he produce his real birth certificate?" two people ask at once. "Here's my birth certificate," says an elderly white woman sitting in front of an American flag. "Where's yours?" "He may or may not have been born in the US," says another man, while yet another asserts emphatically that "he wasn't born in the US." A white man in sunglasses complains, "I don't see any proof." Some of the vloggers are clearly concerned in this section with then-President Barack Obama, who was famously accused of not being eligible to be President of the United States because he was—so claim his detractors—actually born in Kenya. However, the assertion that "you gotta show your ID" is likely a reference to Henry Louis Gates Jr., who refused to show his identification when police came to investigate him for breaking into what was, in fact, his own house. Regarding both cases, the vloggers' call for documentation reflects a desire to ground and stabilize identity in an officially sanctioned government document. The ID card or birth certificate seems to hold the promise of making legible identities that these vloggers find frustratingly obscure.

The vloggers then turn to quantification and neologism to attempt to fix "his" racial identity. "He's just as much white as Black." "He needs to be Black." "What type of Black man says that he is 56% white?" "According to him, he's more than 56% white." "50% of yourself is Black and 50% is white." "So he's more of a white guy. He even said so himself." Some of these are likely references to Obama, who has a white mother and a Black father. Others probably refer to Gates, who announced that genetically he is 56% white. Then a woman says, "He's not all Black. He's Caucoblasian." And a series of voices echoes, "He's Cablasian." These vloggers are clearly discussing Tiger Woods, who coined the term "Cablasian" for himself to reflect his combination of Caucasian, Asian, and Black heritage. Like the emphasis on documentation, this recourse to numbers and racial terminology indicate the vloggers' need to see race as determinable.

Yet, as Bookchin's piece demonstrates, it is not just their racially complex genetic heritage or physical appearance that upsets the vloggers. It is also their cosmopolitanism, which conflicts with dominant notions of Black masculinity tied to "the hood," to a fixed, local, and therefore to a more ostensibly "authentic" Black identity. As noted above, Obama, Gates, Woods, and Jackson all are/were very affluent men, Woods and Jackson particularly so. Meanwhile, Obama and Gates both have a great deal of cultural capital given their elite educations and high-ranking jobs in government and university, respectively. In one section of the piece, the vloggers emphasize the wealth of their subjects: "This dude, was comin' home—" "He came home in his

Escalade—" "Escalade" "Cadillac Escalade" "$80, 000 SUV" "He was driving a 2009 Cadillac SUV" "Driving his Escalade on his million-dollar-plus compound" "At 2:30 in the morning" "He comes home" "Trying to get into his house" "With his hired driver" "With his chauffeur" "His chauffeur" "Who also happens to be a Black man." Here, the vloggers slip between references to Woods and Gates. Woods's involvement in scandal began when he crashed his Escalade into a fire hydrant outside his house at 2:30 A.M. one night; it was later revealed to have been precipitated by an argument with his then-wife, Elin Nordegren, who had discovered that Woods had been unfaithful. When Gates, also late at night, found that the door to his house was jammed, he and his African American driver tried to get into the house another way. Regarding both Woods and Gates, the vloggers emphasize their privilege—the price of Woods's Escalade and home and the fact that Gates has a hired chauffeur. In addition to emphasizing "his" wealth, this focus on "his" car and driver implicitly gesture toward their mobility, "his" ability to go where he likes in his expensive vehicle or hired car.

The vloggers also focus on the fact that the four men in question precisely do not live in the "hood." "Now uh, he lives in . . ." "—let's pick a place like—" "Florida." "Bensonhurst." "Cambridge, Massachusetts." "Which is in like, you know, a suburb area up there." "We've seen it so many times, the brother with the suitcase who moved to the suburbs, don't want to give back to his people in the hood, he just abandons them." "You know, this is a very upscale, very nice neighborhood." "It's a nice neighborhood." "A predominantly white neighborhood." "Suburban, affluential [sic]." "A predominantly white neighborhood, if you will." "In a gated community." "In this Harvard house." "He's got an amusement park in front of his house." "What does he think, he's better than me and you?" . . . "You draw attention to yourself Black man, when you go living in all white neighborhoods, Black man." The vloggers' discourse in this section actively contributes to the policing of these men's identities, reinforcing the problematic notion that certain spaces are for white people only and that Black men must be immobilized within a particular location.

In his analysis of Jay-Z's career, Neal poses the question: "Can a nigga be cosmopolitan?"[52] Neal ultimately answers in the affirmative, suggesting that Jay-Z provides a model for a hip-hop cosmopolitanism. He writes, "A hip-hop cosmopolitanism is undergirded by desires for physical, social, and economic mobility, including . . . a mobility from or even within the essential tropes—playa, pimp, hustler, thug, nigga—that define contemporary mainstream hip-hop masculinities."[53] However, the acceptance of hip-hop cosmopolitanism does not appear to extend to a wider African American cosmopolitanism. The wealth, power, and mobility of Obama, Gates, Woods, and Jackson clearly generate some degree of resentment among the vloggers. Even those vloggers who we would assume not to be racist—for instance, those who appear to be African American—seem to want to fix these men's identities.

Indeed, a number of apparently African American vloggers seem to take genuine pleasure in metaphorically rescinding these men's cosmopolitan identities by opposing it to blackness. In a later section, the vloggers chorus continues: "There's a time and a place to show your blackness." "Now what a person does in their own personal life that's their business, but he messed up when he walked out that door. Now . . ." "—the metamorphosis started happening, right?" "If he wasn't never Black before—" "He, he, he, he's changing colors!" "—the motherfucker is Black as hell right now." "The blackness is coming out of him." "You Black now, honey." "He's Black now, goddammit." There seems to be a certain satisfaction that the vloggers—African American and otherwise—find in putting the Black man "back in his place." As Jacqueline Bell, in her excellent thesis on Bookchin's installation, points out, "the vloggers' descriptions of blackness both rely on and work against an understanding of race as biological . . . 'Color' is identified as changeable—celebrities were always visually identified as African American but only 'became' black . . . when the scandals erupted."[54] While the vloggers implicitly acknowledge the fluidity of blackness as a category, they simultaneously deploy the notion of blackness as part of an attempt to arrest their subjects' identities. In fact, the cosmopolitanism of Obama, Gates, Woods, and Jackson appears to be couched by the vloggers firmly within a discourse of borrowed privilege rather than earned identity. In this sense, the scandals—around Obama's birth certificate, Woods's altercation with his wife, Gates's arrest at his own home, and Jackson's rumored pedophilia—transformed illegible bodies that could not be easily read according to the established tropes of Black masculinity into legible Black bodies in need of renewed surveillance. The slightest hint of "scandal" opens the possibility that this mobile cosmopolitanism may be rescinded and that these men may be transformed back into legible Black men, immobilized both literally and metaphorically. The vloggers themselves thus become part of the surveillance apparatus that seeks to define the acceptable contours of Black masculinity.

Bookchin's piece as a whole, however, refuses to be complicit in this act of surveillance, toying with our own surveillant desires. By refusing to give us the names of the men under discussion, by mixing up the commentary so that we can only rarely be sure who is talking about whom, by editing the vloggers' speech in fragments, by having the vloggers speak simultaneously from multiple monitors, Bookchin reinscribes illegibility at multiple levels. While the vloggers try almost desperately to define and contain their subjects, Bookchin actively works to undo this containment. As she weaves together these multiple intersecting narratives, she returns to "him" his right not to be fully known.

In addition to raising questions about legibility, Bookchin's piece also explores the limits of what can be said about race in the digital era and how technologies such as digital video and video-sharing websites like YouTube allow for certain articulations that might otherwise not be made. While these technologies may be legitimately celebrated as a democratic development that allows more voices to be heard, when this speech becomes derogatory—or denigrating—the politics of these vlogs appears more fraught. In her analysis of Bookchin's installation, Erica Levin notes that, "What [the vloggers] share in common is the act of passing judgment on the public figures they discuss and dissect."[55] Unfortunately, this judgment often takes the form of racist statements that many of us would wish were no longer sayable. At one point in the video, numerous vloggers simultaneously state, "I'm not a racist." Then there is a pause followed by the word "but . . ." This phrase, when spoken within the context of a YouTube video blog, often indicates a double denial of responsibility. First, it denies responsibility for any racist content to follow. Second, because what is said to the video camera and posted on YouTube is not addressed to anyone in particular, it is therefore not responsible to any specific viewer or listener. Armed with this phrase and this technology that offers itself as a silent and implicitly sympathetic interlocutor, vloggers feel authorized to speak about and, more importantly, pass judgment on a variety of subjects. Some make explicitly racist statements: the blond white woman who states that "they have a completely different psychological makeup than we do . . . they're physically wired in a totally different way than we are"; the young white woman who quips, "What's the matter? Can't keep the black dragon in the pants?"; the man with a European accent who snaps, "Don't lie to me, boy!"; the heavyset older white man who says, "In the past, he would have been serving me coffee." These speakers seem to have no awareness that those viewing their vlogs might not share their views. The digital video camera and the video-sharing platform offer no resistance to any assertion. These are monologues, shared publicly, but with no apparent anticipation of debate or dialogue. Bookchin's loop, however, creates an alternative context for this literally irresponsible speech, most likely unanticipated by the vloggers. First of all, her installation offers us as viewers an opportunity to judge the vloggers as they pass judgment on Obama, Gates, Woods, and Jackson. Levin notes that "viewers are invited to respond in kind by finding ways to classify and situate each speaker within a larger social matrix: this one a tea partier, that one a Tiger Woods apologist or perhaps a Michael Jackson super-fan." Second, her installation creates the illusion of a polylogue rather than a monologue, at least gesturing toward the need for conversation rather than unfiltered pronouncements.

The ethics of Bookchin's appropriation are complex. This is not private speech in that the vloggers did put their videos onto YouTube, making them public and therefore opening themselves up to public scrutiny—just like their subjects. Yet, like Charles Ramsey, these are private individuals, not public figures in positions of power. Hence, Bookchin's misuse of their video posts cannot be read as political satire in the same way as can "States of the Union—Bill Clinton" or "The Reagans Speak Out on Drugs." It can, however, be read as a form of social critique, aimed not so much at the individuals whose voices, words, and images she appropriates but rather at the wider discourse on race refracted through these individuals. While we get brief glimpses of each speaker, their individual identities are largely submerged into the polyvocal chorus.

It is worth noting that this justification is similar to that claimed by Dominic Gagnon regarding his appropriation of YouTube videos of Inuit people for *of the North* (see Introduction). He argued that the videos were already online and therefore fair game and that his film was less about the individuals than it was about their acts of online self-representation. The greatest difference between *of the North* and *Now he's out in public and everyone can see*, however, has to do with the respective foci of the clips that Gagnon and Bookchin appropriate. Whereas Gagnon clearly searched for videos of a particular people and place (likely using terms like "Inuit," "Eskimo," or "north"), Bookchin was looking for *commentary* on specific Black public figures. Her video is organized around a set of discursive tendencies rather than an ethnic group or geographic locale. Gagnon's film solicits an objectifying ethnographic and potentially denigrating gaze vis-à-vis the unidentified Inuit people in the clips he appropriated. We are asked to judge not what these people have to say about a topic but, rather, their "way of life" as selectively presented by Gagnon's compilation and editing. Moreover, the viewer is placed in an outside, seemingly omniscient position. In contrast, although it is possible to read a denigrating gaze into Bookchin's piece—some of the speakers do appear naïve, vindictive, or just racist—the denigration does not seem to be aimed at the particular speakers who briefly flit by but rather at the naivety, vindictiveness, and racism of contemporary (online) discourse. What is being ventriloquized is not so much the vloggers themselves but, rather, the racist underbelly of our society, the social unconscious or—more precisely—the social "unconscience" that allows racist things to be thought and said aloud online. Moreover, while the video blogs seem to solicit a complicit gaze—in other words, an audience that simply accepts whatever is said—Bookchin's piece solicits a gaze that is not only cartographic but also dialectical. It is cartographic in that, although it does not aspire to the scope of big data analysis, it does map a wide range of views on Obama, Gates, Woods, and Jackson, offering a cross section of popular opinion. It is dialectical in the sense that by combining these divergent voices in a colloquy, it places the viewer in the position of negotiating and synthesizing the various positions articulated.

The ethics of archival ventriloquism stand to become even more complex with the rise of new technologies that (will soon) allow users to convincingly imitate a particular speaker's voice and vocal patterns. The Jordan Peele video discussed at the opening of this chapter demonstrates that we are already on the cusp of a whole new era of archival ventriloquism. In 2017, Supasorn Suwajanakorn, Steven M. Seitz, and Ira Kemelmacher-Shlizerman of the University of Washington published a paper entitled "Synthesizing Obama: Learning Lip Synch from Audio," alongside which they included the results of their synthesis, a video of Obama in which the image of the former president convincingly appears to match existing, unaltered audio; however, the image was, in fact, a computer-generated simulation.[56] The video image is perceptually convincing, and the content is not absurd; indeed, it matches an unaltered recording of something Obama actually did say. To the casual viewer, there would be no reason to suspect that this is a vocalic body onscreen rather than a recording of Obama's actual speaking body. The same year, a Canadian company also unveiled a new technology called Lyrebird, which can "clone" a voice based on only a minute of indexical audio recording of that voice. This development suggests that "artificial intelligence is making human speech as malleable and replicable as pixels."[57]

Adobe, Google, and Apple have been working on similar technologies. Hence, it is surely only a matter of time before it will be possible to use software to "ventriloquize" another person without any need for him or her to actually have said the words in question, combining synthesized voice recording and manipulated video recording to make videos that look and sound perfectly indexical when they are not. This suggests that problems of "framing," with its intentionally misleading misrepresentations, will become ever more frequent and perceptually convincing. And this means that ventriloquized subjects will have no more agency in the process than actual ventriloquist's dummies, "spoken through" as if their own voices, bodies, and acts of verbal signification no longer belong to them at all. Nevertheless, practices of archival ventriloquism—particularly when they do not obscure their constructed form—continue to serve a productive critical function, revealing latent tendencies about politics and society through voices that unwittingly contain their own undoing.

# 3

# Dislocating the Hegemonic Gaze

In April 2018, a white woman named Jennifer Schulte in Oakland, California called the police because two Black men were barbecuing some meat beside Lake Merritt. Bystander Michelle Snider took a video of Schulte calling the police, which soon went viral, leading Schulte to be dubbed "BBQ Becky" and mocked relentlessly online for calling the police on Black people doing nothing wrong.[1] In addition to the nickname, the incident inspired a series of memes in which the image of Schulte on her cellphone calling 911 is superimposed on a variety of images of Black people.[2] We see her inserted image standing behind Martin Luther King, Jr. as he gives his "I Have a Dream" speech on the Mall in Washington, sitting on the bus a few rows behind Rosa Parks, and watching Barack Obama's inauguration as U.S. President, among many others. Behind these hilarious memes, of course, is a serious critique of how white people like Schulte frequently call the police on Black people for simply carrying out their daily activities—sometimes with violent or even deadly results for innocent Black people. These memes are emphatically *not* fair to Schulte; but on the internet at least, there appears to be a sense that—by making this racist call—she opened herself up to this appropriation. Moreover, the critique, though it does appropriate her image, is arguably aimed less at Schulte per se than at the larger racist social structures of which BBQ Becky's 911 call was a symptom. What interests me here, however, is how the image of Schulte's *body* is placed within other contexts to produce this critique. The point of these memes is not only to mock BBQ Becky but also to use Schulte's now-familiar figure to renew our sense of both the radicalism of the Civil Rights movement and the need for continuing struggle. By interrupting known historical images associated with Black rights, her bodily image renews our recognition of how profound—and unlikely—these moments of resistance and achievement were, given the fact that even now, Black people are subjected to this kind of surveillance.

## Embodied Interruption

The previous chapters have examined ways in which certain instances of "misuse" may potentially violate the rights of those whose recorded voices and/or images are appropriated as well as of audiences who may be duped into misunderstanding. Although these issues remain relevant throughout this book, the next two chapters focus on instances in which misuse is employed for actively ethical ends. In particular, when the gaze solicited by the original recording is read as unethical in some way, the act of subverting its meaning and soliciting a critical gaze takes on an ethical valence. For instance, when a recording reads as soliciting a racist, sexist, homophobic, or otherwise discriminatory gaze, appropriation becomes a possible means of disruption of and resistance to this gaze. In her essay about audiovisual appropriation as a form of "ethical possession," Emma Cocker argues that "the appropriation and re-use of archival material by artists—often including unwanted remnants and discarded moments from the past—presents a potential disruption of the official order of knowledge in favour of counterhegemonic narratives capable of producing new (indeed dissenting or resistant) forms of cultural memory."[3] Hence, one of the main ways in which audiovisual appropriation has been used as an ethical tool has been in the service of interrupting hegemonic discourses that serve the interests of white, patriarchal, heteronormative capitalism while excluding subjects and discourses that do not fit into its dominant categories and narratives.

The Situationist practice of détournement, first theorized by Guy Debord and Gil Wolman in 1956 and practiced primarily in the 1960s, was explicitly a tactic of interrupting the flow of corporate or government media in order to undermine its authority. Jennifer Stob has outlined the specificity of détournement as opposed to audiovisual appropriation more generally. She notes that in détournement the "material removed and altered from its original context must communicate a stance in its new context—it cannot be neutral juxtaposition." The transformations of the original objects are "always explicit, so that the ulterior context of the material appropriated is either suspected or recognized." Moreover, "the original meaning of a particular object or expression is never purged, but rather sublated—contradicted, conserved and enriched in complexity."[4] She further describes détournement as a "subversive optic . . . comparable to a conceptual lens that disperses rather than converges perception within a scopic regime or apparatus, and restricts or unseats the power of vision."[5] She notes that Debord's films often refuse to communicate, undermining the very notion that the visual can convey "reality" in any way or even, perhaps, meaning of any kind. In other words, Debord's films focus primarily on the subversion of established meaning rather than the assertion—or at least the full endorsement—of a new one.

In the 1990s, several decades after Situationism lost its momentum, those who called themselves "culture jammers" continued a practice linked to détournement. Marilyn DeLaure and Moritz Fink have retrospectively defined some of the main characteristics of culture jamming, noting that its appropriations are generally artful, playful, anonymous, participatory, political, serial, and transgressive.[6] One of the attributes that sometimes distinguished 1990s culture jamming from détournement, however, was the emphasis on political critique through play or—in my terms—the solicitation of a playful gaze, even as a critical gaze is also invoked.[7] They write, "In confronting serious issues, culture jammers use humor, pranks, and carnivalesque inversions."[8] This is not to say that Situationist détournement was never funny but, rather, that culture jamming frequently and intentionally deployed humor to make its critique more accessible. In contemporary digital culture, culture jamming—which Mark Dery notes was a "subcultural backlash" against corporate consumer culture—has morphed into a much more widespread practice in which sounds and images are constantly appropriated for a variety of ends, not necessarily the progressive political ones favored in the 1990s. He has noted that digital culture may have rendered culture jamming either irrelevant or ineffectual.[9] Yet, he concludes, even in the digital era, the strategies of culture jamming "inspire us to update the Situationist tactic of 'using spectacular images and language to disrupt the flow of spectacle' (Debord), dreaming up ways to punch through the seamless surface of the matrix to expose the emptiness of its promise."[10] Thus, Dery suggests, culture jamming has continued relevance for progressive political causes—even if many of its strategies have been coopted at times by corporate or even fascist interests (see Chapter 5).

In this chapter, I want to argue that a series of recent films combine a Situationist "subversive optic" that seeks to "unseat the power of vision" and/or the culture jammers' playful transgressions with a practice to which I refer as "embodied interruption," in which the image and voice of the "othered" body undermines the unity and persuasive power of the original document. Of course, in common discourse, interruption is often viewed as an impediment to dialogue or narrative. However, when dialogue is impossible or narrative becomes ideologically calcified or communicative power is inequitable, interruption may become necessary to the production of an ethical discourse. Amit Pinchevski, drawing on Emmanuel Levinas, sees "interruption as bearing a special ethical significance: as a point of exposure and vulnerability upon which the relation with the Other may undergo a profound transformation."[11] Certain works of audiovisual appropriation that reuse existing sounds or images enact an interruption that may serve as such a "point of exposure and vulnerability." By interrupting the flow of one set of images or sounds with other sets, audiovisual appropriation may open a space in which otherness can be encountered without established preconception. Pinchevski also notes that "there is communication only when there is a moment, however, fleeting or minimal, of non-understanding, of disorientation, or even of stupidity with respect to what is said."[12] This moment may be so fleeting that we often do not even consciously acknowledge it.

Yet, in works of audiovisual appropriation, which often ask us to synthesize disparate sounds and images that have no immediately apparent connection, there is always a moment of incomprehension before we make sense of the misuse.[13] Indeed, some such works transform this moment of incomprehension into an opportunity for disrupting habitual ways of thinking about the "other." Pinchevski has written:

> The Other's interruption makes evident what is oppressed and denied by "innate" communal structures: the immanency of a relation transcending similarity and like-mindedness. Rather than having or working to have something in common, this community is realized in the approach and exposure to the foreign: the outcast, the mental patient, the immigrant, the Indian, the stranger, the enemy.[14]

The films discussed here literally and metaphorically interrupt dominant discourses, producing an encounter with iterations of the "foreign" in ways that reveal the rule of "like-mindedness." By interrupting established discourses literally and metaphorically, sonically and visually, spatially and temporally, these films call upon us to rethink the notions of audiovisual traces as "documents" that ostensibly form the basis of future social and historical knowledge. Moreover, by placing bodies that refuse to be reduced to a singular identity into times and spaces—or temporal and spatial structures—wherein they do not easily "fit," these films interrupt any comfortable epistemological relation between viewer and viewed. They not only cast doubt on signification but also solicit an intensely critical gaze vis-à-vis the original recording, which I refer to as a "dislocating gaze."

These films also actively open cracks in signification through which we are confronted with an experience of embodied difference. Indeed, the specificity of the videos discussed here lies in their use of strategies of détournement and culture jamming to reveal the exclusion of particular identities from mainstream discourses and to foreground what their inclusion might entail. They raise issues of how visible and audible bodies may transform our perception of represented time and space, creating hybrid temporalities and spatialities with powerful political implications. The rest of this chapter explores how strategies of embodied interruption in audiovisual appropriation may solicit a dislocating gaze and, as a result, reveal the exclusion from or distortion of minority bodies and identities within certain media spaces. In doing so, they have the potential to produce an ethical awareness of the "other" as present but also irreducible to self.

## Interrupting the White Gaze

Christopher Harris's short film *Halimuhfack* (2016) begins with the image of a Black woman wearing a black dress and red hat that suggest the fashions of the early twentieth century.[15] She is sitting in front of a screen on which we see what appears to be ethnographic footage of Maasai people dancing in traditional clothing (see figure 4). As the seated woman begins to speak, we hear the voice of a woman—who, we may learn from the program notes, is Zora Neale Hurston—answering a man's questions about her work learning, performing, and recording African American folk songs in the US South.[16] However, the lips of the visible speaker and Hurston's voice

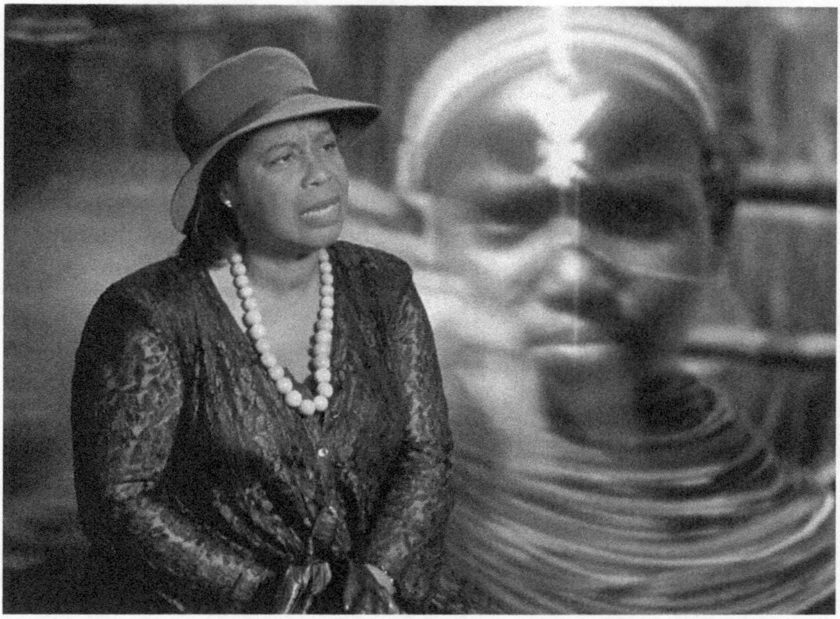

FIGURE 4 Still from *Halimuhfack* (Christopher Harris, 2016). Courtesy of the artist.

slip increasingly out of synch so that it quickly becomes clear that it is not Hurston we are seeing onscreen. After the short conversation with the interviewer, Hurston sings the song "Halimuhfack"; once the song is complete, the soundtrack begins to skip and repeat, distorting her words. The ethnographic images behind the lip-synch performer, which have been on a loop, begin to stutter. Soundtrack and image both break down until they become visually and sonically nonsensical. The film not only refuses to cohere into narrative but also moves increasingly toward incoherence, dislocating the viewer in relation to both time and space.

There are at least three distinct temporalities in effect in *Halimuhfack*. First, there is the temporality of the footage of the Maasai people performing a dance or ritual. Without annotation, this color footage reads as having likely been taken in the mid-twentieth century by white Western ethnographers intent on capturing the Maasai before they became "Westernized," part of the project of "salvage ethnography." The bodies of these filmmakers are notably absent in the footage, but their gaze is emphasized through the repetition of an image of one girl looking back at the camera. That these images are of the Maasai is particularly significant because, as Neal Sobania has explored in depth, the "othering" of the Maasai through visual representation has a long history. He has noted, "Everyone 'knows' the Maasai and Zulu—women in beads with breasts uncovered, in or around their 'primitive huts,' warriors with spears and shields dancing or charging across the open plains."[17] Thus, these images likely also generate a sense of familiarity for the viewer as stereotype. A second temporality is represented by the audio recording of Hurston speaking about her ethnographic documentation of African American songs during the 1930s. As Daphne A. Brooks has noted, this was part of Hurston's larger quest to "celebrate, cultivate, and make more audible to the masses the depth and complexities of Afro diasporic sonic cultures."[18] In the recording, we hear Hurston describe her insider/outsider participant-observer status as she incorporated African American songs into her own embodied inscription of this tradition. As Brooks further observed, Hurston used "embodied and sounded performance as a tool of ethnographic inscription, as an instrument that might put black voices on the (scholarly) record. . . . Her performance doubly inscribes the subjectivity of the black collective whose voices she preserves, as well as her own present, active independent reception."[19] Although Hurston's actual body is not visible in Harris's film, it is audible, demonstrating that her ethnography is not just a documentation of the ethnographic "other" but an embodied performance of that other's artistic practice. Finally, there is the temporality of the body of the performer, poet and author Valada Flewellyn, who lip-synchs to Hurston's words. The synch slips in and out without any effort to convince the viewer that this is Hurston's body onscreen. Indeed, Flewellyn's intentionally imperfect embodiment of Hurston is aligned with the present moment of the making of Harris's film, closer to—though not coincident with—our own moment of viewing. Flewellyn's visible body further accentuates the absence of Hurston's actual body—and of the bodies whose songs Hurston echoes.

Corresponding to this multiplicity of temporalities, a spatial layering is also at work, represented not only by the gap between Flewellyn's lip movements and Hurston's actual recorded voice but also by the gap between the impersonator and the rear projection that appears behind her. The gap between lips and voice gestures toward a form of intentionally flawed ventriloquism that indicates the inability of past and present to match up and make a coherent sense. Moreover, the rear projection creates a literally in-coherent space. Writing about narrative cinema, Laura Mulvey has stated, "Rear-projection's clumsy visibility seems to smuggle something of modernism into the mass medium of modernity, creating an unusual paradox, almost a clash of cultures, within a single space."[20] Although Mulvey indicates that she means "clash of cultures" metaphorically, *Halimuhfack* seems to literalize this clash of cultures, pointing to the gaps between Western culture and African cultures as well as between African and African American identity and even between the highly educated Hurston and her working-class subjects. Mulvey also notes that in Classical Hollywood film, "There is a further incompatibility, a further paradox, inherent to the rear-projection process. The location footage can seem especially 'realistic', almost like documentary film footage, when it intrudes into otherwise wholly-staged narrative dramas."[21] Similarly, in *Halimuhfack*, the footage of the Maasai tribe—contrasted with the obviously staged performance in the foreground—begins to align with the "real." Yet, this offer of the "real" is plagued by interruptions. As the footage is looped and plays over and over again, it loses something of its voyeuristic, ethnographic appeal in its very repetition. Moreover, as the speed of the looping increases, the footage itself grows increasingly grainy and hard to read. On top of that, the sound of Hurston's voice starts to loop so that the lyric "Who do? Who do? Who do working?" is transformed simply into "Hoodoo, hoodoo, hoodoo, hoodoo," which Harris describes in his program notes as an "incantation." As a result, both sound and image track seem to lose their denotative function, transforming into non-sense or literal in-coherence. Through these temporal and spatial layerings and stutterings, the film refuses to satiate our desire for "real" knowledge—historical, ethnographic, or otherwise—which depends on spatial and temporal coherence. Everything we are seeing and hearing is visibly and audibly incomplete, unsynchronized, and actively incoherent.

Jeffrey Skoller has identified a particular tendency within avant-garde films that engage with history, which he has categorized as "shard" films and has linked to Walter Benjamin's ideas of historical materialism and allegory. Benjamin was interested in how the detritus of a past moment can have significance not for reconstructing the actual past but as a means of constructing an understanding of the past through the lens of the present and vice versa. Skoller has written,

> For modern artists, the use of discarded, mechanically-recorded images and sounds has allegorical possibility because they remain unchanged while the original context for their existence passes out of visibility. The temporal untranslatability of the object becomes the embodiment of present meaning and is generative of new possibilities for significance.[22]

Similarly, in *Halimuhfack,* the "discarded" fragments of the Hurston interview and of the Maasai people are revealed in their "untranslatability." Rather than attempting to reconstruct their original context, the film emphasizes the fact that this context has passed out of visibility so much so that we cannot understand these traces as coherent messages from and about the historical past. Writing about another found footage film, Ernie Gehr's *Eureka* (1974), Skoller notes, "the foregrounding of the present moment of the viewer's gaze through the slowing down of the image denaturalizes it and pulls the viewer out of the image of the past and into an acute sense of the present."[23] This denaturalization and emphasis on the present moment of viewing are present in *Halimuhfack* as well. Any immersion in the past is violently sundered through both the "inauthenticity" of the performer and the aesthetics of interruption; our gaze is dislocated in relation to everything we see and hear.

Yet, in *Halimuhfack*—and in Harris's work more broadly—this denaturalization and dislocation through interruption is fundamentally political. In our present moment, Black people are still implicated in scopic and sonic regimes that combine exoticization with denigration, that seek to fix Black bodies and voices in the service of a white gaze (or ear). *Halimuhfack*, however, undermines our sense that we can know or understand African or African American history through audiovisual ethnographic fragments. In particular, by placing the body of the lip-synch performer—who functions as a "temporal other"—into the space of the frame, the possibility of knowledge about the past "untainted" by the present is exploded. The gap between her lip movements and the voice we hear, more than anything else in the film, points to that which we cannot access, cannot possess. It is in the gesture of placing the contemporary Black body within the historicized space of the appropriated document (with its implicit white gaze and ear) and acknowledging its interruption that the political—and ethical—stakes of interruption most keenly emerge. The discourses of ethnography attempt to produce coherence out of the life and experience of the "other"—usually people of color—for a white reader or viewer. While there is no reason to reject all ethnographic discourse outright, it must be constantly interrupted to reveal how representation exerts power over both its subjects and its audience. By offering ethnographic representation of Black people but interrupting it temporally, spatially, visually, and sonically, *Halimuhfack* offers us traces of Black history but reminds us that it is filtered through a particular (usually white) gaze/ear and, moreover, that we have no particular right to this knowledge.

*Halimuhfack* is not funny; indeed, it is unnerving to watch. However, strategies of embodied interruption and the solicitation of the dislocating gaze can also be combined with humor. In fact, audiovisual appropriation is often, though certainly not always, associated with what Susan Sontag termed a "camp sensibility." This makes a certain sense. If we return to Sontag's foundational—though controversial—1964 essay, "Notes on Camp," we find that many aspects of her description of camp can be easily repurposed as a description of a certain strain of audiovisual appropriation—and their solicited form of spectatorship. Sontag noted that "Camp sees everything in quotation marks."[24] Audiovisual appropriation, by definition, places quotation marks around the images and sounds it appropriates. The experience of watching most works of audiovisual appropriation is that of recognizing that at least certain elements derive from a pre-existing source. These elements are quite literally being "quoted." Yet this sense of quotation alone does not constitute camp. Sontag also stated,

> the camp sensibility is one that is alive to the double sense in which some things can be taken. But this is not the familiar split-level construction of a literal meaning, on the one hand, and a symbolic meaning, on the other. It is the difference, rather, between the thing as meaning something, anything, and the thing as pure artifice.[25]

It is an emphasis on exposing the "pure artifice" of the source that constitutes a particular act of audiovisual appropriation as a camp gesture.

In many works, this artifice often derives from a sense of naïveté within the source. What she calls "naïve camp," Sontag notes, "rests on innocence."[26] This is an apt description of many works of audiovisual appropriation in which the appropriationist takes a seemingly earnest, innocent representation and revels in its artificiality or awkwardness, its "seriousness that fails."[27] This search for naïve camp is more or less the premise behind *The Found Footage Festival*, curated by Joe Pickett and Nick Prueher. Their website describes their festival as "a one-of-a-kind event that showcases footage from videos that were found at garage sales and thrift stores and in warehouses and dumpsters across the country."[28] These finds—gathered exclusively on

VHS tapes—range from corporate training videos to exercise videos to home videos. The appeal of most of these videos lies, in part, in the sense of innocence described above. Hence, the fact that these videos derive from the VHS era is important. As Sontag noted,

> Many of the objects prized by Camp taste are old-fashioned, out-of-date, démodé . . . the process of aging or deterioration provides the necessary detachment—or arouses a necessary sympathy. . . . Time liberates the world of art from moral relevance, delivering it over to a Camp sensibility. . . . Another effect: time contracts the sphere of banality. . . . What was banal can, with the passage of time, become fantastic.[29]

Thus, on an exercise video from the 1980s, which at the time might have seemed unremarkable, the coaching of host Judi Sheppard is now "so perky, it borders on psychotic."[30] Pickett and Prueher do not remix their found videos. They simply curate them on their website and DVD series. The mere act of finding and screening these videos now solicits a camp gaze, a slightly tongue-in-cheek appreciation of the "fantastic" elements within them. Some appropriationists, however, have deployed this camp gaze in a more political and, as I will argue, ethically charged manner.

*I for NDN* (2011), a very short, seemingly simple film by Clint Enns and Darryl Nepinak, illustrates some of the complexity of the role camp may play in certain works of audiovisual appropriation.[31] It begins with the sound of a bell and a simple logo of a schoolhouse along with the title "School Craft presents Learn at Home with your teacher Fran Allison." The graphics are rudimentary, and the quality of the video suggests early television transferred to VHS. Fran, a middle-aged white woman with bouffant hair wearing a yellow sweater and pearls, appears sitting in front of a display of flowers and behind a desk on which we see a rack holding several square cards. She speaks to the camera in the exaggerated tones with which an adult may address a child, saying,

> Hello! Remember our friends A and E from yesterday? Well, today we're going to learn the sounds of more letters. . . . Now you know who this is, don't you? Of course. An Indian. And what is the sound you hear at the beginning of the word "Indian." I- i- is the sound of the letter "i" as in "Indian."

When Fran points to a card, instead of a drawing of an Indian, we see a moving live-action image of a man in a T-shirt smoking a cigarette, which has been inserted into the rectangular frame of the card (see figure 5). In fact, this is one of the filmmakers, Darryl Nepinak, who is an indigenous Salteaux man. At first, Nepinak appears oblivious of the woman's voice, but as she repeats the word "Indian," he looks around like he is trying to figure out where the voice is coming from. Fran reappears and continues: "So let's go over the letters we learned so far with this little song," and music begins as she sings,

> The clue to 'a' is in the apple, a-a-apple, a-a-apple. The clue to 'e' is in the elephant, e-e-elephant, e-e-elephant. The clue to 'i' is in the Indian I-I-Indian, I-I-Indian. In apple, elephant, and Indian, begin the words to find the clue.

As she sings, we see a close-up of the three cards bearing the individual letters and three cards bearing, respectively, a drawing of an apple, a drawing of an elephant, and—once again—a moving image of Nepinak. Fran's hand points a stick of chalk at the letters and images as she sings. Nepinak dances happily as she sings about and points to the apple and elephant, but as she points to him, he suddenly stops, looking confused and somewhat irritated. The film then cuts back to Fran saying, "Now we have learned five letters and we can begin our first words." This is followed by the sound of the bell again and a title announcing, "End of Monday lesson." Immediately thereafter, the credits to Enns and Nepinak's film appear accompanied by the original card bearing the drawn image of a stereotypical Indian with headband, feathers, and braids.

Clearly, the gaze solicited by *I for NDN* transforms the *Learn at Home* footage into an instance of naïve camp. To begin with, the fact that Fran is addressing children lends an artificiality to her tone, noticeable to any adult listening. Her earnestness, which would likely appeal to children, is likely to seem excessive to an adult audience. Moreover, our sense of the naivety of the footage is significantly increased because the footage is old. To a contemporary audience, the *Learn at Home* footage—originally aired in the 1960s—now appears campy in part because of its "old-fashioned, out-of-date, démodé qualities": Fran's hair and clothing, the overly decorative setting, the tinny quality of the sound, and the basic graphics. Our sense of distance from the 1960s allows us the detachment to perceive the footage

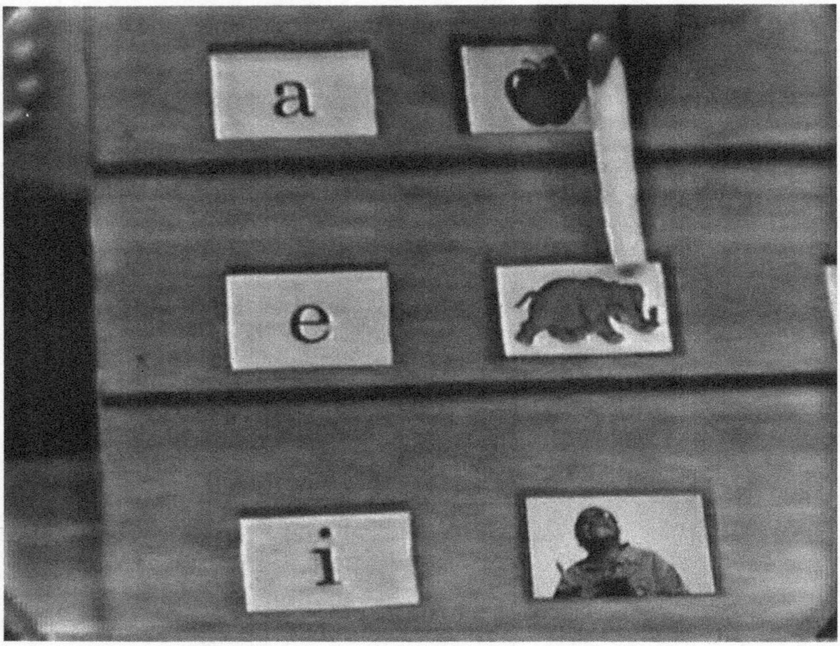


FIGURE 5 Still from *I for NDN* (Clint Enns and Darryl Nepinak, 2011). Courtesy of the artists.

as naïve and therefore potentially nostalgic and charming, evidence of a so-called "simpler time."

However, the insertion of Nepinak's image in place of the drawn "Indian" adds another dimension to the spectatorial experience, transforming what might seem simply naïve into something more revealing. The appearance of a live-action contemporary person in this dated, artificial setting also solicits our identification. Whether or not a given spectator is indigenous, the audience is likely to identify with Nepinak's sense of bewildered frustration at becoming the equivalent of an apple or an elephant in Fran's lesson. In addition, the time and space of *I for NDN* refuses to fully cohere, soliciting a dislocating gaze that does not allow us to look at the *Learn at Home* footage from a comfortable or stable position. Nepinak belongs (more or less) to our here and now, implicating our own time in the objectification of indigenous people. While we may find the *Learn at Home* footage nostalgic and charming to some degree, we are also encouraged to see its complicity with the real harm done to actual indigenous people, then and now. During the 1960s when *Learn at Home* was produced, for instance, many indigenous children were being forcibly taken from their families and often terribly mistreated in "residential schools" in Canada. At the same time, the presence of Nepinak's contemporary body implies the continuity of discrimination against indigenous people in our own time.

Sontag argued that camp is not a form of cynicism or that, if it is, it is a "sweet cynicism." She further suggests that camp requires "underinvolvement" and "detachment," that it does not moralize. It is amoral rather than immoral. Hence, if an appropriation film mocks its object, it ceases to be campy and becomes a form of ridicule. *I for NDN*, however, treads but does not cross the line into ridicule. Part of the reason the film is fun is that it allows us to *enjoy* the naivety of the *Learn at Home* footage—while also making a significant critique. Enns and Nepinak's film does not so much ridicule Fran Allison as it draws attention to the fact that a "simpler time" was also a time in which certain assumptions and expressions that we now see as racist and objectifying were permissible. Indeed, they were not just permissible but also actively and thoughtlessly passed on to children even during a lesson whose purpose was simply to teach them the sound of the vowels. Without actively moralizing, *I for NDN* indicates how thoroughly ideological education is even when it does not notice its assumptions—which is, of course, precisely the definition of hegemonic ideology.

The experience of watching *I for NDN*, then, involves a complex layering of gazes. First, there is the earnest and unironic gaze originally solicited by *Learn at Home*, that of innocent (implicitly white) children learning their vowels. Second, there is the camp gaze that appreciates the naïve, dated, and overly staged aspects of the *Learn at Home* video. Finally, there is the critical, dislocating gaze that recognizes that the footage is, from a contemporary perspective, unwittingly dehumanizing to an entire population. Thus, this film demonstrates how audiovisual appropriation can participate in the enjoyment associated with the experience of camp while simultaneously producing a serious critique.

Although the affective experiences of watching *Halimuhfack* and *I for NDN* are quite different, what unites them is the fact that, through their strategies of embodied interruption and dislocation, they both make visible the white gaze that structured their source materials. The gaze of the ethnographic recordings and interview with Hurston in *Halimuhfack* and the children's educational programming in *I for NDN* were allowed to masquerade as neutral because whiteness has long been the cultural default in

North America. None of these sources is maliciously racist, yet they are revealed as part and parcel of white supremacy precisely because there was no malice involved. By placing the disruptive nonwhite body into the space of these recordings, these two films—and others like them—solicit a dislocating gaze and thereby refuse to let white supremacy retain its apparent coherence.

## Interrupting the Straight Gaze

Whiteness, however, is not the only structuring element underpinning most media; heteronormative patriarchy is also fundamental to most existing representations. Queer artists have long used audiovisual appropriation to deconstruct dominant media representations, overlaying a queer gaze over "straight footage," often in order to impose or bring forth latent homosexual elements in the text. The films of Mark Rappaport, Jerry Tartaglia, William E. Jones, Elisa Kreisinger, and many others, along with films like *The Celluloid Closet* (Rob Epstein, Jeffrey Friedman, 1996) and online slash videos, all participate in this form of queering. William Wees notes of Tartaglia's *Remembrance* (1990), "By offering alternatives to the preferred readings encoded in Hollywood's images of Bette Davis, Tartaglia's film becomes a creative form of reception that recognizes the original, intended use of the images but changes what they mean for someone 'grow[ing] up gay in America.'"[32] As suggested by Tartaglia's focus on Bette Davis, however, this type of queering has often taken place in relation to fiction footage and has usually consisted either of foregrounding queer spectatorship or rewriting narrative as queer narrative. These videos also tend to focus on the overlaying of queer desire on heteronormative texts. I want to focus on two videos that instead of layering queer *desire* over ostensibly straight texts, use the introduction of queer bodies and voices as a form of critique of the representation (or lack thereof) of queer—or at least radically queer—identities onscreen. Like *Halimuhfack* and *I for NDN,* they solicit a dislocating gaze, and in doing so, they transform the time and space of the original text, revealing it as a chronotope hostile to identities that do not fit its norms. And yet, like *I for NDN,* they also manage to be playful and funny in the process.[33]

In some cases, the interruption may take the form of simply inserting gay bodies into an ostensibly heteronormative space, thereby introducing (as

Pinchevski put it) the "foreign" into that space to reveal how the "community" is constructed around—often unacknowledged or invisible—exclusion. Clark Nikolai's *Galactic Docking Company* (2009), for instance, appropriates documentary footage likely familiar to many viewers: NASA technicians and administrators at mission control watching their screens to monitor the launch of a spacecraft in the 1960s. However, in Nikolai's version, what their eyes follow with such eagerness on their screens is not only a spacecraft but also a range of penises and penetrations. Most of these images come from a 1981 gay male porn film, and by inserting these images into the NASA footage, Nikolai's film both sexualizes and queers this footage, rendering it "inappropriate" in relation to both the sober discourse of science and progress and heterosexual social norms.[34]

The film begins with images of spacecraft and mission control operators overlaid with music from the gay porn film *Kansas City Trucking Co.* (Tim Kincaid, 1976), which conjures expectations of seduction rather than scientific demonstration. We see a variety of space vehicles floating through space intercut with images of various white men seated at rows of desks fitted with monitors. At first, the images on the monitors match the images of spacecraft, but suddenly one monitor appears to contain a different image, that of a naked penis. We then see images of other men, some engaged in intense discussion, others simply looking pleased and excited. The film fades to black and then cuts to a close-up of two penises "docking," a term that can refer here to either the process of joining one spacecraft to another or "the act of placing the head of one's penis inside the foreskin of another's penis."[35] On the soundtrack, we hear mission control operators saying things like "Okay, make it smooth. . . . and around we go . . . show us a little style . . . oh, you look good . . ." and so on. A few shots later, the camera tracks into a foreskin until the screen goes black, and then another spacecraft appears as if it is inside the man's penis. We then cut back to mission control, where an eyeline match suggests one man winking at another, followed by another eyeline match that implies that both men are looking at a giant penis floating onscreen. Additional eyeline matches and graphic matches suggest more men watching both spacecraft and penises interchangeably appearing on their NASA monitors. A close-up of a penis tip leaving its foreskin is accompanied by triumphant classical music, which continues over a series of shots of men grinning and laughing, apparently celebrating. Then, on the main screen in the control room, an image of a (toy) spacecraft docking with a penis is superimposed so that the entire NASA operation seems to be a pornographic endeavor. More reaction shots suggest that the men watching the screen are filled with joy—with one exception, an older man who looks skeptical. A few men smoke cigarettes or (even more phallic) cigars, suggesting post-coital relaxation.

Though the dated footage does read as "campy" to some degree, the humor of this film is based less in a camp sensibility than in the incongruity between the source materials and the revelation of ceremony as contrived (see Chapter 2). In addition to the double entendre of "docking," the almost already sexual language of the NASA operators and the visual similarity between spacecraft and penis constitute points of congruity that make the incongruity between the NASA documentary and the gay porn film hilarious. Moreover, the ceremonial aspect of a space shuttle launch, usually a serious and historical topic, is revealed, precisely as a ceremony with its particular rituals. In addition, the fact that we have likely seen this NASA footage many times before further heightens our awareness of both its historical status and the absurdity of this fetishized status. Our attention is fixed on the rapt smiles on the faces of the NASA personnel, one man licking his lips as he looks at the screen—now filled with foreskins rather than space vehicles. Suddenly these gestures become inappropriate or, rather, differently appropriate and, hence, comic.

As a sendup of a nationalistic, patriarchal, and heteronormative institution such as NASA, *Galactic Docking Company* implies a critique of certain societal norms, deflating the sacred status of the U.S. space program. By making use of eyeline matches and matches on action, the film implies a spatial and temporal coherence that is—of course—false. This strategy is not new; the famous submarine periscope sequence in Bruce Conner's *A Movie* (1958) is a much earlier example of this humorous but critical editing technique. However, the use of such editing strategies to suture together NASA footage with gay male porn footage creates a queered space that disrupts our relation to the familiar NASA footage. The space, of course, remains incoherent in the sense that we are fully aware of the false continuities. The dislocating gaze nevertheless asks us to reexamine the implied straight, male, heteronormative gaze implied by the NASA footage.

This kind of false continuity editing is also at play in *Falling in Love . . . with Chris and Greg: Work of Art! Reality TV Special* (2012). This work is part of a series of videos produced by filmmaking duo Chris Vargas and Greg Youmans. In this particular episode, Chris and Greg use simple editing techniques to insert themselves as contestants on Season 2 of the reality television show *Work of Art: The Next Great Artist*. This show, which ran for two seasons on Bravo 2010–2011, generated some controversy for attempting to transform artistic creation into a game show. The Brooklyn Museum, in particular, was criticized for guaranteeing the winner a solo exhibition, despite concerns that the reality show format would likely encourage simplistic, commercialized work that did not deserve to be displayed in a museum.[36] The critique produced through Vargas and Youmans's appropriation is more pointed, focusing specifically on the particular way in which queerness is represented and celebrated on the show. Through added footage of themselves and occasional voiceover dubbing of the appropriated footage, they alter the competition challenge. They reuse footage from Episode 3, "Make It Pop" (aired 26 October 2011), in which contestants were originally asked to "create a piece of pop art that captures the popular culture of their time." In *Falling in Love,* however, the instructions are altered so that the contestants are instead charged with creating "a successful piece of queer art about failure."

*Falling in Love* serves as an instance of détournement or culture jamming in the sense that it explicitly appropriates footage from an existing mass media source and then complicates and politicizes it. By aping the conventions of the reality TV show format and generating a sense of continuity between the appropriated and added footage, the editing of *Falling in Love* might initially allow the added footage to be mistaken for actual footage from the show (see figure 6). Yet, the lower production values of the added footage; the deliberately unconvincing dubbing of the judges' voices (with no attempt to match lips and added voice); and the increasing divergence between Chris and Greg's complex, intellectual ideas and the show's slick and simplistic notion of art production make it difficult to maintain a belief that this is an unaltered excerpt from the original show. The distance between Chris and Greg's thinking and that of the judges becomes increasingly apparent, revealing the gap between two conceptions of what "queer art" is or should be. As the two interlopers present their earnest, conceptual creations about queer life and experience, this gap becomes the source of both comedy and critique in the film.

The film begins by introducing the contestants, the original ones plus Chris and Greg, whose "intro" shots mimic the style of the show. The challenge is then established, and the contestants are shown working on their art pieces or else giving interviews about their work or their thoughts on the other contestants' works. In Greg's first interview, he confesses that he

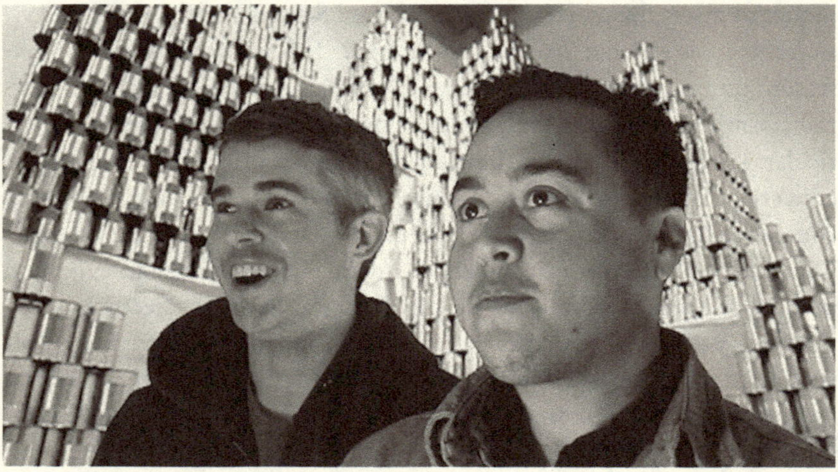

FIGURE 6 Still from *Falling in Love . . . with Chris and Greg: Work of Art! Reality TV Special* (Chris Vargas and Greg Youmans, 2012). Courtesy of the artists.

has been having a hard time on the show because, up until now, his works have been entirely conceptual. He suggests that this may be the first time he is producing something that viewers can see: a set of drawings. Greg's rough pencil drawings include an image of Bette Davis as an adjunct lecturer, who is scorned by her tenure-track colleagues, transforming the narrative of *All About Eve* (Joseph L. Mankiewicz, 1950) into a commentary about how artists and intellectuals are increasingly exploited by neoliberal universities that prefer to hire adjuncts—whom they do not have to offer full-time salaries, benefits, or any form of job security—rather than invest in tenure-track professors. Another one of Greg's drawings presents Norman Bates from *Psycho* (Alfred Hitchcock, 1960) watching Netflix porn DVDs rather than joining the Occupy movement, which suggests how activism is often defeated by inertia or a focus on the self rather than the collective. *Work of Art* judge Simon de Pury—dubbed, of course—seems confused by Greg's ideas but tells him to "keep going," which makes Greg feel like he is on the right track. The discrepancy between Greg's hopeful optimism about the chances of his conceptually rich but aesthetically impoverished pencil drawings winning this glossy television competition generates much of the humor in *Falling in Love.*

In contrast to Greg, Chris appears much more guarded about the show. In an early critique, de Pury appears—through editing that constructs a shot-reverse-shot structure—to listen to Chris's idea about wanting to critique how Chaz Bono has been viewed and labeled in a particular way because he is a trans man in the public eye. Then de Pury—again obviously dubbed—appears to say something callous about being able to tell a trans man by his small hands, performing precisely the kind of judgment that Chris is trying to critique. Chris's final piece is entitled "Small Hands" and is a speeded up version of Bono's appearance on *Dancing with the Stars*, another reality TV show. In this appropriation within an appropriation, Chris explains, Bono's gender is illegible because of the speed at which the image moves, disallowing assessments of his ability to "pass" as male. The judges complain that it should have been slower, completely missing Chris's point. Chris's artwork also points self-reflexivity to Chris's own (constructed) presence on a reality TV show. While there are whole reality TV shows structured around transgender figures (*RuPaul's Drag Race*, for instance), Chris is a transgender man, who does not fit into the reality TV audience's apparent desire for transgender bodies as spectacle—which is, of course, more often associated with transgender women. Transgender men are much more rarely featured. In fact, if one did not know that Chris is transgender, it is not immediately apparent. Yet, perhaps because of this, his (constructed) presence on *Work of Art* inscribes an illegibility into the show, which contradicts its extremely legible and consumable representation of queerness in the form of actual contestant Young Sun Han.

Intercut with Greg and Chris's conversations with de Pury is footage of Young producing his piece of contemporary "pop art," here reframed as "queer art about failure." Young, an attractive and unassuming young Korean-American man, notes that some of his earlier paintings were inspired by the work of Andy Warhol, and he then proceeds to make a painting in Warholian style about Proposition 8. This proposed state constitutional amendment banning same-sex marriage appeared on the ballot in the November 2008 California state elections; it passed, but in 2009 the controversial amendment was ruled unconstitutional in the courts, and same-sex marriages were allowed to proceed in California. Young's painting consists of the phrase "Prop 8" in large, vibrantly colored letters; on the back, there is space for viewers to write comments with markers. The show does include some ambivalence about Young's piece. Original contestant Lola notes that there is a lot of art about Prop 8 but that Young's piece does not really seem to take any particular position on the amendment. Hilariously, Chris is inserted saying "I agree with Lola." However, during the judging period, the judges gush about Young's piece, and it wins the challenge. In contrast, the queer artworks of Chris and Greg are—through dubbing—ultimately deemed "failures" by the reality show hosts, and "not in a good way."

It is perhaps somewhat unethical to place words in the judges' mouths that they did not speak and that make them seem, if not homophobic, at least ignorant of the complexities of queer identity. This is partially offset, however, by the fact that *Falling in Love* is edited in such a way that the insertion of Chris and Greg is quite obvious, and the dubbing is not convincing. Thus, the act of ventriloquism (see Chapter 2) is apparent rather than deceptive. In addition, all the appropriated footage in this film comes from a public text, and reality television is notorious for its own deceptions and exploitations. Arguably, the judges and contestants who agreed to participate in *Work of Art* traded any expectation of dignified treatment for the publicity that comes with being on reality TV.

Moreover, Vargas and Youmans's appropriation of this footage serves an actively ethical function by interrupting the flow of reality television to reveal its attitudes toward queer identity. Young, it becomes clear, is being used to represent gay identity on the show but also to make it palatable to straight audiences or, in other words, to the straight gaze solicited by the show. As Lola notes, Young's Prop 8 painting takes no stance even if his own identity as a gay man suggests that he opposes it. The space for commentary further suggests that his artwork is entirely open to interpretation and that the viewer has no obligation to engage with queer politics beyond a quick scribble. The judges' ringing endorsement of Young's work serves only to further emphasize that the show itself seeks to avoid any genuine political engagement. And, of course, the "presence" of Chris and Greg is what brings this avoidance into relief, making the queer body a disruptive figure rather than simply part of the flow of "liberal" television. As the judges (are dubbed to) disparage Greg and Chris's works, it becomes clear that there is no room for radically queer bodies or politics on this show. This returns us to Pinchevski's notion that a "community is realized in the approach and exposure to the foreign: the outcast, the mental patient, the immigrant, the Indian, the stranger, the enemy." Of course, reality television is based entirely around a structure of ever-increasing exclusion as, one by one, contestants are declared in some way deficient or unfit and removed from the show. The constructed inclusion and then exclusion of Greg and Chris from the show simply highlights how the exclusions begin long before the show—that only certain types of bodies and identities are even allowed to appear onscreen and then, more often than not, those that do not fit an existing set of criteria are—spectacularly—eliminated. Moreover, by using their own "foreign" bodies to reveal their predetermined exclusion, Greg and Chris also make themselves vulnerable in their act of interruption. Although they do control the film to a degree because they are its editors, by opening themselves to our gaze, they also risk being judged themselves. This reciprocity of visibility/audibility and judgment further underscores how this film functions as an ethical commentary on the ways "queerness" is defined and limited in mainstream discourse.

It is crucial to emphasize, however, how funny this film is. The inclusion of Greg and Chris into the space of the show creates a space that does not fully cohere and therefore opens the show to a camp sensibility even if the footage itself is not particularly dated. The chronotope of reality television is quite specific—a group of people sequestered together in a single space or series of spaces and their time structured according to the set of competitions and eliminations that are basic to the format. By adding Greg and Chris into this chronotope but without trying to convince us of their actual presence within it, the film solicits the dislocating gaze, repeatedly making us laugh by suggesting spatial and temporal coherence where we know there is none. As in *Galactic Docking Company*, the combination of congruity and incongruity is part of the pleasure and humor of the film alongside the exposure of the "ceremonial" structure of reality television. Yet, of course, as in *Galactic Docking Company,* the laughter solicited by the film is a critical laughter. In these films, the straight heteronormative gaze assumed by the NASA footage and *Work of Art* becomes visible. Like the white gaze, the straight gaze ceases to be imperceptible background and becomes, instead, a figure available to our critical eye.

## Interrupting the Male Gaze

While radically queer bodies remain absent from most mainstream media, the problem of the representations of women's bodies is perhaps less their absence than their overabundance. However, commercial representations of women continue to operate almost exclusively in the service of a male gaze. Hence, appropriating existing images of women in order to deconstruct the male gaze that structures them appears akin to an ethical imperative. While

Laura Mulvey developed her famous theorization of the male gaze specifically in relation to Classical Hollywood films, appropriation filmmakers have exposed the underpinning presence of the male gaze in media of all kinds and across the entire history of moving image media.[37] Indeed, there are far too many feminist appropriation films that expose the male gaze in pornography, fiction film, television, and other media for me to attempt to survey them all. Rather, I want to focus on ways in which an "othered" body has been used to interrupt the male gaze and make it visible through the solicitation of a dislocating gaze.

Such a strategy emerges forcefully in the filmmaking duo Soda_Jerk's very short film, *Undaddy Mainframe* (2014), which has much in common with both *I for NDN* and *Galactic Docking Company*. The film begins with an image of a 2014 Mac computer desktop replete with application folder and icons atop the classic galaxy desktop image. A window appears on the right side of the screen showing a dated video introduction to online culture for kids, with titles such as "Email" and "Internet" as well as logos for "MTV" and "Yahoo" soaring through digital space alongside the faces of attractive white kids, accompanied by peppy synthesizer music. It is appropriated from *The Kids Guide to the Internet* from 1997, now beloved for its outdated camp value, a fact confirmed by the many comments on YouTube.[38] This is followed by an image of a highly made-up young blonde woman in a red blazer and pearls sitting next to a computer. Again, the source of the footage is the 1990s, in this case "The Komputer Tutor for Komputer Kindergarten," hosted by Kim Komando. In Soda_Jerk's appropriation, however, when Komando appears to begin to speak, her original voice and words are replaced by a "female" computer voice speaking aloud the "Cyberfeminist Manifesto for the 21st Century," first declared by the Australia artist collective VNS Matrix in 1991, which reads as follows:

> We are the modern cunt/ positive anti reason/ unbounded unleashed unforgiving/ we see art with our cunt we make art with our cunt/ we believe in jouissance madness holiness and poetry/ we are the virus of the new world disorder/ rupturing the symbolic from within/ saboteurs of big daddy mainframe/ the clitoris is a direct line to the matrix/ VNS Matrix/ terminators of the moral codes/ mercenaries of slime/ go down on the altar of abjection/ probing the visceral temple we speak in tongues/ infiltrating disrupting disseminating/ corrupting the discourse/ we are the future cunt[39]

In the film, a few words are changed (*probing, infiltrating*), but the text remains otherwise intact despite the awkward cadences introduced by the computerized voice. However, additional images are inserted into the frame as Komando "speaks." For instance, the first four times we hear the word "cunt," an image of a hand grabbing a crotch is momentarily laid over the woman's image, breaking the frame within the frame of the computer screen. When she says, "big daddy mainframe," the male face of a classical statue briefly appears over her face like a mask. When she points to a space above her left shoulder where a computer-related graphic likely appeared in the original, the graphic is replaced by a labeled diagram of a vulva. When we hear the words "VNS Matrix" (pronounced Venus Matrix), she holds up two fingers. Added onscreen text transforms her hand gesture into a "V" that completes the written phrase "VNS Matrix." She then turns to a television monitor and VHS player. As we hear the phrase "mercenaries of slime," the famous image from *The Exorcist* (William Friedkin, 1973), in which the possessed girl Regan pukes slime into the priest's face, appears on the monitor. Next, a hand holding an installation CD—the kind that used to come with software—appears in front of the Mac computer screen. The image on the CD is a low angle shot of a man looking very enthused, his crotch precisely aligned with the hole in the CD. A finger pokes through the CD, creating a phallic joke. Meanwhile, in the window where Komando continues her manifesto, her last iteration of the word "cunt" is accompanied by a shot of a floppy disc drive before the desktop window disappears. As the manifesto ends, the soundtrack returns to the peppy theme from the beginning and a woman sings, "Interactive appetite, searching for a website, a window to the world that to get online [sic]. Take the spin, now you're in, with the technoset. You're going surfing on the Internet." The desktop image is then overlaid by the diagram of the vulva, now turned to precisely match the oval shape of the galaxy.

*Undaddy Mainframe* is part of series of videos entitled "The Lessons." On their website, Soda_Jerk describe "The Lessons" as "a series of short video works where archival history is folded into new constellations, producing virtual proximities between disparate temporal moments."[40] This approach to archival documents is fundamental to nearly all Soda_Jerk's work; through digital compositing, they expertly suture disparate sources into a visually unified but conceptually disjunctive space and time, creating "virtual proximities" that we experience as such. In *Undaddy Mainframe*, a virtual proximity is created, first of all, between the 1990s and 2014, when Soda_Jerk's film was produced. As in the *Learn at Home* footage in *I for NDN,* there is camp value in this old instructional video in which the lower production values, out of style fashions, and outdated content appear naïve and therefore humorous. However, an additional level of humor is, of course, derived from the incongruity between Komando's appearance and what she is "saying." Her appearance speaks to how computer users are framed as male while computer technologies are feminized to appeal primarily to these male users. Even though Komando is a woman giving instructions about computers, she is dressed and coiffed according to traditional feminine standards (figure 7). This is what makes her assertion, for instance, that "we are the modern cunt" seem utterly out of place. Further, the inserted diagram of a vulva that appears as one of her visual aids points to the video's assumed heterosexual male gaze, which seeks either to discipline or to fetishize the female body. While the desire to see the woman's naked body is fundamental to the male gaze, the sudden appearance of a labeled vulva makes a joke of this desire.

In terms of its ethics, this video is perhaps unfair to Komando, who is no dummy, ventriloquist's or otherwise. In fact, she is now a successful radio host whose weekly three-hour call-in show—in which she answers questions about digital technologies—reaches millions of listeners.[41] Yet, in this instance of audiovisual ventriloquism, the target of critique is not so much Komando herself as the mise-en-scene of her show, which seeks to make the presence of a technologically savvy woman unthreatening (to men) through casting, hair, make-up, and clothing. By ventriloquizing Komando, Soda_Jerk reframes her as a cyberfeminist icon, a femme-bot who is not serving the patriarchy but, rather, "rupturing the symbolic from within." One of the members of VNS Matrix, Julianne Pierce, has written,

> Cyberfeminism was about ideas, irony, appropriation and hands-on skilling up in the data terrain. It combined a utopic vision of corrupting patriarchy with an unbounded enthusiasm for the new tools of technology. It embraced gender and identity politics, allowing fluid and non-gendered identities to flourish through the digital medium. The post-corporeal female would be an online frontier woman, creating our own virtual worlds and colonising the amorphous world of cyberspace.[42]

In Soda_Jerk's film, Komando becomes this post-corporeal female and online frontier woman. Moreover, the appropriation serves a broader cri-

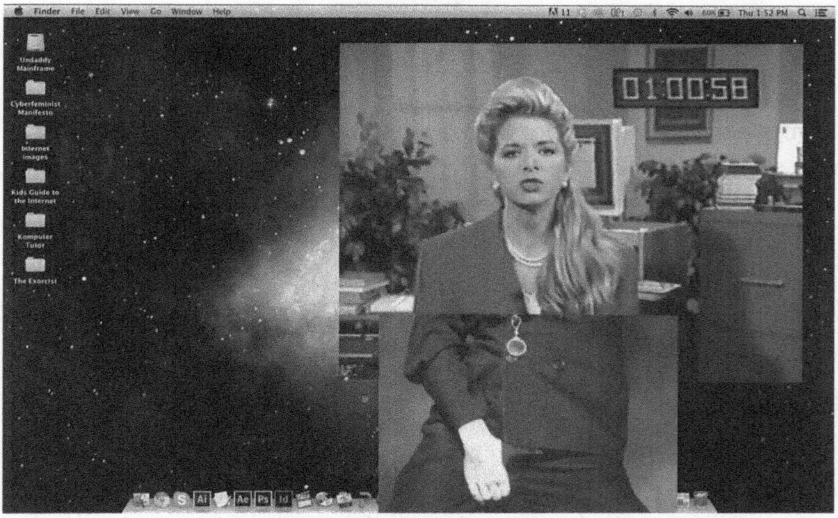


FIGURE 7 Still from *Undaddy Mainframe* (Soda_Jerk, 2014). Courtesy of the artists.

tique, interrupting the flow of corporate, male-dominated tech discourse with the female body, or more precisely with a "cunt." This term, which is generally used by misogynists to reduce women to their genitalia, is reclaimed in the "Cyberfeminist Manifesto" and *Undaddy Mainframe* as "modern," "future," seeing, and creating art.

There are obvious similarities between *Undaddy Mainframe* and *Galactic Docking Company*, most clearly in the introduction of images of and references to genitalia into a seemingly asexual professional space. Yet, they differ in terms of their constructed temporalities. *Galactic Docking Company* queers the NASA footage Nikolai appropriates and thereby suggests a potentially queer past. In contrast, *Undaddy Mainframe* reconstitutes the "Komputer Tutor" footage as a radical feminist call to action and, in doing so imagines a present or future world in which computers are not associated with tech bros but, rather, with uninhibited female bodies, productions, and desires. Despite its brevity and humor, then, the film can be read as a piece of speculative science fiction that proffers an alternative technological utopia in which computerized "personal assistants" like Siri and Alexa are not feminized digital secretaries but a form of feminist malware that has destroyed the patriarchal structures of "the technoset." In this film, the dislocating gaze denaturalizes the current technological moment—here signified by the contemporary Mac desktop—suggesting a parallel technological future in which computer culture is truly egalitarian regarding gender instead of rife with sexism and misogyny.

A very different strategy for interrupting the male gaze within digital culture entails in Jennifer Proctor's short film *Am I Pretty?* (2017). There exists on YouTube—and likely other sharing sites—a whole genre in which individuals, most often adolescent or pre-adolescent girls, post videos of themselves asking the Internet audience at large the simple question "Am I pretty?"—or the converse "Am I ugly?" In *Am I Pretty?* we hear a multitude of young female voices asking various versions of the title question. First, a series of young female voices introduce themselves by first name. They then proceed to explain their situations. One girl explains that most of the boys at her school call her "a slut, a bitch, and a ho, and a whore," though she asserts that she is not any of those things. She goes on to say that they also tell her she is ugly but that that is "just their opinion." Then she asks the viewer to comment on whether she is ugly or pretty. This is followed by a much less confident girl's voice almost whispering, "I have a question. People tell me this all the time, so I don't know. Is it true? People say I'm ugly. So, tell me. Am I?" A number of other girls' voices discuss being bullied, having low self-esteem, having unruly hair or small teeth, or thinking they are fat before they, too, pose the question to an undefined "you" of whether they are pretty or ugly. Several girls also explain that they do not believe their friends who tell them they are pretty, so they are looking for an opinion unbiased by the obligations of friendship. Many also say that they just want "the truth" and that they will not be hurt or offended if the answer is negative. Just a few assert that they think they are, indeed, pretty, and the film ends as one girl announces, "I honestly think I'm beautiful."

Although these videos were ostensibly addressed to the public and posted for the public to see, the youth of these girls, the need for validation implied by their questions, and the naiveté implicit in the very act of making these videos suggests that appropriating these videos does constitute a potential exploitation. Even as the girls in these videos explicitly request an evaluative, judgmental, and objective gaze, it is almost impossible not to imagine that these young makers are seeking a validating gaze. Who among us, if we ask, "Am I pretty?" is not hoping that the respondent will answer in the affirmative? (Videos asking the parallel masculine question, "Am I handsome or ugly?" do exist, but Proctor's film emphasizes the way girls are particularly dependent on affirmations of their beauty.) These girls, who are seemingly hoping that the internet will contradict the bullies who tell them they are ugly (or confirm the flattering opinion of friends who may or may not be telling them "the truth"), do not seem to realize that the worst bullies of the contemporary world are internet trolls; should the trolls decide to respond to such videos, the response is unlikely to be kind, to say the least. Opening these makers to further, potentially cruel scrutiny seems to exacerbate this risk.

Proctor, however, counters this threat by refusing to let us see what we are being asked on the audio track to judge. Instead of the visages that accompany the voices we hear, we see simply a blank, bubble-gum pink screen, which brings to mind Derek Jarman's 1993 film *Blue,* another film (not involving appropriation) that denies our gaze in favor of soliciting intense listening. In *Blue,* we hear Jarman—who was nearly blind and dying of AIDS as he made the film—narrate aspects of his life as we watch a filmstrip dyed a vibrant shade of blue projected on the screen. One of the effects of this occlusion is to align our own gaze with Jarman's blindness in a mimetic approximation of his embodied experience, denying us the ability to see just as Jarman has lost this ability. *Am I Pretty?* is similarly self-reflexive but to different effect. In Proctor's film, the occluded gaze (see Chapter 1) firstly protects the identities of the original makers—a gesture akin to the blurred face usually used by documentary filmmakers or news producers who failed to get permission to use footage of someone's face. Yet, it also actively denies not just our *ability* to look but also our *right* to look, despite the fact that these videos were originally posted online. The film implicitly makes the argument that just because someone, particularly a naïve teen, posts something online, their action does not give us the right to look—or to judge. Through its visual occlusion, *Am I Pretty?* implicates us in the question of whether *availability* to our gaze equals the right to look, a question to which the answer in the internet age is too often and easily assumed to be "yes."

Notably, there is no obvious disruptive body inserted into the text. However, the blank pink screen nevertheless solicits the dislocating gaze associated with the films discussed above. Because we cannot see the speakers, it is very difficult to position them temporally or spatially. Except for the timbres of their voices or their slight accents, there is nothing to tell us where or when they are speaking from. The dislocation here is not a result of juxtaposition but, rather, of a lack of temporal or spatial markers. We cannot get our bearings because we cannot see precisely the thing we are being asked to look at and evaluate. In addition, the disruptive body is precisely the female body that we are conditioned to want and expect to see but, here, remains unavailable to our gaze.

In a related gesture, *What Happened to Her* (Kristy Guevara-Flanagan, 2016) transforms, rather than occludes, our gaze at women's bodies. Notably, in contrast to my other examples, this film appropriates not actuality footage but rather, fiction footage; however, in doing so, it destabilizes the status of that footage as fictional through a dislocating gaze. Guevara-Flanagan's film could be categorized as a supercut (see Chapter 2) in that it combines similar images from many disparate sources: in this case, the image of a dead female body from various fiction films and television shows. The repetition of one female corpse after another creates an awareness—as do many supercuts—of just how prevalent and consistent this kind of image is. Several series of images of dead women with their eyes open floating in the water, of tarps or sheets pulled back to expose a dead woman underneath, of prone women being rolled over to reveal that they are dead and bloody, of (mostly male) voices describing gruesome injuries and mutilations, and so on, demonstrate the redundancy of these morbid tropes. Beyond this simple structure of repetition, however, what invokes the dislocating gaze is the inclusion of a voiceover from an interview with a woman, named in the final credits as Danyi Deats, who once acted as a murder victim. Crucially, we hear Deats speaking but we never see her (unless she is one of the unidentified bodies onscreen, but this is never indicated).

The film begins with an appropriated image from an unnamed film in which a dead woman's body is found in the water by two men ("Holy Christ, it's a dead body!" "Look at that . . . Jesus." "That's a woman, huh?" "She's dead isn't she?") As the camera pans across her half-naked, floating form, the men's voices fade, and Deats's voiceover begins,

> I got the job as the dead body because my girlfriend was trying out for the part. And the casting director just asked me, "Hey, would you be interested in trying out for the part?" And I was like, "Yeah, I'll do it." I was nineteen. I didn't know what I was getting into at the time. I just sort of said "Yes." I just didn't really realize that everyone was going to see me naked from here on out.

The effect of this description on the image track—which proceeds with its visual taxonomy of dead women's bodies—is transformative. What initially read as fiction footage suddenly becomes actuality footage, not of actual death but of the *performance* of death, and specifically female death. Our gaze is suddenly reoriented to think not about the character in the image but, rather, about the actress pretending to be dead. In my introduction, I argued that the ethics of appropriating documentary footage is categorically different from appropriating fiction footage because in fiction footage the people onscreen are performing as others rather than enacting their own selves. However, this film complicates that distinction because it foregrounds the fact that, of course, fiction footage is also simultaneously actuality footage of the actors onscreen. In *What Happened to Her,* this is emphasized by the intimacy of the performances being appropriated since almost every "body" we see onscreen is naked or partially disrobed. Deats continues,

> We were up in Northern California. It was cold out. It was freezing. And then all of a sudden I just had that panicked feeling like, "Oh no, I don't want to do this." And then they just, like, offered me more money and you know, that's how they solve problems in Hollywood. In the beginning, because I was nineteen, I had never been naked in front of like, you know, men. It's an 80 person male crew. . . . At first I felt really nervous, you know, like, "What's going to happen to me?" They never really showed me the full script of what I was getting into.

As she describes being cold and naked, we see images of many different nude women out in the open. The fact that these (living) women are cold is suddenly palpable. Moreover, as Deats speaks about the many men who were on set, we see a series of images of the nearly all-male police crews who generally find the female corpse in such narratives. These police officers, however, suddenly read as actors, as crew members who are fully clothed while the women playing the victims are lying naked on the ground. As a result, the actresses' embodied experience as naked and vulnerable in a public space populated primarily by clothed men becomes tangible to us.

Deats's description of the coercion she experienced also emphasizes the unethical practices that undergird the production of such images. Although we may imagine that actors who play dead bodies are fully cognizant of what they are getting into and are adequately compensated for being cold and naked, Deats makes it clear that this is not always the case. In fact, her descriptions of coping with her experience begin to sound eerily like those of sexual assault victims. She says,

> I didn't have a body double. One person rolls me off a cliff. Another drags me across the ground. I really went into it just not knowing. I had to just kind of put a box around me. I'd be like "I'm not here. All these people aren't here."

And, as the film makes clear, Deats is far from the only one to experience these things. As she speaks, we see a series of different women being rolled off cliffs and dragged across the ground, and we are prompted to wonder what these living actresses were thinking and feeling as their bodies were being thus treated. Although we may usually understand the gaze of the crime film or television show camera as ethical in the sense that it is focused on a paid and performing actor, the ethics of this seemingly sanctioned gaze are put into question by Deats's description of her experience.

The line between fiction and documentary is further blurred by the fact that the film in which Deats was acting was based on an actual murder of a girl by her high school boyfriend. She describes the experience of filming the murder scene:

> The hardest scene was the death scene when he was really like starting to choke me. Because there's like this weird moment when you both don't know if you're going too far. But as he started choking me I really started to kind of think about the girl that it happened to. And I guess that's something that happened to me a lot during the filming. I read a bunch of articles on her. And I just sort of felt like wow, this isn't like a made up story. This really happened to someone. And when he was choking me I was kind of picturing that. It was definitely like the hardest but weirdest moment. I was like wow, this is what happened to her.

Her description of reenacting an actual murder points us back to the fact that even though this is fiction footage, it also refers to a real girl's death, which is being (re)lived by another woman for viewers' entertainment. The confusion of actor/body/actual murder victim is particularly apparent when Deats says, talking about her makeup, "They took the actor who killed me's hands and had to kind of trace it [sic], so that it would be his fingerprints on my throat." Her use of the phrase "the actor who killed me" suggests the existential confusion involved in this kind of performance. The actor remains "the actor" but she refers to him killing her ("me"), not her character. Any attempt we as viewers might make to neatly separate reality and fiction is denied.

The effect of the editing combined with the voiceover in *What Happened to Her* is to perceptually transform the fiction footage of the dead women into actuality footage of real women pretending to be dead for the camera. Thus, the film is far more than a simple interrogation of the male gaze. It is, rather, a reassertion of real, live, agentic female bodies into these fictional (or fictionalized) narratives of femicide. These documentary bodies suddenly interrupt the diegesis, entering into our shared ethical space. One might argue that, if these actresses were exploited in the making of these crime narratives, Guevara-Flanagan is exploiting them all over again by repurposing images of their naked bodies for her critique. There is some truth in this. However, by dislocating our gaze—to reveal the morbid, sadistic male gaze that structures the spectacle of female death again and again—and by making us look at these "bodies" as actresses, as living, feeling human beings, the film can be read as an ethical intervention into an unethical practice that we accept nearly every time we turn on our televisions.

By its very nature perhaps, audiovisual appropriation always involves a dislocating gaze as it stitches together clearly disparate times and spaces into "virtual proximities." Détournement and culture jamming both established this kind of dislocating gaze as a means for political critique of the dominant, capitalist culture. However, the specific strategy of embodied interruption as a means of invoking this dislocating gaze often constitutes both a political and an ethical gesture vis-à-vis those who have been excluded or misrepresented in mainstream media culture. When a disruptive body (or voice) enters a mediated space structured by the white, straight, male, or otherwise hegemonic gaze, this gaze becomes a *figure* that we can suddenly see. It becomes subject to our evaluation and, potentially, our rejection. By opening up possible new ways of looking, the dislocating gaze as evoked by the "other" body suggests possible new ways of framing all bodies, ways that do not serve hegemonic and exclusionary ideologies so often presented as transparent, neutral, and natural.

# 4

# Reframing the Perpetrator's Gaze

What does it mean to align one's gaze with that of photographers or filmmakers who filmed or photographed their subjects with total disregard for their humanity? Can such images be ethically reused? And, if so, how and for what ends? In the previous chapter, I demonstrated how audiovisual appropriation may serve to interrupt hegemonic ideologies that, under cover of neutrality, exclude or misrepresent certain bodies and identities. In such cases, the original recordings do not read precisely as unethical; they appear, rather, as unwittingly biased, distorted, or exclusionary. In other words, they do not seem to be consciously complicit with violence and dehumanization. A different set of ethical issues based on appropriating and misusing found recordings arises when the recordings themselves have been produced by makers whom we know or perceive to be perpetrators of hideous crimes and so are already inscribed with a clearly unethical gaze.

## The Misuse of Perpetrator Images

Footage of their victims filmed by the Nazis, the photographs of their victims taken by the Khmer Rouge at the S-21 prison, many of the infamous

Abu Ghraib photographs and videos, and other images produced specifically to dehumanize their photographed and filmed subjects carry with them the gaze of the perpetrator. Defining the notion of "perpetrator images," Marianne Hirsch has written, "These images illustrate the quality of the perpetrator's look as well as its connection to the perpetrator's deed. When we confront perpetrator images, we cannot look independently of the look of the perpetrator."[1] As a result, to reuse them risks both complicity with the perpetrators and an additional violation of the humanity of the recorded subjects.

Yet, to dismiss them as meaningful historical evidence is also fraught. Frances Guerin has written extensively about the problems of appropriating Nazi film footage. She has noted,

> It is usually agreed Nazi documentary images must be approached with caution. Critics argue that they represent the glorification of the Nazis' criminal advance to totalitarian power, the violence of the German camera, the objectification of the enemy. . . . Thus, the Nazi image is complicit in the dehumanization of the Jews, it embodies all the ideological beliefs that led to World War II and the Holocaust. The violence of these images overwhelms them, eclipses them, and therefore, it is not possible to approach them for their historical evidence, aesthetic innovation, or their other ideological influences. They have no currency as anything but evidence of Nazi ideology.[2]

Guerin, however, counters this argument, suggesting that some Nazi documentary images—specifically amateur Nazi films, in her analysis—do have complex historical value that can be made useful without reinforcing Nazi ideology. She suggests that some "Nazi amateur footage both advances our understanding of documentary film and offers critical insight into the historical events it witnesses." She further asserts such footage has "status as evidence of much more than Nazi ideology."[3] Brad Prager, by contrast, is less sanguine about the usefulness of even amateur Nazi footage. In his analysis of the W. G. Sebald's 1992 novel *The Emigrants*, which includes many photographic images, he notes that Sebald describes but chooses not to reproduce an image produced by the German accountant, amateur photographer, and Nazi Walter Genewein.

> It is as though he feared the still image's power to collapse the gaps of time and space and thought that in looking at it, he might disquietingly or

> accidentally step into the position of Genewein. . . . He may have feared that in reproducing it, he himself would be implicated in the very exploitation that conditioned their production.[4]

Prager argues that, although he was an amateur photographer, "because Genewein was a Nazi and responsible for many deaths, it is difficult not to think of his camera as a metonymic extension of Nazi weaponry."[5] He further notes that when we look at images produced by Nazis, "our imaginations undertake to restore life and a voice to those depicted, yet at the same time we are forced to acknowledge that we cannot accomplish this goal and to consider the possibility that we are taking pleasure in an inappropriate object, one saturated by the photographer's own dark attitudes."[6] In other words, the gaze of the perpetrator cannot, in Prager's view, be easily dismissed in favor of reading "against the grain," no matter how much we might like to do so.

Vincente Sánchez-Biosca, writing about the photographs taken at the S-21 torture center and prison by members of the Khmer Rouge, notes how easy it seems to disregard the gaze of the perpetrator once the images have been reframed, for instance, as the S-21 "mug shots" of their victims have been reframed as evidence of Khmer Rouge crimes.

> The gaze with which all these human beings contemplate us comes not from their victimhood; on the contrary, their condition is pervaded by their status as traitors. It is this which was being registered by the camera. In effect, when they lifted their eyes to the camera and this framed them, they were guilty. We are then surprised by the ease with which, without changing the contents in the frame, our perception of these people is transformed into its opposite. How is it possible to ignore the steady bureaucratic eye which created these photos?[7]

Sánchez-Biosca suggests that it is crucial that the "bureaucratic eye," aligned with the Khmer Rouge's genocidal intent, be continuously recognized: "We must reflect on the original impulse which brought the archive into being, the eye which engendered it."[8] To forget or ignore this original eye opens the possibility of an historical obfuscation that might allow us to unwittingly align ourselves with a dehumanizing—and murderous—gaze.

In general, I share the concerns articulated above about reusing Nazi, Khmer Rouge, or other perpetrator images; replicating the perpetrator's gaze and potentially aligning oneself (or another viewer) with it are deeply unnerving prospects. However, there are times when there is an ethical imperative to reuse perpetrator images to expose and critique their original purpose. This requires an *explicit* engagement with the source of the appropriated footage, acknowledging its previous purposes; and it still risks reinforcing the ideologies inscribed in the footage. This type of misuse is ethically dangerous but also necessary. A dislocating gaze (see Chapter 3) is not, in these cases, sufficient. Rather, such misuse—to read as ethical—entails the overt identification and deconstruction of the original gaze. Without such identification and deconstruction, the appropriation may become complicit with its ethically compromised source material and participate in further dehumanizing the recorded subjects. Nonetheless, when perpetrators produce images in order to dehumanize a group of human beings, "misusing" such images and establishing a "countergaze" can be a profoundly ethical act.

## The Revelatory Gaze

Yael Hersonski's *A Film Unfinished* (2010) is a documentary about an unfinished film shot by the Nazis in the Warsaw Ghetto in 1942 and rediscovered in 1954 in an East German film archive in a series of film canisters labeled "Das Ghetto."[9] These are some of the only existing filmic images of the Warsaw Ghetto. The silent black-and-white images depict, among other scenes, busy streets full of carts and people, elegantly dressed Jewish people shopping or eating a lavish meal in a restaurant, a meeting of the Jewish Council, a circumcision ceremony, Jewish men and women separately taking a ritual bath, lingering portrait shots of individual Jewish men and women, emaciated Jewish corpses lying in the street, and bodies of dead Jewish people being pushed down a chute into a mass grave.

Hersonski's film indicates that, although these images were understood to have been propaganda when they were first found, in the intervening years their status as such was forgotten and the footage came to be regarded as a reliable source depicting ghetto life. The voiceover narration explains: "Ironically, after the war, this film commissioned by the Nazis turned into a trustworthy document for any filmmaker seeking to show what really happened, to tell the untellable. The cinematic deception was forgotten, and the black-and-white images were engraved in memory as historical truth."

Indeed, Stuart Liebman notes that Frédéric Rossif's *Le Temps du ghetto* (1961) and Alexander Bernfes's 1968 BBC documentary about the ghetto "rather naively exploited the images as such."[10] He further argues that, through their reuse, these images became fundamental to our vision of the ghetto: "Almost without exception, the conceptual foundation for their continual recycling . . . was and still is the same: This, the filmed images imply, is the way the Warsaw Ghetto looked; this was the way it was . . . [while] in fact, there is a profound gap between the way the Ghetto appeared to the German cameramen's lenses and the way it was."[11] Hersonski's film sets out to rectify this case of mistaken reception. Other documents—both written and visual—are summoned to reframe the images of "Das Ghetto."

To understand the images properly, the film argues, we need to understand *why* they were produced. "In the absence of a final version of the film," the narrator says, "the intentions of the propagandists can never be determined. One can only surmise." Nevertheless, *A Film Unfinished* carefully attempts to piece together the Nazis' intentions in producing this footage. As Ursula Böser notes in her analysis of the film, inevitably, the "process of audio-visual quotation raises questions about the historicity and origin of the archival footage, about what it was once meant to mean."[12] The question of what this particular footage "was once meant to mean" is crucial because it determines whether we read the footage as a reliable document of the Warsaw Ghetto or not. It is precisely the Nazis' intentions—which cannot be precisely known but are inevitably imagined by the viewer and can be determined to some degree by other evidence—that are at stake in Hersonski's appropriation and rereading of the images.

Böser notes the status of "Das Ghetto's" images as an instance of "perpetrator images."[13] But this is not immediately obvious from the images themselves. Some of the images do read as unstaged actuality, particularly images of starving people begging for food and corpses lying in the street. As the camera lingers on emaciated children and dead bodies, the gaze looking at them might be mistaken for the "humane gaze" theorized by Vivian Sobchack in that they are marked by duration, which could lead us to see them as compassionate (see Introduction). However, our extratextual knowledge of the Nazis' campaign to murder all of the Jewish people in Europe belies this interpretation. A "gaze" that more likely describes these images is another gaze identified by Sobchack: the "professional gaze." Sobchack writes that this gaze is "marked by ethical ambiguity, by technical and *machinelike competence* in the face of an event that seems to call for further and more humane response."[14] These horrifying unstaged scenes suggest this sense of a dispassionate, machinelike recording of a situation that seems to demand compassionate intervention.

Meanwhile, the degree of staging in other images is initially unclear. Many of the scenes from "Das Ghetto" emphasize a disparity between impoverished and starving Jewish residents of the ghetto and those who are better off. Böser asserts,

> Even in its unfinished and silent state the rhetorical structure and propagandistic thrust that underlies the Warsaw footage is readily evident. It is predominantly conveyed through the constant juxtaposition of extremes between or within shots: the film is structured around the contrast between the well-clad and well-fed who live a life of "luxury," and the destitute and emaciated whose bodies are discarded as waste.[15]

Yet, despite the repetition of this juxtaposition, these images could still suggest a professional gaze, purporting to simply "document" the uncaring attitudes of rich Jews toward their poorer fellows. However, as Hersonski's film demonstrates, reading the Nazi camera's gaze in terms of the ethically ambiguous professional gaze is, in fact, far too generous. *A Film Unfinished* reveals the gaze of "Das Ghetto" to be propagandistic and dehumanizing, and a fundamentally unethical form of filmmaking vis-à-vis both the film subjects and the audience.

In *A Film Unfinished*, voice frequently acts as counterpoint to the "Das Ghetto" images. As we watch the silent "Das Ghetto" footage, voiceover narration provides historical context, explaining the origins of the footage and the history of its (mis)use. The status of the footage as documentary evidence, already put into question by the main voiceover, then begins to be further undercut as head of the Warsaw Ghetto Jewish Council Adam Czerniakov's diary entries about the Nazi film crew's activities are read on the soundtrack. Czerniakov notes the various ways in which the Nazi filmmakers coerced Jewish actors into participating in the film through payment or fear. He further describes how some of the scenes were staged. For instance, over corresponding images, we hear a voice reading Czerniakov's diary entry for 3 May 1942: "At 10 A.M. the propaganda crew arrived. They started to take pictures in my office. First, they staged a scene of rabbis and petitioners entering my office, etc. Then they removed all the paintings and charts and brought in a nine-armed candlestick with all the candles lit." As we watch the images overlaid with this narration, their staged and stilted nature becomes glaringly evident. Later, during the circumcision scene, we also hear Czerniakov's entry about the event. He states that the Germans insisted that the procedure be performed in a home rather than a hospital, which would have been customary and, presumably, safer. He also notes that the scene was in jeopardy since it was uncertain if the main "actor," the baby, would live long enough to complete it. Yet the Nazis were determined to film the scene. Czerniakov's spoken diary entries juxtaposed against the "Das Ghetto" footage undercut any claim that the images might represent "typical" Jewish life in the ghetto; rather, these images are revealed as fictional and—in the case of the circumcision scene—utterly inhumane.

Like Czerniakov's diary entries, the transcript of postwar testimony by German cameraman Willy Wist, read aloud on the soundtrack over a stylized reenactment of his deposition, also serves to undermine any sense that the scenes were objective representations of the ghetto. Wist claims he was just filming what he was told to film, stating that he had little direct contact with the Jewish people but that SS officers chose Jewish people for him to film whom they "deemed appropriate for filming." Wist also notes that the Jewish people were "frightened of the SS [so] there were no incidents during filming." These statements emphasize the fact that the film subjects were carefully chosen by the SS for particular reasons and coerced into participating. Wist also admits his sense that the very choice of film subjects revealed a propagandistic intent. "I never knew what the purpose of the films we shot was," he says. "However, it was absolutely clear to me that they were intended for propaganda, particularly because we were focusing on the extreme differences between the rich and the poor Jews." Wist repeatedly attempts to disown the dehumanizing, propagandistic gaze, even complaining at one point that "we didn't have a chance to express ourselves," but he nevertheless acknowledges his participation in constructing a false representation.

In addition to the narrated voices of Czerniakov and Wist, a third historical voice—or set of voices—is summoned to act as counterpoint to the "Das Ghetto" imagery. Emanuel Ringelblum, a Jewish historian who was forcibly resettled in the Warsaw Ghetto, organized a group of Jewish writers, artists, scientists, workers, and even children to document in writing their experiences in the ghetto, thereby creating an archive of Jewish experience known as *Oneg Shabbat*. Excerpts from some of these documents are also read on the soundtrack, some directly addressing the German filmmakers' activities. "They continue filming everything inside the Ghetto," one voice says. "All the scenes are being staged. On Smocza Street, they assembled a crowd of Jews and ordered the Jewish policemen to disperse them." Another voice adds, "In order to achieve a more 'natural' effect, guns were fired in the air to induce people to flee in panic." As we watch these scenes, which might have been read as documentary crowd footage, the narration transforms the footage into a massive performance, albeit one in which the Jewish actors are genuinely frightened. This scene in *A Film Unfinished* ends with a freeze frame in which Hersonski zooms into the background of the image to focus on a German cameraman recording—another blow to the ostensible spontaneity of the event. Clearly, multiple German cameras were in position to film this scene (figure 8). The archival statements, combined with Hersonski's editing, serve to further weaken the "Das Ghetto" images' claim to be straightforward documentation, unmasking the professional gaze as a deceptive propagandistic gaze.

Hersonski's own documentary images also work as counterpoint to the images from "Das Ghetto." For instance, the Nazi footage is frequently interspersed with recent interviews with elderly survivors of the ghetto, who were children or young adults when the "Das Ghetto" footage was produced. As these survivors watch the footage—the light from the screen reflected on their faces—they comment on it, reframing our reading with their personal recollections. The survivors remember the specific locations and some of the people seen in the footage: a street performer named Rubenstein, a woman who frequently stood in the street holding her baby and begging for a piece of bread. They also remember the presence of the film crew, the fear that the Jewish residents experienced when the crew appeared, and the crew's overt interest in filming corpses lying in the street. These reminiscences subvert any pretense to a humane or even professional gaze by further exposing the unequal power relations between the filmmakers and their subjects. Other survivor observations challenge particular images' claim to documentary status. Over scenes of a market, one survivor notes that the Germans "brought geese to the market to prove that Jews were living in reasonable conditions," changing the food we see for sale into props. Over footage showing a well-dressed Jewish woman setting a table with flowers and a teapot in a well-appointed apartment, another survivor comments, "Where did one ever see a flower? We would have eaten the flower. Who could stay in their private apartment with their furniture and their teapot? Who? Only the privileged like Czerniakov." This commentary overtly contradicts

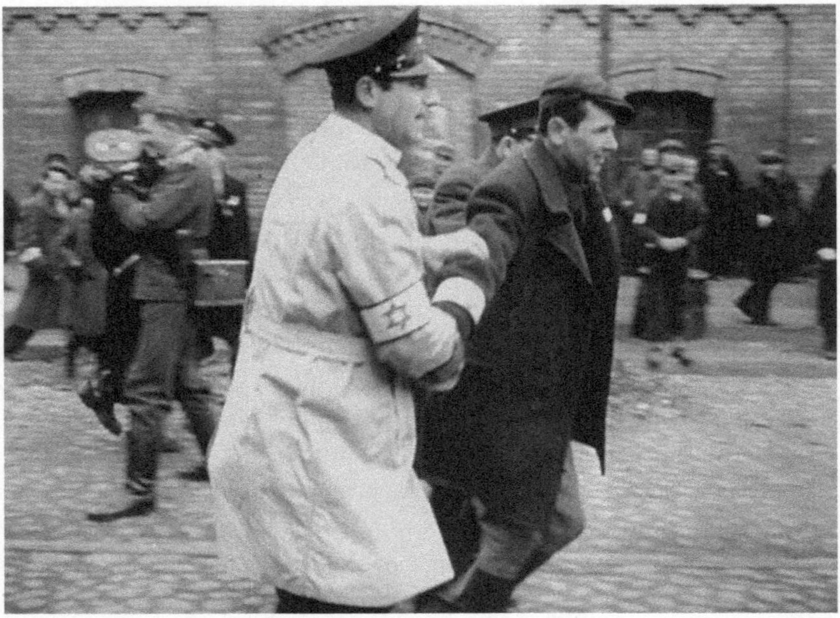

FIGURE 8 Still from *A Film Unfinished* (Yael Hersonski, 2010). Courtesy of the artist.

any pretense to typicality in the footage staged in Czerniakov's apartment. Moreover, a third survivor comments explicitly on the filmmakers' tendency to film the starving beside those who were better off. She says,

> There were many contrasts in the ghetto. Many people kept clean and preserved their dignity. We used to shower and brush our teeth every day. Our mother took good care of us, even though the conditions were impossible. People who are not starving to death don't surrender their humanity.... People did what they could. That was the tremendous contrast and paradox that the Germans had created.

Instead of allowing the footage to read as an indictment against the better-off Jewish prisoners of the ghetto, this commentary establishes their heroism for maintaining their dignity in the face of an impossible situation. Moreover, the survivor points to the fact—obscured by the footage—that the ones to blame for all of the misery are the Germans themselves. A critical gaze is turned back on the Germans through this survivor's viewing of the "Das Ghetto" footage.

While the various forms of testimony do much to expose the Nazis' intentions, the propagandistic, dehumanizing gaze of the Nazi filmmakers becomes even more apparent when additional found footage is inserted into the film. In 1998 in a U.S. Air Force base, forty-four years after the "Das Ghetto" footage was found in East Germany, filmmaker Adrian Wood discovered two additional reels from the same shoot, which included outtakes that, Hersonski's film asserts, the Nazis never meant to be seen. These outtakes *visibly* reveal that the Nazi film crew was not simply filming the reality of the ghetto as it spontaneously occurred but, rather, staging their own vision of that reality. Multiple takes of the same scenes, which Hersonski shows in succession, demonstrate that the film crew instructed Jewish people to perform particular acts in order to convey a preconceived image of the ghetto, one that emphasized the disparity between richer and poorer Jews and constructed a fictional vision of the richer Jews' uncaring attitude toward their poorer neighbors. For instance, we see several takes of a well-dressed woman ignoring a pair of boys dressed in rags as she enters a butcher shop. By staging these scenes and presenting them as documentary evidence, the Nazis attempted to disguise their propagandistic gaze as the professional gaze. However, Hersonski's "misuse" of the outtakes makes the propagandistic, dehumanizing gaze explicit. Indeed, in relation to the staged Nazi footage that has been accepted as unbiased documentation, it asserts a "revelatory gaze," offering us context that fundamentally changes how we view the footage.

Through this revelatory gaze, *A Film Unfinished* fulfills an ethical imperative to demonstrate that the purported documentary intention to record the "real" may conceal more devious intentions, the ostensibly professional gaze disguising the propagandistic gaze. Yet nothing is ethically simple. To reuse these images may still seem unethical in relation to the people depicted in the images, most of whom are dead. Many, if not all, of them were coerced into being filmed. Certainly, those whose dead bodies were filmed never had any say in the matter. To look at these images could be considered a further violation of their dignity and humanity. There is often a certain voyeuristic fascination in viewing the bodies of the poor, the starving, the dead, or the soon-to-be-dead. While the images are mostly anonymous—the names of most of the people filmed are unknown—they are not occluded. We see every detail of the emaciated corpses sliding into their mass grave. Yet there also seems to be an ethical imperative to bear witness; to occlude these images would obscure the extent of the horror of what the Nazis did. Thus, in addition to a revelatory gaze, *A Film Unfinished* also reasserts a humane gaze over and above the dehumanizing gaze of the Nazi filmmakers. In addition to directing our gaze to the German cameramen, Hersonski's use of freeze frames and slow motion also increases the duration of our own gaze at the Jewish subjects. By increasing the duration of the dehumanizing propagandistic gaze, she asserts her own compassionate subjective responsiveness and thereby transforms—or at least attempts to transform—the gaze into its opposite: the humane gaze that bears witness. Through this palimpsest of gazes, footage intended to degrade and demean is reclaimed as a tribute to those who were filmed against their will and then—most of them—sent to die soon after. Viewing the Nazis' footage, which was meant to dehumanize in order to justify mass murder, may to some degree provoke a sense of voyeuristic complicity in the viewer. However, the "misuse" of the footage in the name of historical justice, in my view, warrants its reuse. As she watches the Nazi footage of the dying and dead, one survivor weeps, saying, "Today, I am human. Today, I can cry."

## The Accusatory Gaze

An explicit countergaze is likewise apparent in *You Don't Like the Truth: Four Days Inside Guantánamo* (Patricio Henriquez, Luc Côté, 2010), but the gaze here is somewhat different from the revelatory gaze described above. Whereas *A Film Unfinished* primarily reveals the deceptive intent of the perpetrator images that it incorporates, *You Don't Like the Truth,* rather, shifts the focus of the footage from its ostensible subject to the other figures in the frame. In doing so, it transforms what was figure into ground and vice versa. It thereby becomes a critique of those other figures, who were never meant to be the objects of our gaze. This is similar to how Hersonski's film points to the German camera operators visible in some of the staged Nazi footage, but Henriquez and Côté's film takes this as one of its primary strategies.

*You Don't Like the Truth* consists primarily of footage appropriated from seven hours of interrogation recordings originally produced over four days in February 2003 in the US military detention center in Guantánamo Bay. The subject being interrogated is Omar Khadr, who was at the time a sixteen-year-old Canadian citizen accused of killing an American soldier in Afghanistan. On 27 July 2002, at age fifteen, Khadr was severely wounded during fighting between U.S. soldiers and Taliban fighters in the village of Ayub Kheyl. He was alleged to have thrown a grenade that killed U.S. Army Sergeant 1st Class Christopher Speer. While he was being held at Bagram Airfield, he pleaded guilty to throwing the grenade and was then taken to Guantánamo Bay despite his status as both a minor and a Canadian citizen. The interrogators in the video are members of the Canadian Security Intelligence Service (CSIS). Three surveillance cameras were recording the interrogation producing three types of image: an extreme long shot in which Khadr, a table, and both interrogators are usually visible; a medium shot of Khadr taken through a vent; and a reverse shot of the vent and part of the interrogators' side of the table. The film is divided into four sections: "Day 1: Hope," "Day 2: Fallout," "Day 3: Blackmail," and "Day 4: Failure." In each section, the interrogation footage is alternated with or else accompanied in split screen by later interviews with a variety of people including Khadr's former cellmates Moazzam Begg, Mamdou Habib, and Omar Deghayes; his lawyers Lieutenant-Commander William Kuebler, Nathan Whitling, and Dennis Edney; *Toronto Star* reporter Michelle Shepard; psychiatrists Dr. Raul Berdichevsky and Dr. Stephen Xenakis; a former U.S. intelligence officer and interrogator, Damien Corsetti; and others.

The appropriated interrogation footage is structured, in part, by the "hermetic gaze" associated with secret recordings, which I discussed in relation to Jane Gillooly's *Suitcase of Love and Shame* (see Chapter 1). However, in contrast to the personal footage appropriated in Gillooly's film, which reads as secret due to its intimate address, this footage was explicitly classified as secret by intelligence agencies—until it was determined by a court of law to warrant public scrutiny. A title early in the film notes that "In July 2008, The Supreme Court of Canada authorized the disclosure of a seven-hour video that had been classified as top secret." Thus, we are cued to understand that this footage was never intended by its producers to become public. Moreover, the callous behavior of the interrogators also suggests that they did not expect this footage to be seen by anyone other than an audience entirely aligned with their aims as interrogators. As one of the filmmakers, Patricio Henriquez, put it in a later essay, "The Canadian agents played their roles with an authenticity guaranteed by the absolute certainty that recordings would never be brought to public knowledge."[16] Indeed, the footage was clearly produced without the anticipation that it would be viewed beyond the confines of Guantánamo Bay. The interrogators may have even expected it to be destroyed. As noted in a 2008 report entitled "Captured on Tape: Interrogation and Videotaping of Detainees in Guantánamo," by the Seton Hall University School of Law Center for Policy and Research,

> The CIA is just one of many entities that interrogated detainees in Guantánamo. . . . Each of these entities has identical motives to destroy taped investigations as did the CIA, and each can apply an identical justification to the destruction of tapes: the entity's interest in "protecting" the interrogators.[17]

In the name of protecting the interrogators, these entities, including CSIS, could actually cover up their violation of detainees' rights. The same report notes that some Guantánamo Bay interrogation tapes were, in fact, destroyed. Thus, the hermetic gaze, which never imagines a broad audience—and certainly not a critical one—is clearly at play in this interrogation footage.

When the Canadian Supreme Court ordered the Khadr interrogation footage released to the public, however, the hermeticism of the gaze associated with secret recordings was breached. Significantly though, in the released footage the heads of the interrogators are obscured by floating black circles that continuously mask their faces as they move around. In addition, in several sections, we see Khadr speaking but the audio goes suddenly silent, alerting us to the fact that we are being sonically shut out. The film notes in a title, "Invoking security reasons, CSIS requested and obtained from the court the right to erase some audio from the video released to the public." Hence, even before it became available to public view and for appropriation, the footage had already been altered by its "author," the security apparatus affiliated with Guantánamo Bay. As a result, vestiges of the hermetic gaze persist even in the appropriation.

Yet, the hermetic gaze is not the only one at work in the interrogation footage. The ostensible purpose of recording interrogations in Guantánamo Bay is to produce a record of any useful intelligence in the "war on terror," in other words, information that can be used to stop or capture terrorists. It is also, presumably, meant to be used to convict the people who are being interrogated. The gaze of the hidden cameras—unmoving, with no one physically behind them—seems to be neutral, simply documenting the interrogation. Yet, the fact of their hiddenness and their very presence in this hermetic space belies this neutrality. As Joseph Pugliese notes in his reading of the footage taken from the camera hidden behind the barred vent,

> The persistence of this bar in the field of vision forecloses the possibility for the filmic lens/spectator's eye to be transparent and invisibilised. It materialises the voyeuristic relation of this "peephole" looking into the anguish of the target subject, thereby bringing into scopic focus the asymmetries of power that mark this relation; in this asymmetrical scopic relation, Khadr has no visual right of reply to his unknown and invisibilised spectator.[18]

Within this asymmetrical structure of scopic and audial power, it is evident that the cameras' purpose is to trap, to extract information, and—ultimately—to condemn the one at the center of the frame. Although there is no actual human body immediately behind the camera, the interrogation room cameras are aligned with what I call an "extractive gaze." In itself, obtaining information from someone is not necessarily dehumanizing; however, the extractive gaze seeks to transform human beings into information regardless of the consequences for the human beings themselves. This gaze evinces no sympathy or empathy. Its duration, unaffiliated with any human body, does not signal a humane gaze with its "subjective responsiveness" but rather simply the gaze of a computer with essentially unlimited storage space. Nor is this just a "professional gaze" that documents without bias or specific agenda. The camera is present as a prosthesis to the interrogators—and may be deleted if it becomes a danger to the interrogators themselves.

The extractive function of the camera is reinforced by the behavior of the interrogators, whom we hear and partly see onscreen. In the beginning, they allow Khadr to think that they are Canadian diplomats who are there to help him get out of Guantánamo. They gain his trust by telling him they are Canadian, removing his handcuffs, offering him a Subway sandwich, and so on. Yet, as *You Don't Like the Truth* reveals, they want only to extract information from him that will help convict him or lead to other supposed terrorists. Over the course of the film, it becomes increasingly evident both to Khadr and to the viewer that these interrogators do not care about Khadr as a human being with rights, but only about the information they can obtain from him. Their extractive gaze is fundamentally dehumanizing. Although it records Khadr's very human response to his mistreatment, this is incidental to his value as "intelligence."

*You Don't Like the Truth,* however, both reveals this extractive gaze and asserts a different gaze, retraining our attention. The focus of the original video is Khadr. This is obvious from the way he is centered in the frame. He is the object of the original gaze of the cameras, aligned with the security apparatus as a whole rather than any individual maker. Yet, despite the blacking out of his face, the figure that is foregrounded in this film is the unnamed interrogator, who comes off as callous, cruel, and incompetent. In his review of the film for *The Guardian,* Peter Bradshaw writes, "This almost unbearably painful documentary features what could be the most hateful villain to appear in the cinema this year. And he is just a disembodied voice."[19] Indeed, even as the black circle makes his face invisible, over the course of the documentary the anonymous and faceless lead interrogator becomes the central focus through his voice. This takes time. In the first section of the film, "Hope," Khadr appears genuinely happy to see the interrogators, thinking that they are there to help him. And, in the beginning, the lead interrogator seems like a decent person to both Khadr and the viewer. He starts the "interview," saying,

> If at any time you don't understand what I'm saying or you want it clarified a bit, just don't hesitate to ask. And if I'm not getting what you're saying. You know, just a normal conversation. I don't want you to feel like you have to come up with an answer if you really don't know.

Khadr responds positively, answering most of the interrogator's questions willingly, even as they veer towards his father's possible affiliation with Osama bin Laden. However, in the footage from the second day included in the section "Fallout," it becomes clear to both Khadr and the viewer that this is not a normal conversation and that the lead interrogator only wants Khadr to give them information. When the interrogators come in, Khadr is clearly upset and says there is something he is afraid to tell them. "Promise me you're gonna protect me from the Americans," he says. The lead interrogator refuses to make this promise, insisting that Khadr tell him what he is afraid to say without any guarantees, asking, "Why don't you just tell us what it is you have to say?" This is the moment in which the lead interrogator's lack of empathy for Khadr first becomes apparent. Khadr tells the interrogator that he confessed to the Americans only because they tortured him at Bagram Airfield, where he was held after the firefight in which he was wounded and Speer was killed. Soon after, Khadr takes off his shirt to show the interrogator the scars he bears from the firefight, crying as he describes his mistreatment by the Americans. The interrogator responds, "[Your wounds] look like they're healing well to me. I'm not a doctor but I think you're getting good medical care." "No, I'm not. You're not here," Khadr responds. Later, when Khadr—who lost sight in one of his eyes and sustained major injuries all over his body during the firefight—says, sobbing, "I lost my eyes. I lost my feet. Everything." The interrogator replies, "No, you still have your eyes and your feet are still at the end of your legs." Khadr responds, "You don't care about me. Nobody cares about me." Pugliese reads this scene, writing, "In the face of Khadr's attestation of his trauma of fragmentation and loss, the interrogator replies with a clinical observation that fails to register the psychic reality of Khadr's suffering."[20] In fact, it is likely that this sense of detached "clinical observation" in the face of Khadr's pain that produces—at least in a viewer who has any sympathy for Khadr—the greatest sense of horror. In *You Don't Like the Truth,* a later interview with Damien Corsetti—a former U.S. soldier who was charged with mistreating and assaulting prisoners at Bagram and whose nicknames included "Monster" and "The King of Torture"—is intercut with this footage as he watches it on a computer screen (figure 9). He says, "This is exactly why as an interrogator, you wouldn't want cameras in the interrogation room. We fought that off both at Bagram and at Abu Ghraib. We didn't want cameras in there." This statement, especially coming from someone like Corsetti, validates our sense that the interrogator in the footage, bolstered by the belief that this footage will never become public, knows that he is abusing Khadr—but just doesn't care. What the documentary asks us to attend to is less Khadr himself than the interrogator, whom we cannot see but whose words and complete lack of "subjective responsiveness" reveal his inhumanity vis-à-vis Khadr.

Yet, what is ultimately being figured in the documentary is less the lead interrogator than the "security" apparatus of which he is just a small part. This becomes clear when, moments later, the interrogators leave Khadr crying in the room, telling him they will continue the interrogation once he has gotten himself together. We watch for several minutes as Khadr, alone, sobs, calling for his mother over and over. This is intercut in the film with others watching the footage after the fact—including his mother, his former cellmates, his Canadian lawyer Nathan Whitling, and Dr. Berdichevsky. The ethics of appropriating this footage is especially complex in that watching it feels like a violation of Khadr's privacy during a moment of great vulnerability. At the same time, of course, his privacy was already violated by the presence of the cameras of which he may or may not have been aware. Dr. Berdichevsky notes in the film that Khadr was watched and observed during this segment by the interrogators for about sixteen minutes, to see

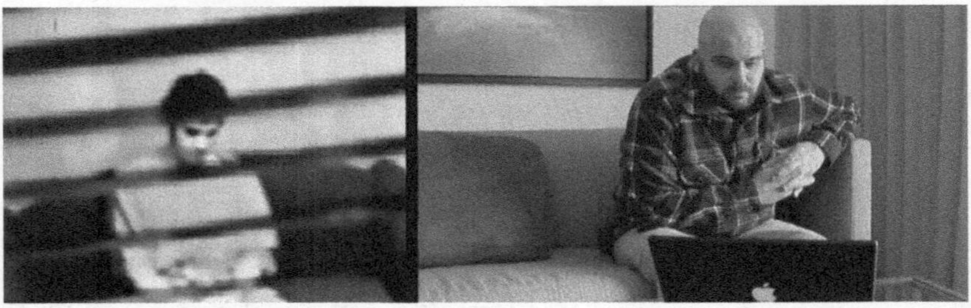

FIGURE 9 Still from *You Don't Like the Truth: Four Days Inside Guantanamo* (Patricio Henriquez, Luc Côté, 2010).

whether there was an opportunity when Khadr was psychologically susceptible so that they could go back and continue the interrogation. Framed through this commentary, then, what is figured in Henriquez and Côté's appropriation is not so much Khadr crying—although that is certainly apparent and upsetting to a sympathetic viewer—but rather the extractive gaze of the surveillance camera and the system it represents, which can look upon a child crying for his mother with no feeling at all.

The latter two sections of the film, "Blackmail" and "Failure," reinforce our negative impression of both the lead interrogator and the system he serves. As he fails to get the information he wants, the interrogator becomes increasingly petulant. At one point in the section called "Failure," Khadr is explaining that he lied earlier because he was afraid of being tortured again.

> INTERROGATOR . . . It's never gonna get any worse for you now, but—
>
> KHADR It may get worse.
>
> INTERROGATOR In what sense?
>
> KHADR More torturing. Get put in an isolated room with no stuff.
>
> INTERROGATOR Get put in an isolated room with no stuff? I wouldn't consider that to be torture.
>
> KHADR I don't think you could handle that for one night.
>
> INTERROGATOR No? Well, I mean, fortunately I'm not in a position where that has to be something I have to worry about. I'm not here to change positions with you and I'm not here to tell you what your life is about right now because, quite honestly, that doesn't apply to me.

Rather than taking seriously Khadr's fears, the interrogator dismisses them. Then, when Khadr attempts to make the interrogator imagine being in a similar position, the interrogator dismisses this very possibility as well. The film then cuts to Dr. Berdichevsky, who says,

> I think it's one of the most cruel things that you can possibly say to anybody who's in that kind of a predicament. He's really saying, "You know what? You're the product of your circumstances and I don't have anything to do with it. So yes, we are both from Scarborough, you're a man, I'm a man, but you know what? When it comes to this, we're not equal." And he's proud in saying, "I'm not in trouble. You're in trouble. And what happens to people in trouble. They can be put in detention, they can even be tortured. . . . Fortunately, I don't have to worry about it."

Indeed, what is most disturbing about this exchange is the interrogator's explicit denial of his and Khadr's shared status as human beings. The idea that he does not even need to contemplate what it would be like to "change positions" with Khadr, that Khadr's fears do not "apply to" him undermines the very basis of empathy, which is the ability (and willingness) to imagine oneself in the position of another. Simply by showing this exchange, the film foregrounds the interrogator's lack of basic empathy, and the commentary by Berdichevsky further affirms this lack.

The gaze the documentary asserts over and above the hermetic, extractive gaze of the appropriated interrogation footage is similar to the "disclosing gaze" that I discussed in relation to the surreptitious recordings appropriated in *Shut Up Little Man: An Audio Misadventure* (see Chapter 1). Yet, what I want to emphasize here is how *You Don't Like the Truth* retrains our attention on those who created the footage as perpetrators of a crime. Within the context of this film, these images are revealed as, precisely, perpetrator images. It is one thing to take surreptitious recordings of your unruly neighbors, as in *Shut Up Little Man*; it is another to record the violation of a child's basic human rights—as well as his legal ones. Beyond disclosing and revealing, the gaze of this film also accuses. Hence, it solicits an "accusatory gaze" that explicitly seeks to use footage created by the security apparatus against itself, accusing both low-level interrogators and the high-level bureaucrats who authorized this type of interrogation of violating Khadr's rights. In fact, the footage from this interrogation likely played a role not only in Khadr's eventual repatriation to Canada but also in his civil suit against the Canadian federal government for infringing upon his rights under the Charter of Rights and Freedoms. The lawsuit was settled in 2017 with a

$10.5 million payment and an apology by the federal government.[21] Even as we may feel that we are aligned with the gaze of the perpetrator and that we may once again be violating Khadr's rights by watching him in some of his most defenseless moments, the accusatory gaze—which actively asserts the wrong done to him—may at least mitigate this sense of ethical violation. The purpose of the appropriation is to demonstrate the injustice of his experience and to bring his terrorizers to justice—or, if not justice, at least to make them audible (if not fully visible) for our judgment.

## The Reformative Gaze

*A Film Unfinished* and *You Don't Like the Truth* are both documentaries that make their reframing of perpetrator footage explicit. In contrast, *Sara Nokomis Weir* (Brian L. Frye, 2014) is an experimental film that does not so much appropriate perpetrator footage but, rather, appropriates a previous *appropriation* that can be seen as potentially unethical or even a perpetration of concealed violence. Frye's film demonstrates that layers of use, reuse, and misuse can easily multiply, making the unpacking of their ethics even more difficult. At the same time, the stakes of Frye's film are literally a life—and the fairness of the US judicial system in which audiovisual evidence is playing an increasingly important role in courtrooms, which suggests that examining these layers is worthwhile.

In 1995, Douglas Oliver Kelly was convicted of murdering 19-year-old Sara Nokomis Weir two years before. In the penalty phase of the trial, the jury was shown a twenty-minute video that compiled snapshots and home videos of Sara Weir taken throughout her life. It was accompanied by a voiceover spoken by her adoptive mother, Martha Farwell, narrating the events on the image track, and music by Enya in the background. The jury sentenced Kelly to death. Kelly's lawyer then appealed the death sentence, arguing that the jury should not have been allowed to see the video because it was prejudicial. The California Supreme Court upheld the verdict. Kelly's lawyer then appealed to the U.S. Supreme Court, which refused to review the case. As a result, Kelly remained on death row. This victim impact video has raised much debate among legal scholars about the legalities of victim impact videos in general. However, the question of ethics—which might help clarify the legal issues—has been less clearly articulated.

In form, the video presented in *People v. Kelly* is quite similar to that of the "memorial tribute video," a form that has become one of the primary cultural forms through which mourning is enacted in contemporary society among those who have access to even simple computer technology. These videos are often shown at funerals or posted online. There are now many businesses that will compile images for you and add music, as well as online services that—for a monthly fee—offer pre-existing templates to which you simply add photos or video clips. These videos can be viewed as works of audiovisual appropriation because the images usually do not appear to have been produced with the intention of placing them in a memorial tribute video. In other words, they have been repurposed regardless of who is reusing them. Yet, while the by-definition unsanctioned appropriation of images of a dead person can raise ethical questions, the ethics of these appropriations generally seem unproblematic because these videos are usually produced or commissioned by a relative or friend of the deceased to celebrate and mourn for them. Moreover, even when they are posted online, they read as intended to be viewed primarily by people who knew and cared about the deceased. Yet, when this format appears as evidence within the context of a capital case, the ethics become much more complex.

Like funerals, trials are about memory and the past. Unlike funerals, however, they are dedicated to reconstructing past actions in order to determine who did what to whom and who is to blame, as well as to mete out punishment. Witnesses present testimony and evidence as to what happened. Narrated memories and the evidence that substantiates them are thereby transformed into "facts," on the basis of which the jurors must determine guilt or innocence and sometimes a sentence. But while memory is closely aligned with affect, trials are supposed to exclude emotion. Juries are supposed to make their decisions relying only on evidence and reason. This is particularly true in death penalty cases. In 1977 in *Gardner v. Florida*, the U.S. Supreme Court stated that "it is of vital importance to the defendant and to the community that any decision to impose the death sentence be, and appear to be, based on reason rather than caprice or emotion."[22] Yet, the line between reason and emotion becomes exceptionally blurry in relationship to victim impact evidence. As Todd Butler has noted, "Critics in both the United States and Canada have long insisted that . . . [victim impact statements] inappropriately interject passion into juridical deliberation and thereby transform presumptively objective court processes into mechanisms for revenge."[23] Many of these critiques have been made about victim impact *testimony*. They become even more salient in relation to victim impact *videos*. Louis-Georges Schwartz has shown that, since their earliest introduction into courtrooms, moving images have raised concerns about their potential to produce emotion. "Formally, the cinema encourages the use of motion pictures to produce subjectivity and affect, but the courts proscribe such effects. Evidentiary films and videos must function as nonsubjective seeing and any affect they contain must be screened out as prejudicial."[24] However, as Schwartz demonstrates, the line between affect and fact is often muddied by moving images.

Moreover, unlike most other forms of courtroom evidence, the goal of victim impact evidence is not to help jurors determine what happened or the guilt or innocence of the defendant. It serves, rather, to demonstrate "the loss to the victim's family and to society which have resulted from the defendant's homicide."[25] Victim impact evidence has been allowed in US courts during the penalty phase of a trial since the U.S. Supreme Court ruled in *Payne v. Tennessee* in 1991, overturning *Booth v. Maryland* and *South Carolina v. Gathers*, which had previously precluded the use of victim impact evidence. According to Justice Sandra Day O'Connor, whose opinion in *Payne* concurred with the majority, "there is no strong societal consensus that a jury may not take into account the loss suffered by a victim's family or that a murder victim must remain a faceless stranger." She further noted that the "State may decide also that the jury should see 'a quick glimpse of the life the petitioner chose to extinguish' . . . to remind the jury that the person whose life was taken was a unique human being.'" O'Connor added, however, that victim impact evidence should be excluded when it is deemed "unduly inflammatory" and therefore prejudicial.[26]

As legal scholar Emily Holland notes, "Video was not, seemingly, a form of victim impact evidence that the Supreme Court contemplated in *Payne*."[27] Holland further demonstrates that because Payne provided courts with little guidance in determining what victim impact evidence is too emotional or prejudicial to be allowed, courts are inconsistent in terms of what kind of victim impact video is permitted.[28] The U.S. Supreme Court has not ruled on this matter, declining to hear arguments in *People v. Kelly*, the trial in which Farwell's victim impact video was presented and Kelly was sentenced, as well as another case involving a victim impact video, *People v. Zamudio*. Nevertheless, two justices argued in writing that the court should have granted review of these cases. Justice John Paul Stevens wrote that "the videos added nothing relevant to the jury's deliberation and invited a verdict based on sentiment, rather than reasoned judgment." He also argued that they "vastly exceed[ed] the 'quick glimpse' the Court's majority contemplated when it overruled *Booth*." Justice Stephen Breyer, who would also have granted review in *Kelly v. California*, stated regarding the Weir video that "it is this minimal probity coupled with the video's purely emotional impact that may call due process protections into play."[29] Thus, it is clear that the debate about the admissibility of victim impact videos, particularly in death penalty cases, remains unresolved.

Legal scholar Regina Austin has written about the close relationship between the form of certain victim impact videos, including the one shown in *People v. Kelly*, and the memorial tribute videos shown at funerals and posted online.[30] She also notes how victim impact videos' "limited probative value"—value as proof—is countered by its affective force. Drawing on Roland Barthes, she has written,

> Seeing the victim on screen—happy and oblivious to her or his fate in what seems to be the here and now—makes viewers uncomfortable because they know that the victim will never be that way again. It is a bit like watching a ghost. No one can stop time or turn back the clock. The "angst" that the viewers experience has been described as an "intolerable nostalgia" stemming from the "present absence" of the victim.[31]

While this sense of angst and nostalgia may not be ethically problematic in certain circumstances, in the courtroom in which a jury is deliberating whether or not to sentence a defendant to death, the ethics of appropriation are complicated by the extremely high stakes.

In the case of the victim impact video shown in *People v. Kelly*, the gaze originally solicited by the photographs and videos of Sara Weir reads as the familial, preservationist gaze associated with what Richard Chalfen has termed "home mode documents."[32] In other words, these images read as having been taken purely as a prosthesis to personal and family memory, as a means of preserving a fragment of a happy moment for future remembrance to be shared exclusively among friends and family members. These images do not appear to anticipate a public viewing and certainly not one occurring within a legal context. It goes perhaps without saying that they do not read in any sense as perpetrator images. The second gaze, that solicited in the act of appropriation, seems—on its surface—to be a "memorial gaze," the same gaze associated with memorial tribute videos, which serves to idealize and commemorate the deceased. However, the context in which this video was intended to be shown belies this apparent gaze. It solicits a literally "judgmental gaze" in the guise of a memorial gaze. This masquerade is not entirely apparent from the text itself. If viewed online, for instance (and the original victim impact video is currently available on YouTube), without reading the accompanying text that explains its production, this masquerade may not be clear.[33] The only reference to the trial is a brief mention at the end. Over images of men riding horses through a mountainous landscape (the only images in the video that do not include Sara Weir), Farwell says: "As time goes by, I try very hard not to think of Sara in terms of this terrible tragedy that we've had to deal with here in court, but rather of her in a place like this." This reference to the "terrible tragedy that we've had to deal with here in court" is the only line that indicates the intended viewing context of the video. This reference, however, points to the offscreen space in which the video was meant to be shown and obliquely introduces the defendant into the video.

In most of the films in this study, the question of the ethics of appropriation is primarily about the rights of the film subject—in this case, Sara Weir—and to some degree the rights of the audience. Yet here, there is another subject to whom there is an ethical obligation: the defendant Douglas Kelly. In regard to Sara Weir, whom Kelly violently and horrifically murdered, one might argue that the appropriation of Sara's image into the victim impact video is an actively ethical act, demanding justice for her in her absence. In regard to Douglas Kelly, however, the judgmental gaze has the potential to become a vengeful, murderous gaze. The victim impact video asks the implied viewer—the juror—to kill Kelly by proxy. Kelly most likely did commit this hideous act. Hence, whether or not one supports capital punishment may determine one's view of the ethics of this appropriation. Yet, regardless of one's stance on the death penalty, there is something ethically disturbing about this video. I would suggest that it is the particular editing of the images and the inclusion of Enya's music that generate the affective form that transforms the gaze from a simply judgmental one, which could be a fair judgment, to a vengeful one, which is most likely not a fair judgment—at least not within the context of the United States legal system.

The ethics of this first appropriation are brought into relief by Frye's film, *Sara Nokomis Weir.*[34] To make this film, Frye appropriated the image track of the victim impact video from *People v. Kelly,* removed the original soundtrack, and added a soundtrack composed of parts of the oral discussion of the video that took place during Kelly's appeal to the California Supreme Court. The juxtaposition between image track and soundtrack in Frye's film functions primarily to reveal the inadequacy of current legal discourse when it comes to discussing the affective dimensions of audiovisual material. Toward the beginning of Frye's film, accompanying images of Weir as a baby, we hear Evan Young, the lawyer for the appellant Douglas Kelly, note that although courts do allow victim impact evidence, this does not mean that there are no limits on "emotional evidence." She argues that the video violates due process because it is too long, providing more than the "quick glimpse" allowed by *Payne*. However, the following discussion of the video's length does little to clarify what constitutes a quick glimpse of a life that lasted nineteen years. Young argues that "one would have to say that twenty-plus minutes is a very long time to be looking at these kinds of images." One of the judges counters her assertion, saying, "It was just showing the victim at different points in her development from a small child to being a young woman at the time she was murdered. And maybe that's why it was long because it showed her at different stages of her life." For viewers of Frye's film, watching Weir change from a baby into a young child during this exchange emphasizes the fact that the notion of a "quick glimpse" is entirely subjective.

Beyond the court's neglect of the subjectivity involved in determining what counts as a "quick glimpse," the soundtrack of Frye's film also indicates the court's inability to adequately account for what video can and cannot actually convey to a jury. Few would disagree with the argument that "video evidence always conveys information beyond what spoken testimony alone can, as visual information always adds something to purely verbal information."[35] However, the precise nature of this "something" is less than clear in the oral discussion of Kelly's appeal. Later in Frye's film, we hear prosecutor Stephanie Brenan attempting to defend the admissibility of the video by claiming that it showed who Weir was as a "unique individual," referring to language in *Payne*. Brenan argues that "it was a brief glimpse to see what her personality was like, in the small parts of the video we saw that she was a shy—." The judge interrupts her, asking, "And why was that important in the context of this particular case?" Brenan falters as she replies, "It was important in the context of this particular case to see *who she was*. . . ." The judge then offers Brenan some help, suggesting that perhaps the video shows Weir's particular "vulnerability," a term Brenan then uses repeatedly. The

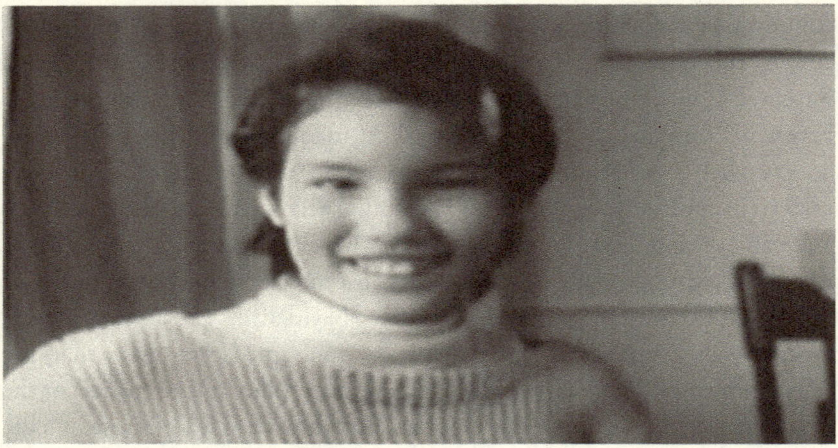

FIGURE 10 Still from *Sara Nokomis Weir* (Brian L. Frye, 2014).

judge then asks how the video conveys this vulnerability. Brenan refers to two of the home videos included in the victim impact video: one taken at her mother's wedding in which Weir tries to avoid being photographed, which Brenan says demonstrates that she was camera-shy, and another of a school singing performance in which Weir's posture suggests to Brenan that Weir was uncomfortable during her solo. In Frye's film, we see these images as Brenan speaks about them, so that we can witness these possible indications of Weir's personality. Although we can see what Brenan is talking about, her overemphasis on the empty phrase "*who she was*" again indicates the inadequacy of these words to convey our complex experience of watching these images.

As Frye's film shows, the lawyers' and judges' arguments fail on several levels because they do not know how to competently discuss the complexities of video representation. First, their arguments assume that photography and video, as indexical media, can unequivocally convey intangible things such as a personality or vulnerability. As Schwartz notes, "Once motion pictures are constituted as an index of the real, they can also function to suggest a fact rather than showing that fact directly."[36] Although we can infer certain things about Weir from the video clips, her "vulnerability" is not something actually visible. Second, they are unable to account for the particular qualities of the recordings appropriated into the victim impact video. In fact, what is at work in this particular video is not simply its indexicality or what Schwarz refers to as its "persuasive supplement."[37] While the indexicality of the imagery does serve as a persuasive supplement, the perception of the images as home mode documents is also relevant. It is not only Weir's innocence that is relevant here but also the perceived "innocence" of the images themselves. It matters that, as viewers, we perceive that the snapshots and home movies were not made to serve as courtroom evidence. We can surmise from their amateur quality and their banal content that they were produced, like most home mode documents, as a prosthesis to personal memories, a means to record and re-experience happy moments of family life (figure 10). The perception that images intended solely for personal and family reminiscence have been repurposed as evidence in a murder trial further emphasizes the fact that neither this young woman nor her family anticipated what would happen to her. Neither could they anticipate that the prosthetic personal memories of her recent childhood could so suddenly be transformed into a public document. The innocence of the images, their lack of anticipation of a public viewing context, reinforces the sense of Weir's innocence and its violent disruption. Third, the lawyers and judges are unable to articulate how the editing of the victim impact video generates a set of effects, namely, the sense that we are witnessing Weir's transformation across time. Visualizing the passage of time, especially from childhood to adulthood, often generates a feeling of sadness and loss even in viewers who were not present for the imaged events. Being able to "see" years passing as they are inscribed on a young girl's face as she grows speaks to our own experiences of growing and aging, watching our own loved ones grow and age, and knowing we cannot go back in time.[38] The knowledge that Weir was brutally murdered at the age of nineteen further intensifies the sense that some things, once lost, are gone forever. Neither we nor the jurors in *People v. Kelly* were personally acquainted with Sara Weir. Yet the act of witnessing these home mode images, edited together in this temporal sequence, offers us a sense of privileged access not to *information* about her but—seemingly—to a series of *memories*. While Farwell's narration of the events may have given the jury the impression they were learning factual information, as Frye's film demonstrates, there is no need for her mother's narration, because the details of the events are unimportant. It is the sense of proximity and intimacy, of being drawn into another family's daily life over the course of years that makes us feel like we "remember" Sara rather than "knowing about" a victim named Weir.

Frye's film also indicates that the lawyers and judges lack the vocabulary to articulate the function of sound—particularly music—in the victim impact video. Although Frye's film replaces the original music and voiceover narration with the recorded deliberations of the California Supreme Court, these deliberations include a discussion of the original soundtrack. In this discussion, there is little dispute about Farwell's voiceover, which both the lawyers and the judges seem to agree was "matter-of-fact" and descriptive rather than emotional. The focus of debate, rather, is the use of Enya's music. Young makes the argument that the music was "very emotional." However, one of the judges replies that he did not find that the music was "tied to great emotions." Later on, Brenan, the prosecutor, argues that the music was appropriate because it was chosen for a particular reason: because it was what Weir liked and was listening to around the time she died. No one in the courtroom, though, makes any meaningful argument about what precisely makes the particular music "emotional" or not. In contrast, writing about *People v. Kelly,* music scholar Lily Hirsch offers a much more detailed analysis of Enya's work:

> Enya's music generally lends itself to commemoration, given the music's connection to spirituality and Celtic culture, which is imbued with mystic overtones. The music itself has ethereal qualities that derive from its repeated, legato melodies—the backbone of Enya's craft—and from the use of synthesizers, keyboards, and voice, including simple layered vocal effects that emanate from Enya's lone voice. In addition to the unearthly dimension of this sound augmentation, the liberal application of reverb makes the music sound as if it plays in a vast open site, such as a hall or church.[39]

As Hirsch demonstrates, the particular qualities of a piece of music—the tempo, instrumentation, and audio effects—as well as its cultural associations are part of what may determine whether the listener will experience it as "emotional" or not. While Farwell may have chosen Enya's music because it was what Weir was listening to around the time she died, this music does have particular qualities and associations that make it a popular choice for commemorative occasions. Moreover, it is not simply the use of Enya's music that is at stake but rather the use of musical accompaniment itself. There is something about setting disparate images to music that acts to unify them, transforming them into something more than a series. Even music that is not considered "overly emotional" may produce a sense of unity and proximity and will likely affect the viewer's experience of the image track. Carol Vernallis has written, "the music-video image . . . foregrounds the experience of movement and of passing time. It attempts to pull us in with an address to the body, with a flooding of the senses, thus eliciting a sense of experience as internally felt rather than externally understood."[40] I would argue that in the victim impact video, music functions to intensify the affect produced by the editing on the image track, further foregrounding the sense of "passing time" and of proximity. As a result, the sense of "remembering" Sara becomes an even more intensely embodied experience through the addition of music.

The question, then, is whether this sense of "remembering" rather than just "knowing about" the victim of a crime should be a part of the jury's experience and deliberation. These two different kinds of relationships to the past—and the dead—are both valid forms of experience. However, it remains to be determined whether the sense of "remembering" something one did not experience firsthand has a place in the courtroom. This question has no easy answer, but Frye's film makes clear that there is a dire need for a more nuanced legal vocabulary for evaluating this kind of audiovisual text. Kelly, however horrible his crimes, may be on death row because his lawyer could not adequately critique the powerful affective force generated by this victim impact video. Frye's film acts to reveal the literal lethality of the gaze solicited by this previous appropriation, aimed not at Weir but at her killer. There are no perpetrator images here, but there may still be a perpetrator's gaze, solicited by the victim impact video and aligned with a legal system that sends a man to death based on "evidence" its representatives do not know how to adequately assess.

Yet Frye's film is also embroiled in the ethics of audiovisual appropriation. On the one hand, re-appropriating home mode recordings of Weir, who obviously had no say in the matter, could be read as a violation of her privacy. It is one thing for her mother to repurpose them, another thing for Frye, who never met her, to do so. On the other hand, these home mode documents had already been repurposed as public, courtroom evidence in the form of the victim impact video. Is Frye appropriating a series of home mode recordings or a victim impact video? Of course, he is doing both, but I would argue that he is primarily appropriating an appropriation, that the object of his film is less Weir than the victim impact video itself. Over and above the preservationist gaze of the original recordings and the judgmental/vengeful gaze of the victim impact video, *Sara Nokomis Weir* imposes a "reformative gaze" that seeks to redress a possible wrong or to prevent such wrongs against others in the future. Although Frye's film does not take an explicit stance vis-à-vis the legality or ethics of the victim impact video, by pointing out the inability for the court to adequately discuss the video, the film implies that the legal system requires revision. Frye's film attempts to reestablish an ethical gaze over and above the one solicited by the victim impact video, one that asks us whether this is the kind of "evidence" that we wish to allow a jury to see when a human life is at stake. It is therefore, in my view, like *A Film Unfinished* and *You Don't Like the Truth,* an acutely ethical intervention.

There are obvious overlaps between the revelatory, accusatory, and reformative gazes; they are not mutually exclusive. Each of the films discussed above reveals, accuses, and seeks reform in some fashion. They differ mainly in whether they emphasize revelation, accusation, or reformation—a difference of degree rather than kind. These films all participate in a larger gesture of reparation in which something originally unethical is reclaimed for an ethical purpose, clearly exposing the perpetrator's gaze in order to make it available for critique and perhaps restitution.

If the perpetrator's gaze is not exposed and clearly criticized, however, the danger of reusing the footage may outweigh its reparative value. In his detailed study of the many reuses of a segment of archival footage shot in Liepaja in 1941 by German marine soldier Reinhard Wiener on an amateur film camera, Tobias Ebbrecht-Hartmann demonstrates the way the same piece of footage can be overlaid by a reparative gaze—or not. The footage in question involves silent images of a mass shooting of several groups of Jewish men by German soldiers. Ebbrecht-Hartmann reads the original gaze of this footage as a preservationist gaze aligned not with sentimental remembrance but with the logic of the "trophy." However, he suggests that this gaze has since been overlaid with a variety of other gazes: in the trial of Nazi Adolf Eichmann, in *Eichmann and the Third Reich* (Erwin Leiser, 1961), and in *The 81st Blow* (Haim Gouri, David Bergman, Jacques Ehrlich, Ghetto Fighters House, 1974). He has written,

> The footage transformed from a secret wartime trophy to evidence when it was used in trials against perpetrators, and became a visual document circulating through various films after it was edited into Leiser's cinematic indictment. But while Leiser still used it in his film as "pure" visual evidence of the crime, *The 81st Blow* reframed the footage from the victim's perspective: by merging it with the voice of a surviving witness, the German

> onlooker's perspective is overwritten. But the competing perspectives still coexist in this particular alliance of a perpetrator's gaze and a victim's voice.[41]

In other words, to translate this into the terms of my study, in these other texts, a revelatory and accusatory gaze was asserted, transforming "trophy" into evidence against the Nazi killers. Ebbrecht-Hartmann has noted, however, that the very same footage was reused in the German television documentary *Holokaust* (Philip Remy, 2000) to authenticate the trauma of a German soldier, Karl-Heinz Mangelsen, who witnessed the killings:

> First, Mangelsen is authenticated as a witness, then the background of the incidents in Liepaja is exemplified, and finally the interviewee is identified as traumatized. His emotional collapse is the final warrant for the German witness' credibility and his "trauma" is verified through the archive film that is edited in between his testimony. Thus the footage is finally transformed into an emotional tool for creating "traumatized" images.[42]

Ebbrecht-Hartmann gestures toward the sick irony in using footage of the mass killing of Jewish people to validate the trauma of a German soldier. Although Mangelsen may have been traumatized by the event, the reuse of these perpetrator images to illustrate the experience of another perpetrator (or, at very least, a complicit bystander) reinforces the unethical gaze embedded in the original footage. At Eichmann's trial, in *Eichmann and the Third Reich,* and in *The 81st Blow,* the revelatory and accusatory gazes were in effect, working over and against the original gaze of the perpetrator. In *Holokaust,* revelation and accusation are disregarded in favor of an emotional appeal on behalf not of the victims, but of the German soldier standing by. Such a misuse revictimizes the human beings whom we see being violently murdered in the footage. Their greatest, fatal trauma becomes backdrop for the much lesser trauma of a witness. An ethical misuse of perpetrator images must involve an active call for justice for the victims. Without such a call for justice, any reuse becomes abuse and an act of renewed violence.

# 5 Abusing Images

There are moments when we are confronted by a work of audiovisual appropriation and something tells us simply, "No, this is not right." This can occur in visiting the hallowed halls of a major museum or looking through the results of a simple web search. But what is it, precisely, that prompts this response? How can we locate the exact structures of experience that lead us to reject the ethics of a certain appropriation? Of course, these structures will vary for different audiences. These reactions of rejection, I argue, occur specifically when a given viewer experiences identification with the people recorded but senses that the appropriationist does not—or at least not in the same way or to the same degree. When this is the case, the appropriation will read to that viewer as an act of inexcusable exploitation. This chapter explores several cases in which at least some viewers have found a particular appropriation ethically offensive—in other words, have felt that these texts failed to meet an ethical standard—and seeks to articulate why this may have occurred.

## Eliciting the Endangered Gaze

The 2017 Whitney Biennial included *Open Casket*, a painting by white artist Dana Schutz, whose inspiration for the painting was an existing photographic image of a murdered Black child, Emmett Till. Critics argued that Schutz made inappropriate use of an image that belonged to a group of people to which Schutz did not belong, and they therefore regarded the painting as an instance of cultural appropriation and exploitation. In response, defenders advocated freedom of speech, and antagonisms escalated. While several writers offered close analyses of the painting, whether to critique or defend it, it seems to me that the debate has less to do with the painting's actual form and much more to do with the perceptions about the gaze it solicited from its viewers. Hence, I want to look at how *Open Casket* may be read in terms of a gap between the gaze *solicited* by the painting and the actual—and variable—gazes *elicited* from its viewers. Drawing on the work of Courtney Baker in particular, I examine the multiple layers of the gaze at work in and around this text in order to interrogate whether or not it solicits a "humane gaze" with its implication of a reciprocal humanity—and, even if it does, whether this solicitation is enough, ethically speaking, when differently embodied viewers may experience the painting in radically different ways.

To reiterate a passage from my introduction, Vivian Sobchack has written that "the humane gaze . . . *visibly and significantly encodes in the image its own subjective responsiveness to what it sees.*"[1] She has suggested, for instance, that sustained duration is often one of the formal elements that "visibly and significantly encodes" the humane gaze. This sense of encoded "subjective responsiveness" is aligned with what Baker has referred to as "humane insight" (which she contrasts to the "gaze"). Baker has written,

> Whereas the gaze ignores or denies the humanity of the person being looked at, humane insight seeks knowledge about the humanity of that person. It is an ethics-based look that imagines the body that is seen to merit the protections due to all human bodies. Humane insight describes a decision to identify the body being looked at as a human body, a gesture that is integral to the formation of our social interactions. It is a look that turns a benevolent eye, recognizes violations of human dignity, and bestows or articulates the desire for actual protection.[2]

Terminologically, I am not making the same distinction between "look" and "gaze" that Baker does, but rather linking Sobchack's idea of the humane gaze with Baker's notion of humane insight. Like Sobchack's humane gaze, Baker's concept of humane insight suggests that looking at an image of actual human death can incite an empathetic response in the viewer who fully recognizes the humanity of the person imaged. However, in works of audiovisual appropriation, this subjective responsiveness or humane insight must be encoded both in the appropriationist's choice of existing material and in the editing or arrangement of that material.

The reading of the appropriationist's gaze is very much at stake in the controversy surrounding *Open Casket.* Schutz based her painting on a famous photograph of the body of Emmett Till, a 14-year-old African American boy who in 1955 was falsely accused of making lewd remarks to a white woman, Carolyn Bryant, and was brutally murdered by Carolyn's husband Roy Bryant and his half-brother J. W. Milam. Emmett Till's body, including his face, was horribly disfigured, but his mother Mamie Till decided to hold an open casket funeral and allowed his body to be photographed. Emmett Till's murder and the photograph of his body in his casket subsequently helped galvanize the Civil Rights Movement. His death remains a central event and the photograph of his body an important record within African American history. The Schutz painting replicates the overall composition of the photograph, but the effect of the large, color brushstrokes diverges dramatically from that of the original black-and-white indexical image. In response to the inclusion of *Open Casket* in the Whitney exhibit, African American artist Parker Bright stood in front of the painting for many hours with the words "Black Death Spectacle" written in permanent marker across the back of his white T-shirt. Subsequently, Black-identified, biracial British artist Hannah Black authored a letter to the Whitney Museum calling for the painting to be taken down and destroyed, a letter signed by numerous Black artists, including Bright. In response to Black's letter, Cuban American artist Coco Fusco wrote an essay entitled "Censorship, Not the Painting, Must Go: On Dana Schutz's Image of Emmett Till." Without agreeing with either stance, I want to argue here that implicit in both the critiques and defenses of the painting is a differential understanding of the gaze encoded in the original image, of the gaze solicited by Schutz's appropriation, of the gaze—or gazes—actually elicited by Schutz's appropriation, and of the relationship between these.

There is some debate about precisely who was addressed by the photograph of Emmett Till's body, of whom Mamie Till Mobley intended to see her dead son and how she hoped they would look upon him. Josephine Livingstone and Lovia Gyarkye suggest in *The New Republic* that in deciding to allow her son's body to be viewed at the funeral and in permitting his body to be photographed, Mobley sought to align the viewer's gaze with her own. They have written,

> By controlling the way that his body looked, Mobley was able to define its legacy. Although he was taken from her, the way lynched Americans were taken from their families, she was able to invert the final stage of public murder, which is *spectacle*. Her action was both brave and a strikingly effective piece of visual rhetoric, accomplished in the depths of appalling grief. [Claudia] Rankine quotes Mobley: "Let the people see what I see."[3]

According to Livingstone and Gyarkye, the gaze solicited by Mobley and, hence, by the photograph of Emmett Till's body is one of bearing witness, an evidentiary gaze that testifies to the horror of racist brutality. Mobley wanted viewers to see what she saw, to look through the eyes of a mourning mother of a young innocent boy, who had been violently murdered. Christina Sharpe argues that the original intended audience for the photographs of Emmett Till's body—there were more than one—did not include white people because they were published first in *Jet* magazine.

> Mamie Till Mobley makes the decision, against much advice, to have those photographs of her son published. It was not mainstream media—or white media—that published those images. It was *Jet* magazine. And those images had nothing to do with white consciousness. They were for Black people, because *Jet* was a Black publication. They weren't meant to create empathy or shame or awareness from white viewers. They were meant to speak to and to move a Black audience.[4]

Coco Fusco, however, has noted that Mobley may not have intended the audience for her son's image to be exclusively Black.

> According to Emmett Till's cousin Simeon Wright, who was with him the night of his capture and attended his funeral, Mamie Till said "she wanted *the world* to see what those men had done to her son". There was no exclusion of non-black people implied. . . . The trial of Till's murderers was filmed and shown widely, as were photographs of his funeral. Those photographs

> galvanized the Civil Rights Movement: activist leaders strategically and adeptly circulated them to encourage blacks *and* whites in the North to join the struggle, and in order to shame politicians by casting doubts on America's adherence to its democratic ideals.[5]

Fusco has suggested that even if the image was initially published in *Jet,* Mobley's intended audience for the image went far beyond the Black readers of that magazine, that she wanted the image to address white people as well as Black. In truth, it is difficult to know precisely who Mobley wished to see the photograph. Nevertheless, there is little question that she wanted the photograph to serve as evidence and as a motivation for change. Unlike other images of Black death, such as lynching photographs taken by white people to celebrate the murder of Black people, this image was not meant to glorify or spectacularize Black death but to demonstrate, to prove, to accuse, and perhaps to shame.

In appropriating the photograph of Emmett Till's body and transposing it into painting, Schutz's critics implicitly argued, she imposed a different gaze upon it from the one solicited by Mobley. Livingstone and Gyarkye have suggested that over and above the evidentiary gaze of the photograph, Schutz introduced an overly "creative" and "subjective" gaze upon Emmett Till's body.

> Mobley wanted those photographs to bear witness to the racist brutality inflicted on her son; instead Schutz has disrespected that act of dignity, by defacing them with her own creative way of seeing. Where the photographs stood for a plain and universal photographic truth, Schutz has blurred the reality of Till's death, infusing it with subjectivity.[6]

By painting the photograph, by using her own hand to represent his body in a nonindexical medium, they argue, she erased the truth function of the image. Further, she imposed her own subjectivity on an image that has come to feel, at least to many African Americans, sacred. The deictic function of the indexical image that Roland Barthes describes is fundamental to this sacred status. He wrote, "the Photograph is never anything but an antiphon of 'Look,' 'See,' 'Here it is;' it points a finger at certain *vis-á-vis,* and cannot escape this pure deictic language."[7] The photograph of Emmett in his casket served as a call to "look" and "see" the horror of what had been done to him.

It is worth noting, however, that photographs hardly constitute a "plain and universal photographic truth." The indexicality of the photographic image points to the factuality of Emmett Till's dead and mangled body, but "truth" is linked to meaning, which is always a matter of debate. The dominant meaning of the image developed over time, as it became a symbol of the Civil Rights Movement, but that meaning is not inherent in the image itself. Moreover, had Schutz appropriated the photograph through mechanical reproduction rather than approximation through painting, would her artwork have seemed any less "disrespectful" to those who found it so? Reusing an indexical image of Emmett Till would likely have been regarded as even more egregious because it would have felt even closer to actually appropriating Emmett Till's body. Audiovisual appropriation through mechanical reproduction—because it maintains an indexical relation to the referent—generally raises much more pressing ethical questions than other types of appropriation like allusion. Arguably, Schutz's painting *alludes* to the photograph of Emmett Till's body rather than directly appropriating it. One could, then, read this as a form of respectful distance—an instance of the partially "occluded gaze"—rather than the flippant imposition of creativity and subjectivity.[8]

Meanwhile, in contrast to Livingstone and Gyarkye, Sharpe suggests that the issue is less one of creativity or subjectivity than of abstraction. "[Mobley] insists that the violence that [Emmett Till] has been subject to be seen, unobscured. It seems to me that what Dana Schutz has done is to take that unobscured violence and make it abstract. Mamie Till wanted to make violence real."[9] Here Sharpe suggests that Schutz's painted reference to the indexical image without its indexical pull eliminates the evidentiary value that was so crucial to its rhetorical function within the Civil Rights Movement. From this perspective, it is not Schutz's subjectivity so much as the erasure of the photograph's indexicality in its transfer to painting that goes against Mobley's original wishes for the image. Fusco, however, points out that some of Schutz's critics "assert (without explanation) that abstraction in and of itself is illegitimate for representing a traumatic figure, a claim that ignores key 20th-century aesthetic debates about the problems with realistic depictions of extreme violence."[10] Indeed, realism—in contrast to abstraction—is not inherently a more ethical approach.

Yet the imposition of creativity, subjectivity, and abstraction were not the only criticisms aimed at the painting. Its perceived affect was also criticized. Livingstone and Gyarkye wrote,

> Schutz is not a solemn artist, which is partly why *Open Casket* feels so intrusive. The paint of Till's face dances like it is alive; he is made decorative when he was brutalized. The colors of his coffin are bright and pretty when in reality only a black-and-white photograph of him survives. An artist who wishes to work with such a charged subject needs to approach with unmitigated rigor in order to succeed. In her body of work, Schutz does not demonstrate a rigorous sensibility.[11]

In addition to being creative and subjective, Schutz's gaze—and hence the gaze solicited from the viewer of the painting—is also read as not "solemn" or "rigorous." Many of Schutz's other paintings are indeed absurdist or even comic. However, there is nothing in *Open Casket* to suggest humor. Livingstone and Gyarkye read the color of the image as "decorative" but, of course, the black-and-white photograph was already an abstraction of a world in color. Arguably, the colors of the painting may be truer to "reality." The call for "unmitigated rigor" and a "rigorous sensibility" (whatever those might be), then, seem to be less about the form of the painting than about the writers' perception of Schutz's affective stance vis-à-vis the image—or her paintings more generally. They read a flippant gaze over and against the solemn gaze solicited by the original image.

It is important to note that many of the charges mentioned above could also be directed at Henry Taylor's painting of Philando Castile's body, based on a video image taken during and after Castile's murder by a police officer, entitled *THE TIMES THAY AIN'T A CHANGING, FAST ENOUGH!* This painting was also included in the Whitney Biennial but did not receive nearly as much criticism as *Open Casket*. In fact, Taylor's "creativity" and "subjectivity" were lauded. "As any artist would, Taylor took artistic liberties with that moment," Alicia Eler wrote of the painting, noting also that "Taylor's decision to isolate and then combine a few freeze frames from the video into a singular composite image was deliberate—it slows down the moment, making space for contemplation and in-person reflection rather than just reacting online."[12] Here, Taylor's artistic intervention in repainting and reconfiguring the video image of a murdered Black man is celebrated for inviting a more contemplative gaze than the original. The two paintings deal with similar subject matter and are both "creative," "subjective," and "abstract." Taylor, however, like Castile, is a Black man.

This brings us to the problem of the whiteness of Schutz's gaze. Indeed, the difference in response to Taylor's painting indicates that the fundamental objection to Schutz's painting is not just that her gaze is creative, subjective, or abstracting, but that it is a white gaze. In her open letter to the Whitney, Hannah Black wrote,

> That even the disfigured corpse of a child was not sufficient to move the white gaze from its habitual cold calculation is evident daily and in a myriad of ways, not least the fact that this painting exists at all. In brief: the painting should not be acceptable to anyone who cares or pretends to care about Black people because it is not acceptable for a white person to transmute Black suffering into profit and fun, though the practice has been normalized for a long time.[13]

Here, Black reads Schutz's gaze as a white gaze characterized by "cold calculation" and motivated by "profit and fun." Her letter suggests that for any white person to gaze upon an image of Black suffering is a form of violence so terrible that the gaze must be eliminated. Fusco argues, however, that "It is reductive and inaccurate to claim that all treatment of black suffering by white cultural producers is driven by commercial interests and sadistic voyeurism. Black overlooks an important history of white people making anti-racist art, often commissioned by Civil Rights activists."[14] Indeed, in *Humane Insight,* Baker traces the history of the use of images of Black suffering and death for anti-racist ends by both Black and white activists. This suggests that to conclude, a priori, without specific reference to the form of the painting that it must be racist because the artist is white is to impute a singular, racist, exploitative gaze to all white artists who wish to engage with issues of racism. And this does seem overly reductive, essentializing, and censorious. Yet, this does not mean that the critics of Schutz's painting were wrong.

One thing that both critics and supporters of *Open Casket* largely failed to consider is the different gazes elicited from Black and white viewers by the original photograph, not by design but by factual context. Elizabeth Alexander wrote,

> For black writers of a certain age, and perhaps of a certain region, a certain proximity to Southern roots, Emmett Till's story is a touchstone. It was the basis for a rite of passage that indoctrinated these young people into understanding the vulnerability of their own black bodies, coming of age, and the way in which their fate was interchangeable with Till's.[15]

This observation—when extended from Till's story to his image—gives new meaning to Sobchack's notion of the endangered gaze. Sobchack describes the "endangered gaze" as one encoded in an image when the photographer or filmmaker shares the same danger as the photographed or filmed subject in the same immediate space.[16] Of course, in relation to the photograph of Emmett Till's body, the endangered gaze is not encoded in the gaze of the photographer; in other words, the photographer for *Jet* taking pictures at the funeral was not in any immediate danger. Instead, this sense of danger is solicited from the Black *viewer* of the image by its content. This was intentional where most lynching photographs were concerned; they were produced, in part, to make Black people afraid. In the case of Emmett Till's photograph, this was not the intention so much as a byproduct, yet it was unavoidable for Black viewers of this image. In other words, the endangered gaze is not encoded in the act of photographing but is nevertheless elicited in the act of looking at the image—but only for Black viewers who have lived the experience of being visibly Black in a racist society.

While Schutz herself or a white viewer of either Emmett Till's photograph or *Open Casket* may experience subjective responsiveness or humane insight, they do not experience a sense of personal endangerment—of bodily identification and vulnerability. Schutz herself admitted that she does not know what it is like to be Black but said that she identified with Mamie Till as a mother. Yet even the claim to a shared "maternal gaze" neglects a crucial difference between the Black maternal gaze and the white maternal gaze. While mothers of all ethnicities worry for their children's health and safety, Black mothers—then and now—have much more to fear, particularly for their sons. In an article entitled, "Dear White Moms," Keesha Beckford explains her fear for her Black son, a fear that white moms may vaguely understand but do not experience in the same way because their children—though they may face many dangers—are not at risk of being called the n-word or of being racially profiled and, as a consequence, shot by police.[17]

Whiteness, of course, is not really about skin color. It is about, at least in one respect, a sense of safety. The white gaze is a protected gaze. The fear for one's own body or one's own children's bodies when one looks at an image of a murdered child is what distinguishes the subjectively responsive, humane but still ultimately distanced white gaze from that of the (vicariously) endangered Black gaze. The distinction here is not between the humane gaze and the racist gaze that does not recognize the humanity of the murdered child.

Rather, it is a more subtle but still important distinction between the endangered and the distanced, the vulnerable and the protected. The problem is that the gaze encoded at the moment of Schutz's appropriation is precisely *not* an endangered gaze; it is a protected gaze. And this did not match the actual gaze elicited from Black viewers of both the original photograph and, by extension, of the painting itself. Taylor's appropriating gaze, unlike that of Schutz, encoded his own experience of vicarious endangerment, of shared vulnerability. Looking at Castile, Taylor knew it might well have been him dying in that car. Black viewers could therefore rest assured that the solicited gaze encoded in Taylor's painting and their own actual elicited experience coincided. The lack of coincidence between solicited and elicited gazes is, in my view, where the greatest problem with Schutz's painting lies.

In fact, Schutz's painting is not a "black death spectacle." Though the spectacularization of Black people's death in American history and contemporary society is a very serious problem that needs to be addressed, *Open Casket* is a weak instance of such spectacularization. I have seen other uses of Emmett Till's photographed body online that are truly horrifying, and Schutz's painting reads as, at worst, naïve, insensitive, and misguided and, at best, an attempt to produce humane insight, to convey the horror and tragedy of Emmett Till's murder in a new form. This is not to excuse Schutz, but just to point out that the painting is hardly a racist caricature or diatribe. This, I think, is why many writers—even those sympathetic to her critique—found Hannah Black's call to destroy the painting hyperbolic. The critiques of *Open Casket* imply that the painting solicits a dehumanizing gaze, the extreme opposite of the ethical humane gaze. Looking at reproduced images of the painting (because I was not able to view the original), however, I do not find this reading very persuasive. I would argue that what is really at stake in this incredibly fraught debate is the shared vulnerability that is differentially experienced by viewers of different races. I suggest that critics of the painting were responding to the fact that both Schutz and the predominantly white viewers of the painting at the Whitney may experience both horror and sympathy for Emmett Till but by definition do not share the sense of pervasive bodily danger that Black viewers share with Emmett Till and his mother—and that this experiential inequity was at the heart of the controversy.

Hence, the question should not be framed in terms of "Should white artists be allowed to appropriate images of people of other races or ethnicities?" This question is too easily transposed into questions of freedom of expression, which places those who are uncomfortable with or upset by the text in question in the position of censor. It also disallows the possibility that a white artist might produce artworks that solicit humane insight, that might increase our sense of one another's humanity. The much more complex questions that we need to ask are the following: "When we are asked to align our gaze at a pre-existing image with that of the appropriationist, how are we being asked to look? What sort of gaze is being *solicited* and what sort of gaze is actually being *elicited*? Does the work elicit different gazes from differently embodied viewers? And, if so, do these differential gazes, despite their difference, increase our sense of *shared* vulnerability and therefore shared humanity or do they further obscure it? Can we live with the fact that some viewers will experience a sense of shared vulnerability with the recorded subject while others don't?"

It seems to me that for Bright and Black, the anger at the prospect of a white artist looking at Emmett Till's photograph without experiencing this vulnerability and—by extension—of white viewers similarly disavowing this sense of vulnerability outweighed the possibility that the painting could solicit a deepened sense of shared humanity. And it is hard to imagine that there were not spectators who—at least until the controversy began—just strolled on by. They may also have walked right by Taylor's painting on the floor above. The fact is that we cannot guarantee the gaze of the viewer, regardless of the content of the painting or the intent of the artist. As Baker points out, "The gallery space continues to be a space in which any number of looks is possible, including the look that takes pleasure in the spectacle of death."[18] But the issue is less the race of the appropriationist per se than it is a question of the structures of looking that are solicited and elicited by the work, as well as the space of exhibition and the wider social arena in which certain bodies are in more danger than others. Undeniably, different viewers are going to have different relationships to the image and so there is risk in any act of exhibition, but an articulation of the different gazes in effect—solicited and elicited—may help us evaluate when this is a risk worth taking.

There is, however, a sequel to this controversy. In 2018, Somali-Australian artist Hamishi Farah exhibited his painting of Dana Schutz's young, living son, *Representation of Arlo,* at LISTE art fair in Basel, Switzerland. Farah's painting, like *Open Casket,* is formally based on an existing photograph, which Farah may have found online.[19] It is a realist but stylized painting of a toddler with white skin, pink cheeks, and blond hair wearing a T-shirt and cradling an unidentifiable object in his arms. In terms of both style and content, it would be entirely banal and uninteresting except for its title and source material, which can only be gleaned from contextual writings. In fact, it was largely overlooked until Silke Hohmann in German magazine *Monopol* referred to it as a form of "revenge art" ("Kunst al rache"), which led to a broader discussion of the ethics of the painting.[20] Art critic Olamiju Fajemisin stated that, "it became the general consensus that Farah, in depicting Schutz's still-living son, had actively invaded the artist's privacy—a violation of both person and confidentiality, despite the fact Farah's reference image had already been published online."[21] Fajemisin read the controversy as revealing of "a white fragility complex," arguing that, "This biased gaze only proved that the public sees a Black child as just another body, yet views a white child who suffered no harm worthier of privacy and respect."[22] This is possible. Nevertheless, I do find *Representation of Arlo* unethical. Schutz's appropriation of Emmett Till's image was ethically disturbing for the many reasons detailed above, but violation of his privacy was not one of them. The image of Emmett Till's mangled body in his casket was always intended for public view, its publication authorized by his grieving mother in order to demonstrate the inhumanity of a society that could allow such a thing to happen to her child. Schutz undeniably misunderstood what this image meant to African American people, but it was always a public image. However, the image of Schutz's young son—even if it could be located online, though this has not been confirmed—on which Farah's painting was ostensibly based reads as never having been intended for public view. It is an intimate, personal image addressed to a limited audience composed of those who care for this little boy. To infringe upon his and his family's private space to make a political point is fundamentally an act of violation. One may argue, as Fajemisin implicitly does, that this violation is justified in the name of making a statement about white privilege in the art world. But Farah does nothing to acknowledge the humanity of Arlo himself. Although the painting is not an indexical reproduction of the photographic image, it does not occlude or anonymize the little boy (see Chapter 1). Rather, Farah purposely exposes his name and face. The issue is not the difference between the image of a Black child and a white child, as Fajemisin suggests, but between an image intended for public contemplation (and condemnation) and an image clearly intended only for private viewing. Moreover, the gaze solicited by Farah's painting—over and above the loving preservationist gaze suggested by the source photograph—reads to me as mocking, if not quite vengeful. And asking a viewer to look at a child—of any background or skin color—through a mocking gaze is a form of abuse.

## Soliciting the Endangered Gaze

The strongest critiques of *Open Casket* imply that the painting elicits a dehumanizing gaze, the extreme opposite of the humane gaze that underpins every ethical gaze described in this book. If this is so, however, then there are degrees of the dehumanizing gaze. Schutz may have inadvertently elicited a dehumanizing gaze or, more aptly, the *specter* of the dehumanizing gaze that constantly and materially threatens Black people in American society. It was in part her failure to confront this specter that made *Open Casket* so offensive to so many. In some works of audiovisual appropriation, by contrast, the dehumanizing gaze is intentionally solicited, and it explicitly seeks to transform its human subjects into objects, to eliminate any sense of empathy with them.

This is frequently accomplished through structures of humor. However, make no mistake—humor is frequently a cover for the intent to dehumanize. In December 2017, the style guide for the neo-Nazi website, *The Daily Stormer*, was leaked to *Huffington Post* writer Ashley Feinberg. As detailed in a *New Yorker* article the next month, the style guide was quite clear about using humor as a smoke screen for genuine hatred:

> "The unindoctrinated should not be able to tell if we are joking or not," the author writes, in a section called "Lulz." "This is obviously a ploy and I actually do want to gas kikes. But that's neither here nor there." For legal reasons, the guide continues, writers shouldn't openly incite violence; "however, whenever someone does something violent, it should be made light of." The ultimate goal is to "dehumanize the enemy, to the point where people are ready to laugh at their deaths."[23]

Here, *The Daily Stormer* makes it clear that it intends to make jokes that dehumanize but that can be brushed off as "just a joke," even though the violent intent ("to gas kikes") is real. At the same time, within digital culture more broadly, there is also a practice of trying to be as offensive as possible to impress one's online friends. These producers may not be as set on dehumanizing their subjects as the writers of *The Daily Stormer*. Yet, they participate in the same kind of humor to the point that it is impossible to distinguish who means it from who does not.

Anne Frank memes are image-text combinations that actively and intentionally mock and dehumanize a murdered Jewish child. In contrast to Emmett Till, there is no image of Anne Frank's dead body, but there are numerous extant images of her that were taken before her capture by the Nazis, found in a family album after her death and since then widely circulated. Anne Frank memes make use of these images while consistently referencing her death as something to be mocked and enjoyed. While anti-Semitism is hardly the only form of vile and violent discriminatory discourse online, it is pervasive and extreme. In fact, the "prime directive" of *The Daily Stormer* style guide is that 'All enemies should be combined into one enemy, which is the Jews.'"[24] In light of that statement, it is not all that surprising that Frank is a common target of meme humor and that the memes appropriating her name and/or image are used to mock not only her but also the Holocaust and the deaths of Jewish people more generally.

Of course, jokes about the Holocaust are nothing new. In 1983, Alan Dundes and Thomas Hauschild published an essay entitled "Auschwitz Jokes," in which they documented and analyzed a collection of German jokes about the Holocaust, provoking some criticism for having printed the jokes even though they had, of course, not produced them themselves. In this essay, they noted,

> Nothing is so sacred, so taboo, or so disgusting that it cannot be the subject of humor. Quite the contrary—it is precisely those topics culturally defined as sacred, taboo, or disgusting which more often than not provide the principal grist for humor mills.[25]

From this perspective, the Holocaust is the perfect topic for a certain kind of joke. Dundes and Hauschild also indicate that while some jokes may be told by the very objects of those jokes—i.e., Jewish people telling Jewish jokes—some will likely only be told by those outside the group. Such jokes are not a form of gallows humor, which are jokes told by those who are about to die to alleviate their anxiety. Rather, these jokes are told only by the executioners or would-be executioners.[26] They fall within the category Freud identified as tendentious jokes, which he argues "are able to release pleasure even from sources that have undergone repression." He continues, "Tendentious jokes exhibit the main characteristic of the joke-work—that of liberating pleasure by getting rid of inhibitions."[27] By allowing its teller to overcome repression, the Holocaust joke offers the speaker—and potentially the listener—pleasure.

Dundes and Hauschild identify several common tropes of Auschwitz jokes, for instance, their focus on gassing, burning, and Jewish people transformed into ashes as well as soap. I cite three of these jokes for reference:

> "How many Jews can you fit in a Volkswagen? Fourteen. Two in the front, two in the back, ten in the ashtray."[28]

> "Two [Jewish] children are sitting on top of a roof near a chimney. A passerby asks, 'What are you doing up there?' 'We are waiting for our parents.'"[29]

> "A child plays with a cake of soap. Granny says, 'Keep your fingers off Anne Frank.'"[30]

When I first saw an Anne Frank meme, I will admit I was horrified. I had no idea such things existed and, naïve as I apparently am, I was genuinely stunned. However, as Dundes and Hauschild's study demonstrates, what is perhaps the most salient characteristic of Anne Frank memes is their utter unoriginality. They are the Internet-age visual version of the jokes that Dundes and Hauschild wrote about in the 1980s, some of which they believe date back to the 1960s. The memes follow the logic of these pre-existing verbal jokes almost to the letter. However, even if the pleasure in overcoming repression is the same, the visual element of the meme intensifies the ethical violation involved in the Anne Frank joke.

Internet memes have been defined in various ways, but I will use Asaf Nissenbaum and Limor Shifman's definition: "groups of digital items (such as images or videos) that share common characteristics, are created with awareness of each other, and are distributed online by multiple participants."[31] I also draw on Ryan Milner's analysis of image memes and the "logic of lulz," which he describes as an "irony-laden communicative practice,"[32] borrowing Whitney Phillips's notion of "lulz" as "a detached and dissociated amusement at others' distress."[33] In his discussion of image memes, Milner articulates how a particular image—usually a photograph—"becomes a visual template . . . an 'image macro' or 'stock character macro'. From an established template, participants add unique text to make a joke."[34] Transforming anyone into a "stock character macro" might be a bit unethical in that it abstracts a person's identity, transforming him or her into a "character" rather than acknowledging him or her as a unique individual. Yet, the ethical ramifications of using Anne Frank—as opposed to say living, public figures like Barack Obama or Donald Trump—as a stock character macro are particularly troubling. Of course, observing mainstream ethics is precisely *not* of interest to the people who make these memes. The violation of generally accepted ethics is in many cases their goal. However, I want to spell out the specific ethical norms they are violating—and the ethical ramifications such a violation entails—even if the meme-makers have no interest in adhering to such norms.

Image-text memes take a relatively consistent form. An image is overlaid with text. The text at the top sets up some kind of expectation, which the text at the bottom then subverts. The text also works in dialogue with the image, which is often of a recognizable or stereotypical figure—the "stock character." Often, such memes work through an ironic structure in which the juxtaposition between image and a two-part text generates a double meaning. For instance, in a meme of Donald Trump, we see an image of Trump giving a speech. The top text reads "I misspoke," which sets up the expectation of apology or correction. The bottom text, however, reads ". . . for 40 minutes." The latter alters (or doubles) our perception of the top text and produces a critique of Trump's constant lying. This meme constitutes a satirical use of irony for political critique.

At the same time, there often is a larger question of irony; it may be uncertain whether the meme is meant to be taken as a serious statement or just a joke. As Milner points out about memes, "the blur between irony and earnestness makes room for discourse otherwise impermissible."[35] This observation has been codified as Poe's Law, which states that it is often impossible to know online, without some clear indication of the author's intent such as a smiley emoticon, whether the author is being sincere or ironic.[36] Nevertheless, as Milner also notes, memes that rely on stereotypes frequently reinforce those stereotypes, assuming the perspective of the dominant group: white, male, and Christian. He has written,

> Even if . . . it's hard to assess ideological intent in discourse, racist labels and attributions still discursively trapped a minority identity through antagonistic stereotype. . . . In the voices excluded, in the humour employed, and in perspectives forwarded, an outgroup was consistently implied. Poe's Law or

> no, lulz or no, the discourse was antagonistic. Further, it was antagonistic to an outsider counterpublic not vocally present to counter.[37]

Anne Frank memes play not precisely on Jewish stereotype but rather on the historical association of Jewish people and Anne Frank with the Holocaust; this extratextual knowledge is fundamental to "getting" an Anne Frank meme. The outgroup, however, is implied to be Jewish people.

Anne Frank memes often fall into three groups: gassing memes, hiding memes, and self-reflexive memes.[38] Many of the memes make use of a single image of Anne, which is the latest known and extant photo of her taken in 1942 and was found in her family's photo album. This image is now easily available for download and appropriation online. Some memes make use of earlier photographs of her, also found in her photo album. A few do not make any visual reference to her but only refer to her name.

Some gassing memes take a relatively simple form. In the original image, we see Anne in black and white wearing a blouse and jacket, smiling and looking at something to the left of the camera, and standing against a light-colored background. In some memes, the only alteration to the image besides minor cropping is the addition of text. In other memes, Anne's head has been excised from its original photographic context and laid over a standard "meme" background consisting of blocks of various shades of gray that seem to radiate from behind her head. Text is then added to this image as well. Like most memes of this type, the text operates in the form of setup above and punch line below. Examples of such text include: "Someone must've left the oven on / Cuz I smell gas," "Opens up pizza shop / All gas powered," "What's that burning? / Oh it's my family," "This one time at camp / We got so baked," and "[Sniff Sniff] / Did someone leave the oven on?" The humor—at least the intended humor—in the memes lies in several places. First, it arises in the contrast between the banal setups and the delayed reference to the gassing and cremation of millions of Jewish people—including Anne and most of her family—in Nazi death camps. Second, it derives from the contrast between this reference to mass murder and Anne's innocent, smiling face. If humor lies in economy and recognition of a relation in the juxtaposition of unexpected elements, these memes are successful.

The same image of Anne has also been used in several more visually complex gassing memes. In two of these, we see Anne's face superimposed over a box for a children's Easy Bake Oven. In one meme, this is the only alteration to the box. In a second, Hitler's face has also been added to the box and the name of the product has been changed to "Easy Bake Jew Oven." The first is, from the perspective of humorous economy, more effective. The humorous shock comes not from text but simply from the juxtaposition of Anne's face with a child's toy, which is also an oven, referencing the Nazi crematoria. No additional text or image of Hitler is necessary. "Easy Bake Jew Oven" is comedy overkill, spelling out the joke for the viewer too much. Another example, the "Anne Franks" hotdog meme, is a play on Kosher Hot Dogs (sometimes labeled "Beef Franks") as well as, of course, on Anne Frank's surname. Not content with this simple play on words, however, the producer of this meme added the phrases, "The hotdog you cook in the oven," and "Now hiding at your local grocer" to make sure that we get the reference to Anne's experience hiding from the Nazis and the crematoria.

In addition, we have visual versions of the ashes joke, which also play on internet clickbait genres. In one example, we see the headline "25 Shocking Celebrity Weight Changes: a look at fad diets celebrities have used to shed or gain weight fast," accompanied by icons for various social media platforms. This is followed by what looks like a before/after set of photos. However, instead of a fat person next to their thinner self, we see the 1942 photo of Anne alongside an image of a pile of ashes. In a second example, the image of Anne is absent. We see the clickbait-style headline, "Leaked Anne Frank nudes." The punch line is that instead of a naked girl, we just see several piles of ashes.

Several other gassing memes turn on a pun on "concentration," which references the act of concentrating one's attention as well as the Nazi concentration camps in which Jewish people and others were murdered. One imagines a conversation between Hitler and Anne in a comic strip format, in which Anne is having trouble with her homework and Hitler tells her she needs more concentration. Another takes a more traditional meme format, colorizing Anne's portrait and adding the text "Has ADHD / Gets treatment at concentration camp."

Another type of Anne Frank meme references Anne's experience hiding from the Nazis. Some of these use the same image of Anne but add different text. One reads "Gonna go outside / #YOLO," plus a "comment" that says "Anne frankly, I thought she should have stayed home." The "humor" in this meme seems to derive from the notion of updating Anne's experience to the hashtag age. By adding #YOLO, which stands for "You only live once," a kind of internet-age version of "Carpe Diem," Anne is reframed as a contemporary teenager. However, the humor turns on the knowledge that Anne hid from the Nazis and was eventually found and deported to a Nazi death camp. The comment makes a pun of her name (a common trope) and suggests that she should have stayed hidden. A sort of narrative of Anne as an impulsive teen who is to blame for her discovery by the Nazis—which is, of course, a false narrative—is imposed. The irony of the phrase "you only live once" depends on the knowledge that Anne was murdered, that she is dead. Another hiding meme makes use of a different portrait of Anne along with the text, "I played hide and seek before it was cool." The meme producer has added glasses and a hat that reference the *Where's Waldo?* books wherein which the reader must look for Waldo, who wears this hat and glasses. Reframing Anne as Waldo equates Anne with a cartoon despite the indexicality of the photographic image appropriated into the meme. While perhaps less tendentious than the gassing memes, these memes nonetheless make a mockery of Anne's forced hiding.

A few of the memes are self-reflexive about their offensiveness but simultaneously undermine their claim to conscience by also making a joke. One takes yet another portrait of Anne and adds the text, "This meme is offensive / Anne frankly I won't stand for it." A similar one takes the more common portrait of Anne with the typical meme background and adds the text, "I'm sick of these Holocaust jokes / Anne frankly, they need to stop." Both of these suggest a critique of Anne Frank memes, but then proceed to make a pun on her name, indicating that the critique is facetious. Another meme does not include Anne's face but rather places Anne within the context of an LOLcat meme. Over the image of a very sad-looking cat, we see the text "Too many jokes about Anne Frank / Feels bad." Although this meme suggests a possibly more sincere critique of Anne Frank memes, the fact that it uses an LOLcat to make its critique suggests an ironic, distanced stance.

One effect of the Anne Frank meme is, like tendentious verbal jokes, the articulation of what is unsayable in most contexts, in other words, the overcoming of repression. In his study of the remediation of Anne Frank's name and diary, David Wertheim has noted,

> a common complaint of critics of Anne Frank's remembrance has been her sanctification. Much of the reception of the diary of Anne Frank indeed has religious overtones. She has become a source of moral and religious values—of meaning—and has sometimes literally been described as a saint.[39]

In her study of RIP trolling, Whitney Phillips has shown that trolls often justify their trolling by stating that their target is not, say, a murdered teenage girl, but rather the exploitation of her murder by the wider public on platforms such as Facebook.[40] Likewise, it is possible to read Anne Frank memes as not targeting Anne herself but, rather, her posthumous sanctification. In this reading, it is the sanctimonious image of Anne Frank that has become repressive, and Anne Frank memes overcome this repression. Glossing Freud, Michael Billig suggests that "the joke provides a setting in which one can be freed of the demands of pity."[41] In this sense, the makers of Anne Frank memes are rejecting the discourse of pity that has been built up around their subject.

A second (and most likely intentional) effect of such memes, however, is to offend those who do not subscribe to the same values as the meme-makers. Within the cultures of certain parts of Reddit and 4chan, for instance, the worst "crime" is not being offensive but being offended, in other words, being a "snowflake" with "no sense of humor," a person who "cannot take a joke." Anne Frank meme-makers seek to offend, and yet the implications of their memes can also be disavowed as "just a joke." Writing about KKK jokes, Billig observes,

> These jokes, that are not just jokes, mock restraints against racist violence. They celebrate such violence, encouraging that it should be imagined as enjoyment without pity for the dehumanized victims. The harm of such violent fantasy can be denied—it's not real after all. As with much humour, there is ambivalence, as assertion and denial are both present with no need to resolve the contradiction.[42]

By mocking "restraints against racist violence," the makers of Anne Frank memes attempt to make it laughable to feel any sort of pity or empathy towards the actual person whose image has been appropriated into the meme. If there is a target other than Anne Frank in these memes, I would argue that it is empathy itself as manifested through a relation to an indexical trace. If one reads the memes this way, then the meme-makers do have a point. Anne herself is not present; she is dead and gone. And yet, it is the indexicality of the photographic image that both makes these memes work as jokes and also calls for empathy with an actual though absent person.

Indeed, one major difference between the verbal Anne Frank jokes cited above and an Anne Frank meme is the use of Anne's indexical image (in most cases). Even though her image has become almost divorced from her identity through its pervasive use and repetition, the indexical pull of the image cannot be entirely negated—though it can apparently be ignored. Like Emmett Till, Anne Frank was a child who was murdered; hence, the appropriation of her image for humor is ethically reprehensible despite the commentary on Anne Frank's iconic, sanctified status that may (or may not) have been intended by the meme-makers. The mocking gaze of the meme-maker laid over the loving, preservationist gaze of the original photographer brings this ethical violation into relief. The contrasting gazes solicited by this kind of appropriation, then, is both the potential source of humor for some and the potential source of horror for others.

Yet, like *Open Casket*, these memes likely elicit different gazes from different viewers, even among those who are likely to be horrified by them. After I first presented some of these memes at a conference, a fellow Jewish academic came up to tell me how upset and offended he was by the memes. He asked me point blank, "Are you Jewish?" When I answered in the affirmative, he seemed relieved. Had a non-Jewish scholar presented an analysis of these memes it might—along the same lines as Schutz's *Open Casket*—have suggested that I could appreciate their offensiveness without actually *identifying* with their threat. When I see an Anne Frank meme, I am also looking at (by looking through) a gaze that sees me and my children as ashes—and laughs.

Notably, I found that, in contrast to something like *Open Casket,* Anne Frank memes are rarely discussed—at least outside of the communities that enjoy them. They generate no public controversy and are mentioned only when, for instance, a Jewish journalist receives one on Twitter. There are two likely reasons for this. First, memes are produced anonymously. One can sometimes identify who posted or reposted them, but the actual author usually remains unknown, so there is no one to criticize for their production. Second, the internet is an unruly place, so even if a meme is taken down from one place, there is no way to stop it popping up somewhere else. A meme cannot be destroyed. So, even though most people may agree that these are anti-Semitic, racist objects, there is not much point in opposing them. Any opposition will just lead to further production and circulation since generating offense is one of the main purposes of such memes. One can only shrug and repeat the mantra "Don't feed the trolls."

Yet, it is worth examining how Anne Frank memes have also been "weaponized," sent to Jewish journalists who run afoul of the right wing as a form of intimidation and threat. After reporter Julia Ioffe published a critical profile of Melania Trump in *GQ*, she faced a hailstorm of anti-Semitic messages and tweets, some of which she retweeted to demonstrate the abuse she was enduring. Although I can no longer locate the meme, her retweets included the first instance of an Anne Frank meme that I saw. In addition, Ioffe received another version of weaponized anti-Semitic appropriation, an image of her face photoshopped onto those of concentration camp prisoners in a Nazi era photograph.[43] Photoshopping someone's face onto a recognizable image has become another common way in which audiovisual appropriation is used to try to scare the person whose image has been thus inserted. Whereas with *Open Casket* Schutz, in her ignorance, may have *elicited* an endangered gaze from Black viewers, I truly believe that she did not *solicit* it. The people who produce or send these anti-Semitic memes actively solicit the endangered gaze from their targets. The purpose of the appropriation is to make the target whose image has been appropriated feel unsafe.

In a related example of audiovisual appropriation as weapon, cultural critic Anita Sarkeesian—who aroused the anger of online gamers with her feminist critiques of video game representations—was harassed with images of her face pasted into pornographic images (in addition to suffering many other abuses). Then, as if that were not enough, someone created a video game called "Beat Up Anita Sarkeesian" in which the player could punch Sarkeesian's appropriated image and produce visual injuries.[44] (Fortunately, this game appears to have been deleted.)[45] These kinds of texts produce not simply a dehumanizing gaze—though they certainly do that—but an actively hateful gaze, a malevolent, threatening, and even violent gaze. The aim of their misuse is, precisely, abuse. Moreover, by actively inviting players to "beat up" a woman's photographic image, it solicits not only a gaze but an action, albeit a virtual one.

The trouble is that we can have arguments about ethics only within a group whose members already share a commitment to similar values, such as racial and gender equality and justice. The people who produce Anne Frank memes or appropriate female critics' images into violent images or games exist outside of the ethical sphere most academics like myself take as more or less given. We cannot shame them as we can shame Schutz and the Whitney Museum. Even by writing about these memes, I give them further exposure, which is precisely what their makers want. There is likely no way to prevent such unethical appropriations; we can only identify and analyze them. As internet trolls—and certain world leaders—try to push the boundaries of what is sayable in terms of racist, sexist, homophobic and other dehumanizing discourses, we who hold a different set of values need to constantly be articulating the ethical lines that we wish to maintain, regardless of those who will inevitably disregard them.

The reversible nature of photographic and digital recording, the fact that we could always find ourselves on the other side of the lens, should incite us to always imagine ourselves—or perhaps our loved ones—in the sounds and images that we appropriate or the appropriated sounds and images that we consume. The simple questions—"What if that were me? What if that were my father or my child?"—offer at least a faint map upon which to trace a path regarding what can ethically be misused and for what ends. Online trolls, of course, will never ask these questions, because—it seems—they simply do not care about other people. But for those of us who do care, we must constantly remind ourselves that just because a recording is already "out there" does not mean that those who have been recorded have no claim upon it. Instead, we must map the layers of the gaze and the relationship between them so as to consciously decide whether a given appropriation is justified. Every reuse is always a misuse, but the effort to chart the layered gaze can help us steer an ethical course.

# Filmography

*The 81st Blow* (Haim Gouri, David Bergman, Jacques Ehrlich, Ghetto Fighters House, 1974)
*Am I Pretty?* (Jennifer Proctor, 2017)
*Aufschub* (Harun Farocki, 2007)
"Barack Obama Singing 'Call Me Maybe' by Carly Jepsen" (baracksdubs, 2012)
"The Bed Intruder Song" (The Gregory Brothers, 2010)
*Blue* (Derek Jarman, 1993)
"Brian Williams Raps 'Rapper's Delight'" (Jimmy Fallon, 2014)
*The Celluloid Closet* (Rob Epstein, Jeffrey Friedman, 1996)
*The Civil War* (Ken Burns, 1990)
*The Daily Show with Jon Stewart* (Comedy Central, 1999–2015)
"Dead Giveaway" (The Gregory Brothers, 2013)
*East of Borneo* (George Melford, 1931)
*Eichmann and the Third Reich* (Erwin Leiser, 1961)
*The Exorcist* (William Friedkin, 1973)
*Facing Forward* (Fiona Tan, 1999)
*The Fall of the Romanov Dynasty* (Esfir Shub, 1927)
*Falling in Love . . . with Chris and Greg: Work of Art! Reality TV Special* (Chris Vargas and Greg Youmans, 2012)
*A Film Unfinished* (Yael Hersonski, 2010)
*Galactic Docking Company* (Clark Nikolai, 2009)
*Ghost of Yesterday* (Tony Gault, 2012)
*Halimuhfack* (Christopher Harris, 2016)
"Hitler Sings The Jeffersons Theme" (FuntToob, 2009)
*Holokaust* (Philip Remy, 2000)
*Home Stories* (Mathias Muller, 1990)
*I for NDN* (Clint Enns and Darryl Nepinak, 2011)

"Inauguration 2013: A Bad Lip Reading of Barack Obama's Inauguration" (Bad Lip Reading, 2013)
*It's Like That* (Southern Ladies Animation Group, 2003)
*The Jeffersons* (CBS, 1975–1985)
*Kansas City Trucking Co.* (Tim Kincaid, 1976)
*The Kids Guide to the Internet* (1997)
"The Komputer Tutor for Komputer Kindergarten" (Kim Komando, c. 1990)
*Millhouse: A White Comedy* (Emile de Antonio, 1971)
*Mondo Cane* (Gualtiero Jacopetti, Paolo Cavara, Franco Prosperi, 1962)
*A Movie* (Bruce Conner, 1958)
*Near the Big Chakra* (Anne Severson, 1971)
*Night and Fog* (Alain Resnais, 1955)
*Now he's out in public and everyone can see* (Natalie Bookchin, 2012)
"Obama Mixtape 1999" (The Gregory Brothers, 2015)
*of the North* (Dominic Gagnon, 2015)
*Our Nixon* (Penny Lane, 2013)
"Palin's Breath" (Wreck and Salvage, 2011)
"The Reagans Speak Out on Drugs" (Cliff Roth, 1988)
*Remembrance* (Jerry Tartaglia, 1990)
*Rose Hobart* (Joseph Cornell, 1936)
*Sara Nokomis Weir* (Brian L. Frye, 2014)
*School Craft: Learn at Home* (Fran Allison)
"Shut Up Lil' Man!" (Mike Mitchell)
*Shut Up Little Man!: An Audio Misadventure* (Matthew Bate, 2011)
*Sink or Swim* (Su Friedrich, 1990)
*Sisters & Brothers* (Kent Monkman, 2015)
*Speechless* (Scott Stark, 2008)
"State of Union . . . Not Good" (Edo Wilkins, 2002)
"States of the Union—Bill Clinton" (Aaron Valdez, 1997)
*Suitcase of Love and Shame* (Jane Gillooly, 2013)
*Tearoom* (William E. Jones, 2007)
*Technology/Transformation: Wonder Woman* (Dara Birnbaum, 1978–79)
*Telephones* (Christian Marclay, 1995)
*Le Temps du ghetto* (Frédéric Rossif, 1961)
"These Hands" (RomneyComms, 2012)
*The Triumph of the Will* (Leni Riefenstahl, 1935)
"U Didn't Build That" (Hugh Atkin, 2012)
*Undaddy Mainframe* (Soda_Jerk, 2014)
*Video Proof: The NAACP Awards Racism—2010* (Andrew Breitbart, 2010)
*What Happened to Her* (Kristy Guevara-Flanagan, 2016)
*Work of Art: The Next Great Artist* (Bravo, 2010–2011)
*You Don't Like the Truth: Four Days Inside Guantanamo* (Patricio Henriquez, Luc Côté, 2010)
"You Won't Believe What Obama Says in This Video!" (Buzzfeed, Jordan Peele, 2018)

# Acknowledgments

Many conversations with brilliant friends and colleagues have been essential to the emergence of the ideas in this book; without their thoughts, questions, and encouragement this project would never have come to fruition.

Selmin Kara and Daniel Marcus first gave me the opportunity to explore questions of ethics and audiovisual appropriation in an essay published in their collection, *Contemporary Documentary*; this became the kernel from which *Reuse, Misuse, Abuse* was born. Along the way, at conferences and symposia, the work benefited from the stellar feedback of Courtney Baker, Né Barros, Lauren M. Cramer, Efrén Cuevas, Zoë Druick, Allyson Field, Kristen Fuhs, Filipe Martins, Eleni Palis, Patrik Sjöberg, Andrej Slavik, Malin Wahlberg, and Janet Walker. More broadly, the entire Visible Evidence community has been instrumental in developing this work. Jennifer Proctor and Jaymie Heilman generously volunteered to read some early chapter drafts and offered invaluable feedback.

My gratitude goes to the many filmmakers who spoke or corresponded with me about their films as I struggled to articulate their ethical complexity, in particular Natalie Bookchin, Clint Enns, Brian L. Frye, Tony Gault, Jane Gillooly, Christopher Harris, Yael Hersonski, Penny Lane, Clark Nikolai, Jennifer Proctor, Soda_Jerk, Scott Stark, and Greg Youmans.

I would also like to thank Alexandra Juhasz and my other anonymous reader for their insightful and immensely helpful comments on the early drafts of the book, as well as my two editors at Rutgers, Leslie Mitchner and Nicole Solano, for supporting the project. Thank you also to the University of Alberta Faculty of Arts for their subvention in support of the book's publication.

As always, I must thank the brilliant and inimitable Vivian Sobchack for talking through my ideas with me through many conversations. Her incisive comments never fail to make my work stronger, clearer, and more precise. I do not exaggerate when I say that she has been the guiding light of my scholarship, as well as my dear friend.

Finally, I want to thank my family: my parents, Ruthellen Josselson and Hanoch Flum, for having always supported my every endeavor; Jonathan Cohn, the person I want always to be standing by my side; and Kai and Audrey Baron-Cohn, who give me a reason to believe in making the world a more beautiful, just, and ethical place.

# Notes

## Introduction

1 Robert Everett-Green, "Debate Rages on over Dominic Gagnon and Consent in the Age of YouTube," *The Globe and Mail,* 25 March 2016.
2 Jorge Barerra, "Tanya Tagaq 'Out for Blood' over 'Racist' Experimental Documentary by Quebec Filmmaker," *Aboriginal People's Television Network,* 25 November 2015.
3 For a discussion of this history of indigenous misrepresentation and responses to it, see Faye Ginsburg, "Isuma TV, Visual Sovereignty, and the Arctic Media World," in *Arctic Cinemas and the Documentary Ethos,* ed. Lilya Kaganovsky, Scott MacKenzie, and Anna Westerstahl Stenport (Bloomington: Indiana University Press, 2017), 254–274.
4 Everett-Green, "Debate Rages."
5 CBC, "Tanya Tagaq Threatens Legal Action against 'Racist' Quebec Film 'Of The North,'" *Huffington Post Canada,* 25 November 2015.
6 "of The North: Un groupe de cinéastes dénonce un cas apparenté à la censure," *Voir,* 25 February 2016. https://voir.ca/cinema/2016/02/25/of-the-north-un-groupe-de-cineastes-denonce-un-cas-apparente-a-la-censure/ [Original in French].
7 CBC, "Tanya Tagaq Threatens."
8 Ezra Winton, "Curating the North: Documentary Screening Ethics and Inuit Representation in (Festival) Cinema," *Art Threat,* 17 December 2015.
9 Jonathan Culp, "Trashing Culture: Dominic Gagnon's art of appropriation," *Now,* 6 January 2016.
10 See also Michelle Stewart, "Of Digital Selves and Digital Sovereignty: *of the North,*" *Film Quarterly* 70, no. 4 (2017): 23–38; and Bruno Cornellier, "Extracting Inuit: The *of the North* Controversy and the White Possessive," *American Indian Culture and Research Journal* 40, no. 4 (2016): 23–48.
11 National Film Board of Canada, www.nfb.ca/film/sisters_brothers/.

12 As part of the Truth and Reconciliation Project, the Canadian government is now committed to naming as many of the children who lived in and may have died in residential schools as possible. For more, see *Canada's Residential Schools: Missing Children and Unmarked Burials, The Final Report of the Truth and Reconciliation Commission of Canada, Volume 4* (Montreal & Kingston: McGill-Queen's University Press, 2015).

13 Lawrence Lessig, *Remix: Making Art and Commerce Thrive in the Hybrid Economy* (New York: Penguin, 2008), 28.

14 Lessig, 76.

15 Lev Manovich, "Remix Strategies in Social Media," in *The Routledge Companion to Remix Studies,* ed. Eduardo Navas, Owen Gallagher, and xtine burrough (London: Routledge, 2015), 142.

16 See, for instance, Stefan Sonvilla-Weiss, "Good Artists Copy; Great Artists Steal: Reflections on Cut-Copy-Paste Culture," in *The Routledge Companion to Remix Studies,* ed. Eduardo Navas, Owen Gallagher, and xtine burrough (London: Routledge, 2015), 54–67.

17 Guy Debord and Gil Wolman, "A User's Guide to Détournement (Debord and Wolman, 1956)," in *The Situationist International Anthology,* ed. Ken Knabb (Berkeley, California: Bureau of Public Secrets, 2006), 15.

18 I use the inclusive term "audiovisual appropriation" to specify my focus on the mechanical reproduction and reuse of indexical visual records including photographs, film, and video; of audio recordings; and of recordings that include both image and sound. The term "recordings" likewise signals that these objects may include images—photographs, films, or videos—and sound. The salient point is that they are indexical traces of the profilmic world.

19 Jaimie Baron, *The Archive Effect: Found Footage and the Audiovisual Experience of History* (London: Routledge, 2014), 23.

20 In addition to Lessig's *Remix Culture*, see, for instance, Patricia Aufderheide and Peter Jaszi, *Reclaiming Fair Use: How to Put Balance Back in Copyright* (Chicago: University of Chicago Press, 2011); and Kembrew McLeod and Peter DiCola, *Creative License: The Law and Culture of Digital Sampling* (Durham: Duke University Press, 2011).

21 *Campbell v. Acuff-Rose Music* (92-1292), 510 U.S. 569 (1994).

22 Bill Nichols, *Representing Reality: Issues and Concepts in Documentary* (Bloomington: Indiana University Press, 1991), 77.

23 Nichols, *Representing Reality*, 77.

24 Thomas Elsaesser, "The Ethics of Appropriation: Found Footage between Archive and Internet," *Found Footage Magazine* 1 (October 2016), 37.

25 John Stuart Katz and Judith Milstein Katz, "Ethics and the Perception of Ethics in Autobiographical Film," in *Image Ethics: The Moral Rights of Subjects in Photographs, Film, and Television*, ed. Larry Gross, John Stuart Katz, and Jay Ruby (London: Oxford University Press, 1988), 121.

26 Lorelle A. Babwah, "Climbing in Our Windows & Snatching Our Likenesses Up: Viral Videos & the Scope of the Right of Publicity on the Internet," *North Carolina Journal of Law & Technology* 12 (2010): 57.

27 J. Thomas McCarthy, *The Rights of Publicity and Privacy*, 2nd ed. (Eagan, Minnesota: Thomas Reuters, 2009), 1:3.

28 Babwah, "Climbing in Our Windows," 57.

29 Elsaesser, "The Ethics of Appropriation," 34.
30 Sarah Cooper, *Selfless Cinema?: Ethics and French Documentary* (London: Legenda, 2006), 23.
31 Cooper, *Selfless Cinema?*, 92–93.
32 Sarah Cooper, "Looking Back, Looking Onwards: Selflessness, Ethics, and French Documentary," *Studies in French Cinema* 10, no. 1 (2010): 58.
33 Martha Nussbaum, *Love's Knowledge: Essays on Philosophy and Literature* (Oxford: Oxford University Press, 1992), 173.
34 Cooper, "Looking Back, Looking Onwards," 23.
35 Nichols, *Representing Reality*, 103.
36 Jane Stadler, *Pulling Focus: Intersubjective Experience, Narrative Film, and Ethics* (New York: Continuum, 2012), 5.
37 While, of course, my own experience as a viewer cannot be generalized to all viewers, in the tradition of Vivian Sobchack's work, cited throughout this study, I use my own embodied, as well as intellectual, response to these films as a jumping-off point for an analysis with wider philosophical implications.
38 Nichols, *Representing Reality*, 76.
39 Vivian Sobchack, "Inscribing Ethical Space: Ten Propositions on Death, Representation, and Documentary," in *Carnal Thoughts: Embodiment and Moving Image Culture* (Berkeley: University of California Press, 2004 [1984]), 243.
40 Sobchack, "Inscribing Ethical Space," 249.
41 Sobchack, "Inscribing Ethical Space," 253.
42 Judith Lancioni, "The Rhetoric of the Frame: Revisioning Archival Photographs in *The Civil War*," *Western Journal of Communication* 60, no. 4 (1996): 407.

## Chapter 1 (Re)exposing Intimate Traces

1 "intimate, adj. and n." *OED Online*. March 2020. Oxford University Press. https://www-oed-com.login.ezproxy.library.ualberta.ca/view/Entry/98506?rskey=jpe8Ry&result=1&isAdvanced=false (accessed April 17, 2020).
2 "intimate, v." *OED Online*. March 2020. Oxford University Press. https://www-oed-com.login.ezproxy.library.ualberta.ca/view/Entry/98507?rskey=UpqDjd&result=2&isAdvanced=false (accessed April 17, 2020).
3 This ethical question intersects with certain debates about "orphan films," whose ownership and provenance are unknown and which, therefore, have no owner to pay for their preservation. However, I am less focused here on preservation per se than on the ethics of reuse of existing footage in a new text. For a detailed introduction to the issues surrounding orphan films, see Dan Streible, "The Role of Orphan Films in the 21st Century Archive," *Cinema Journal* 46, no. 3 (Spring 2007): 124–28.
4 Vivian Sobchack, "Inscribing Ethical Space: Ten Propositions on Death, Representation, and Documentary," in *Carnal Thoughts: Embodiment and Moving Image Culture* (Berkeley: University of California Press, 2004 [1984]), 253. See my Introduction for further discussion of "subjective responsiveness."
5 Frances Guerin, "Introduction," in *On Not Looking: The Paradox of Contemporary Visual Culture,*" ed. Frances Guerin (New York: Routledge, 2015), 1.
6 Sobchack, "Inscribing Ethical Space," 253. See my Introduction for Sobchack's elaboration of the "humane gaze."

7 I have written elsewhere about the appropriation of home movies as a form of "archival voyeurism." See Jaimie Baron, *The Archive Effect: Found Footage and the Audiovisual Experience of History* (London: Routledge, 2014), Chapter 3.
8 Colin J. Bennett, "In Defense of Privacy: The Concept and the Regime," *Surveillance & Society* 8, no. 4 (2011): 486.
9 *Katz v. United States*, 389 U.S. at 361 (Harlan, J., concurring) (1967).
10 Efrén Cuevas, "Change of Scale: Home Movies as Microhistory in Documentary Films," in *Amateur Filmmaking: The Home Movie, the Archive, the Web*, Laura Rascaroli, Gwenda Young, and Barry Monahan, eds. (Bloomsbury Publishing USA, 2014): 144.
11 "seclude, v." *OED Online*. March 2020. Oxford University Press. https://www-oed-com.login.ezproxy.library.ualberta.ca/view/Entry/174485?redirectedFrom=seclude (accessed April 17, 2020).
12 Steve Anderson, *Technologies of History: Visual Media and the Eccentricity of the Past* (Hanover, New Hampshire: Dartmouth College Press, 2011), 90.
13 Rachel Stevens, "Our Nixon," *Millennium Film Journal* 59 (Spring 2014), 17.
14 Anderson, *Technologies of History*, 97.
15 Efrén Cuevas, "Home Movies as Personal Archives in Autobiographical Documentaries," *Studies in Documentary Film* 17, no. 1 (2013): 17–29.
16 All quotations from Tony Gault from email correspondence with the filmmaker, 9 February 2013.
17 Martha Nussbaum, *Love's Knowledge: Essays on Philosophy and Literature* (New York: Oxford University Press, 1992), 148.
18 Marcel Merleau-Ponty, *The Phenomenology of Perception*, trans. Colin Smith (London and New York: Routledge, 2002 [originally published in French, 1945]), 35.
19 Merleau-Ponty, *The Phenomenology of Perception*, 371.
20 Jennifer Barker, "Out of Sync, Out of Sight: Synaesthesia and Film Spectacle," *Paragraph* 31, no. 2 (2008): 241.
21 Barker, "Out of Sync, Out of Sight," 251.
22 "explicit, adj. and n." *OED Online*. March 2020. Oxford University Press. https://www-oed-com.login.ezproxy.library.ualberta.ca/view/Entry/66634?rskey=eLUnfT&result=2&isAdvanced=false (accessed April 17, 2020).
23 David Finkelstein, *Film Threat*, 2 November 2008. http://filmthreat.com/uncategorized/speechless/.
24 Laura Mulvey, "Visual Pleasure in Narrative Cinema," *Screen* 16, no. 3 (Autumn 1975): 6-18.
25 Finkelstein, http://filmthreat.com/uncategorized/speechless/.
26 Jennifer Bean, "Technologies of Early Stardom and the Extraordinary Body," *Camera Obscura* 16, no. 3 (2001): 46.
27 Mark Hansen, "The Time of Affect, or Bearing Witness to Life," *Critical Inquiry* 30, no. 3 (2004): 621.
28 Hansen, "The Time of Affect," 622.
29 Sissela Bok, *Secrecy: On the Ethics of Concealment and Revelation* (New York: Vintage Books, 1989), 10–11.
30 Bok, *Secrecy*, 6.
31 See also my analysis of *You Don't Like the Truth: Four Days Inside Guantanamo* (Patricio Henriquez, Luc Côté, 2010) in Chapter 4.

32 Bok, *Secrecy,* 91.
33 Bok, *Secrecy,* 97.
34 Bok, *Secrecy,* 100.
35 Phone interview with Jane Gillooly, 20 September 2014.
36 One might argue that a living, mentally competent relative of Tom or Jeannie might have given consent for Gillooly's use of the recordings. However, I am skeptical of the notion of third-party consent, at least as ethical grounds. These recordings belonged exclusively to Tom and Jeannie, so the permission of a relative would not mean actual consent on the part of the recorded subjects (even if a relative's consent might constitute more solid legal grounds for Gillooly should she ever be sued). This is another reason that "consent" does not seem to me to be an adequate criterion for evaluating the ethics of many audiovisual appropriations.
37 John Stuart Katz and Judith Milstein Katz, "Ethics and the Perception of Ethics in Autobiographical Film," in *Image Ethics: The Moral Rights of Subjects in Photographs, Film, and Television*, ed. Larry Gross, John Stuart Katz, and Jay Ruby (London: Oxford University Press, 1988), 128.
38 Scott MacDonald, "Cine-Surveillance: 3 Avant-Docs Interviews with Amie Siegel, Sharon Lockhart, Jane Gillooly," *Film Quarterly* 66, no. 4 (2013): 40.
39 As noted in my Introduction, in referring to audio recordings, the visual term *gaze* is not quite appropriate, but there is no audial equivalent in English of a "gaze."
40 Jane Gillooly website, www.janegillooly.com/films/suitcase-of-love-and-shame/.
41 Phone interview with Jane Gillooly, 20 September 2014.
42 Mark Alice Durant, "Jane Gillooly," *Saint Lucy*. http://saint-lucy.com/conversations/jane-gillooly/.
43 Michel Chion, *Audio-Vision: Sound on Screen*, trans. Claudia Gorbman (New York: Columbia University Press, 1994), 32.
44 Chion, *Audio-Vision,* 128.
45 Krista Ratcliffe, "Eavesdropping as Rhetorical Tactic: History, Whiteness, and Rhetoric," *JAC: A Journal of Rhetoric, Culture, and Politics* 20 (no. 1): 90.
46 Macdonald, "Cine-Surveillance," 38.
47 See George Cothran, "Shut Up, Little Man: The squalor and acrimony of the lives of a couple of hard-drinking retirees are dwarfed by the avarice that their celebrity has inspired in others," *The San Francisco Weekly,* 2 August 1995. www.sfweekly.com/sanfrancisco/shut-up-little-man/Content?oid=2132286.
48 In addition to the films discussed below, there have been numerous comic illustrations, a play called "Shut Up! Little Man" written by Gregg Gibbs, and later a movie called *Shut Yer Dirty Little Mouth* (Robert Taicher, 2001). The recordings have also been sampled in several songs including "Shut Up, Little Man" by The Wipeouters, a side project of members of the band Devo.
49 "illicit, adj." *OED Online*. March 2020. Oxford University Press. https://www-oed-com.login.ezproxy.library.ualberta.ca/view/Entry/91445?redirectedFrom=illicit (accessed April 17, 2020).
50 See, for instance, Katherine Biber and Derek Dalton, "Making Art from Evidence: Secret Sex and Police Surveillance in the Tearoom," *Crime, Media, Culture* 5, no. 3 (2009): 243–267; and James Polchin, "The Men in the Bathroom: Reflections on William E. Jones's *Tearoom,*" in *On Not Looking,* Frances Guerin, ed., 77–101 (New York: Routledge, 2015). I have also discussed this film at length in *The Archive Effect*

and in Jaimie Baron, "Translating the Document Across Time and Space: William E. Jones's Tearoom," *Spectator* 30, no. 1 (Spring 2010): 51–54.

51 Charles Acland, "Imaxtechnology and the Tourist Gaze," *Cultural Studies* 12, no. 3 (1998): 438.

52 Acland, 440.

53 Kyle Powys Whyte, Evan Selinger, and Kevin Outterson, "Poverty Tourism and the Problem of Consent," *Journal of Global Ethics* 7, no. 3 (2011): 338.

54 Annabelle Honess Roe, *Animated Documentary* (New York: Palgrave Macmillan, 2013), 90.

55 Cothran's article adds more details that reveal Haskett's life, in particular, to be even more depressing than Bate's film acknowledges. Haskett was apparently unable to work due to extreme anxiety and constant suicidal thoughts.

## Chapter 2 Speaking through Others

1 BuzzFeedVideo, "You Won't Believe What Obama Says In This Video!" www.youtube.com/watch?v=cQ54GDm1eL0&list=WL&index=3&t=0s.

2 For a more detailed discussion of the videos in this chapter that appropriate footage of Barack Obama, see Jaimie Baron, "Ventriloquizing Obama, or, the Ethics of Archival Ventriloquism," in *Media Ventriloquism,* ed. Jaimie Baron, Jennifer Fleeger, and Shannon Wong Lerner (Oxford University Press, forthcoming).

3 Steven Connor, *Dumbstruck: A Cultural History of Ventriloquism* (Oxford: Oxford University Press, 2003), 13-14.

4 Connor, *Dumbstruck,* 35.

5 Connor, *Dumbstruck,* 36.

6 The definition of the term "archival" has been the subject of much debate. For a book-length discussion of the notion of the "archival," see Jaimie Baron, *The Archive Effect: Found Footage and the Audiovisual Experience of History* (London: Routledge, 2014).

7 Connor, *Dumbstruck,* 14.

8 Henri Bergson, *Laughter: An Essay on the Meaning of the Comic* (New York: Macmillan, 1911), 29.

9 Bergson, *Laughter,* 34.

10 There may also be repetition or looping within the appropriation, which constitutes a third form. For a longer discussion of Bergson and audiovisual appropriation, see Jaimie Baron, "(In)appropriation: Productions of Laughter in Contemporary Experimental Found Footage Films," in *Sampling Media,* ed. Laurel Westrup and David Laderman (London: Oxford University Press, 2014): 168-182.

11 Neil Schaeffer, *The Art of Laughter* (New York: Columbia University Press, 1981), 9.

12 Paul Arthur, "The Status of Found Footage," *Spectator* 20, no. 1 (Fall 1999–Winter 2000): 62.

13 Johan Huizinga, *Homo Ludens* (London: Routledge, 1998 [original pub. 1938]), 13.

14 M. H. Abrams, *A Glossary of Literary Terms* (Orlando, FL: Holt, Rinehart and Winston, 1985), 166.

15 Byron Russell, "Appropriation is Activism," in *The Routledge Companion to Remix Studies*, ed. Eduardo Navas, Owen Gallagher, and xtine burrough (New York: Routledge, 2014), 220.

16 Lisa Colletta, "Political Satire and Postmodern Irony in the Age of Stephen Colbert and Jon Stewart," *The Journal of Popular Culture* 42, no. 5 (2009): 859.
17 Bergson, *Laughter,* 6.
18 "denigrate, v." *OED Online*. March 2020. Oxford University Press. https://www-oed-com.login.ezproxy.library.ualberta.ca/view/Entry/49972?redirectedFrom=denigrate (accessed April 17, 2020).
19 Valdez's Vimeo description of the video notes that it was "made with an old clunky tape to tape editor." https://vimeo.com/2717623.
20 www.supercut.org/about. The site is no longer functional but can be accessed via the Wayback Machine: https://web.archive.org/web/20110803233634/http://supercut.org/.
21 Tom McCormack, "Compilation Nation: The History and the Rise of the Supercut," *Moving Image Source,* 25 April 2011. www.movingimagesource.us/articles/compilation-nation-20110425.
22 Aaron Valdez, "States of the Union—Bill Clinton," https://vimeo.com/2717623.
23 Cliff Roth, "The Reagans Speak Out on Drugs," www.youtube.com/watch?v=La5jrfobfTM.
24 Edo Wilkins, "State of the Union . . . Not Good," www.youtube.com/watch?v=6WtuYcn6N3A.
25 Wreck and Salvage, "Palin's Breath," http://wreckandsalvage.com/about/.
26 MSNBC, *The Daily Rundown,* 25 March 2010. www.youtube.com/watch?v=qs75zKxJxVY.
27 McCormack, "Compilation Nation."
28 Jon Bershad, for instance, described the video as "Creepy/Funny." See Jon Bershad, "Creepy/Funny Video Edits Down Palin's Speech To Just The Exasperated Breaths," *Mediaite.com,* 13 January 2011. www.mediaite.com/online/creepyfunny-video-edits-down-palins-speech-to-just-the-exasperated-breaths/.
29 Bergson, *Laughter,* 143.
30 Miriama Young, *Singing the Body Electric: The Human Voice and Sound Technology* (London: Routledge, 2016), 58.
31 baracksdubs, "Barack Obama Singing 'Call Me Maybe' by Carly Jepsen," www.youtube.com/watch?v=hX1YVzdnpEc.
32 "Brian Williams Raps 'Rapper's Delight,'" www.youtube.com/watch?v=7CYJ73pVpVc.
33 Rachel Hall, "Missing Dolly, Mourning Slavery: The Slave Notice as Keepsake," *Camera Obscura* 21, no. 1 (2006): 72.
34 For an excellent, related discussion of "vocal whitewashing," see Jennifer O'Meara, "Identity Politics and Vocal "Whitewashing" in Celebrity Lip Syncs," in *Media Ventriloquism,* ed. Jaimie Baron, Jennifer Fleeger, and Shannon Wong Lerner (Oxford University Press, forthcoming).
35 Bad Lip Reading, "Inauguration 2013: A Bad Lip Reading:—A Bad Lip Reading of Barack Obama's Inauguration," www.youtube.com/watch?v=fpwhA-LdOHo.
36 Mats Carlsson, "The Strange Object of the Voice: A Bad Lip Reading," *Senses of Cinema* 67 (July 2013). http://sensesofcinema.com/2013/feature-articles/the-strange-object-of-the-voice-a-bad-lip-reading/.
37 For a brief discussion of this video published previously, see Jaimie Baron, "The Art of the (In)appropriate," in *Misdirect Movies*, ed. Andrew Bracey and John Rimmer, 16–19. Manchester: Cornerhouse Publications, 2013.

38 FuntToob, *Hitler Sings the Jeffersons Theme,* www.youtube.com/watch?v=J3YRWhg4YaA&skipcontrinter=1.
39 These include *Hitler Sings the Pokémon Theme Song* (www.youtube.com/watch?v=hbNo5ijvyfU), *Hitler Sings Numa Numa* (www.youtube.com/watch?v=xMITLLA3Syg) and *Hitler Sings the SpongeBob Squarepants Theme Song* (www.youtube.com/watch?v=PptJMfp0M9U).
40 Bergson, *Laughter,* 44.
41 Calvin Pryluck, "Ultimately We Are All Outsiders: The Ethics of Documentary Filmmaking," in *New Challenges for Documentary*, ed. Alan Rosenthal and John Corner (Manchester: Manchester University Press, 2005), 206.
42 Donald Bogle, *Toms, Coons, Mulattoes, Mammies, and Bucks: An Interpretive History of Blacks in American Films* (Continuum, 1994), 8.
43 Colletta, "Political Satire and Postmodern Irony," 857.
44 The Gregory Brothers, *Obama Mixtape: 1999 - Songify the News Special Edition,* www.youtube.com/watch?v=eq1FIvUHtt0.
45 Shayla C. Nunnally, *Trust in Black America: Race, Discrimination, and Politics* (New York: New York University Press, 2012), 4.
46 Nunnally, *Trust in Black America,* 4.
47 The White House, "Remarks by the President at a Campaign Event in Roanoke, Virginia," www.whitehouse.gov/the-press-office/2012/07/13/remarks-president-campaign-event-roanoke-virginia.
48 RomneyComms, "These Hands," www.youtube.com/watch?v=sNHeTwoy5vI.
49 The excerpt eventually found its way into YouTube artist Hugh Atkin's "U Didn't Build That." In this musical verbal collage, the quote is once again recontextualized but with an eye to pointing out the way its previous misuse was intentionally used to mislead. To the beat of MC Hammer's "U Can't Touch This," Obama raps a new set of lyrics, explicitly referencing Shirley Sherrod: "Mitt Romney strikes me so hard/ Makes me feel like Shirley Sherrod/ Out of context, those words aren't mine/ The private sector's doing fine." The chorus repeats the phrase "You didn't build that." Thus, we can see that here verbal collage became a weapon to combat strategies of framing. www.youtube.com/watch?v=bQu2SVFF-cU.
50 Mark Anthony Neal, *Looking for Leroy: Illegible Black Masculinities* (New York, NYU Press, 2013), 4.
51 Neal, *Looking for Leroy*, 5.
52 Neal, *Looking for Leroy*, 35.
53 Neal, *Looking for Leroy*, 37.
54 Jacqueline Bell, *Vloggers, Celebrities, Gods and Kings: The Politics of Publicness in Natalie Bookchin's* Now he's out in public and everyone can see (master's thesis, University of Southern California, 2013), 43.
55 Erica Levin, "Toward a Social Cinema Revisited," *Millennium Film Journal* 58 (2013): 35.
56 Supasorn Suwajanakorn, Steven M. Seitz, and Ira Kemelmacher-Shlizerman, "Synthesizing Obama: Learning Lip Sync from Audio," *ACM Transactions on Graphics (TOG)* 36, no. 4 (2017): Article 95.
57 James Vincent, "Lyrebird claims it can recreate any voice using just one minute of sample audio," *The Verge,* 24 April 2017.

## Chapter 3 Dislocating the Hegemonic Gaze

1 Christina Zhao, "'BBQ Becky,' White Woman Who Called Cops on Black BBQ, 911 Audio Released: 'I'm Really Scared! Come Quick!'" *Newsweek,* 4 September 2018. www.newsweek.com/bbq-becky-white-woman-who-called-cops-black-bbq-911-audio-released-im-really-1103057.

2 BBC, "BBQ Becky: Woman Photoshopped into black history after barbecue complaint," *BBC News*, www.bbc.com/news/newsbeat-44167760.

3 Emma Cocker, "Ethical Possession: Borrowing from the Archives," in *Cultural Borrowings: Appropriation, Reworking, Transformation,* ed. Iain Robert Smith, 92–110 (Scope, 2009): 100.

4 Jennifer Stob, "Détournement as Optic: Debord, Derisory Documents and the Aerial View," *Philosophy of Photography* 5, no. 1 (2014): 20.

5 Stob, 21.

6 Marilyn DeLaure and Moritz Fink, "Introduction," in *Culture Jamming: Activism and the Art of Cultural Resistance,* ed. Marilyn DeLaure and Moritz Fink (New York: New York University Press, 2017): 12–24.

7 See Chapter 2 for an extended discussion of the playful gaze.

8 DeLaure and Fink, 16.

9 Mark Dery, "Foreword," in *Culture Jamming: Activism and the Art of Cultural Resistance,* ed. Marilyn DeLaure and Moritz Fink (New York: New York University Press, 2017): xii.

10 Dery, xv.

11 Amit Pinchevski, "The Ethics of Interruption: Toward a Levinasian Philosophy of Communication," *Social Semiotics* 15, no. 2 (2005): 212.

12 Pinchevski, 227.

13 This may be true of all editing, of course, but it is often more pronounced in the case of audiovisual appropriation.

14 Pinchevski, 231.

15 A version of this analysis can also be found in Jaimie Baron, "Christopher Harris' Experimental Audiovisual Historiography," in *History in Images: Towards an (Audio)Visual Historiography,* eds. Peter Aronsson, Andrej Slávik, and Birgitta Svensson (Stockholm: Royal Swedish Academy of Letters, History and Antiquities, 2020): 191–200.

16 According to the Library of Congress website on which this recording can be streamed, this interview took place in Federal Music Project Office in Jacksonville, Florida, on 18 June 1939. The man interviewing Hurston is identified as Herbert Halpert. www.loc.gov/item/flwpa000014/.

17 Neal Sobania, "But Where Are the Cattle? Popular Images of Maasai and Zulu across the Twentieth Century," *Visual Anthropology* 15, no. 3/4 (July 2002): 313.

18 Daphne A. Brooks, "'Sister, Can You Line It Out?': Zora Neale Hurston and the Sound of Angular Black Womanhood," *Amerikastudien / American Studies* 55, no. 4: African American Literary Studies: New Texts, New Approaches, New Challenges (2010): 619.

19 Brooks, 623.

20 Laura Mulvey, "Rear-Projection and the Paradoxes of Hollywood Realism," in *Theorizing World Cinema,* eds. Lúcia Nagib, Rajinder Dudrah, and Chris Perriam (IB Tauris, 2011), 208.

21 Mulvey, 212.

22 Jeffrey Skoller, *Shadows, Specters, Shards: Making History in Avant-Garde Film* (Minneapolis: University of Minnesota Press, 2005), 5.

23 Skoller, 13.

24 Susan Sontag, "Notes on Camp," in *Camp: Queer Aesthetics and the Performing Subject: A Reader*, ed. Fabio Cleto (Ann Arbor: University of Michigan Press, 1999 [original 1964]): 56.

25 Sontag, 57.

26 Sontag, 58.

27 Sontag, 59.

28 The Found Footage Festival, www.foundfootagefest.com/about-fff/.

29 Sontag, 60.

30 The Found Footage Festival, www.foundfootagefest.com/2013/01/jazzercise/.

31 For a related analysis of this film published in French, see Jaimie Baron, "Un « Indien » dans les archives : le document trouvé et l'image composite," *Decadrages: Cinéma, a travers champs: Cinéma de re-montage 34–36* (Fall 2016/Spring 2017): 56–64.

32 William Wees, "The Ambiguous Aura of Hollywood Stars in Avant-Garde Found-Footage Films," *Cinema Journal* 41, no. 2 (2002): 7.

33 I use the term *chronotope* as theorized by Mikhail Bakhtin, "Forms of Time and Chronotope in the Novel," in *The Dialogic Imagination: Four Essays*, trans. Caryl Emerson and Michael Holquist (Austin: University of Texas Press, 1982).

34 For a related discussion of this film, see Jaimie Baron, "(In)appropriation: Productions of Laughter in Contemporary Experimental Found Footage Films," in *Sampling Media*, ed. Laurel Westrup and David Laderman, 168–182 (London: Oxford University Press, 2014).

35 "Docking," *The Urban Dictionary*, www.urbandictionary.com/define.php?term =docking.

36 Carolina A. Miranda, "Bravo's *Work of Art* Riles Up the Art World," *Time*, 4 August 2010.

37 Laura Mulvey, "Visual Pleasure and Narrative Cinema," *Screen* 16, no. 3 (Autumn 1975): 6–18.

38 "The Kids Guide to the Internet," www.youtube.com/watch?v=A81IwlDeV6c.

39 VNS Matrix, "Cyberfeminist Manifesto for the 21st Century," www.sterneck.net /cyber/vns-matrix/index.php.

40 Soda_Jerk, "Undaddy Mainframe," www.sodajerk.com.au/video_work.php?v =20140724231348.

41 See Kim Komando's website www.komando.com/.

42 Maria Fernandez and Faith Wilding, "Situating Cyberfeminisms," in *Domain Errors!: Cyberfeminist Practices*, eds. Maria Fernandez, Faith Wilding, and Michelle M. Wright (Brooklyn, New York: Autonomedia, 2002), 23.

## Chapter 4 Reframing the Perpetrator's Gaze

1 Marianne Hirsch, "Surviving Images: Holocaust Photographs and the Work of Postmemory," *The Yale Journal of Criticism* 14, no. 1 (2001): 26.

2 Frances Guerin, "The Energy of Disappearing: Problems of Recycling Nazi Amateur Film Footage," *Screening the Past* 17 (2004), http://tlweb.latrobe.edu.au /humanities/screeningthepast/firstrelease/fr_17/FGfr17.html.

3 Guerin, "The Energy of Disappearing."
4 Brad Prager, "On the Liberation of Perpetrator Photographs in Holocaust Narratives," in *Visualizing the Holocaust: Documents, Aesthetics, Memory*, ed. David Bathrick, Brad Prager, and Michael D. Richardson (Rochester, New York: Camden House, 2008), 22.
5 Prager, 22.
6 Prager, 19–20.
7 Vicente Sánchez-Biosca, "Perpetrator Images, Perpetrator Artifacts: The Nomad Archives of Tuol Sleng (S-21)," *Cinema & Cie International Film Studies Journal* 15, no. 24 (2015): 104.
8 Sánchez-Biosca, 104.
9 For a related discussion of *A Film Unfinished,* see Jaimie Baron, "The Ethics of Appropriation: 'Misusing' the Found Document in *Suitcase of Love and Shame* and *A Film Unfinished*," in *Contemporary Documentary*, ed. Selmin Kara and Daniel Marcus (London: Routledge, 2015): 156–170.
10 Stuart Liebman, "The Never-Ending Story: Yael Hersonski's *A Film Unfinished*," *Cineaste* 36, no. 3 (2011): 15.
11 Liebman, 15.
12 Ursula Böser, "*A Film Unfinished*: Yael Hersonski's Re-representation of Archival Footage from the Warsaw Ghetto," *Film Criticism* 37, no. 2 (2013): 38.
13 Böser, 39.
14 Sobchack, 255.
15 Böser, 42.
16 Patricio Henriquez, "Some Images of the Unseen: On the Making of the Film *You Don't Like the Truth: 4 Days Inside Guantánamo,*" trans. Mark Abley, in *Omar Khadr, O Canada,* ed. Janice Williamson (Montreal: McGill-Queen's University Press, 2012), 114.
17 Mark Denbeaux, Joshua W. Denbeaux, et al., "Captured on Tape: Interrogation and Videotaping of Detainees in Guantánamo," *Seton Hall Law Review* 41 (2011): 1309.
18 Joseph Pugliese, "Apostrophe of Empire: Guantánamo Bay, Disneyland," *Borderlands E-Journal: New Spaces in the Humanities* 8, no. 3 (December 2009): 13.
19 Peter Bradshaw, "*Four Days Inside Guantánamo*—Review," *The Guardian,* 6 October 2011. www.theguardian.com/film/2011/oct/06/four-days-inside-guantanamo-review.
20 Pugliese, 14.
21 Michael Spratt, "Dislike of Khadr settlement does not entitle critics to disregard law or facts," *Canadian Lawyer,* 24 July 2017. www.canadianlawyermag.com/author/michael-spratt/dislike-of-khadr-settlement-does-not-entitle-critics-to-disregard-law-or-facts-3695/.
22 *Gardner v. Florida* 430 U.S. 349 (1977).
23 Todd Butler, "Victim Impact Statements, New Media Technologies, and the Classical Rhetoric of Sincerity," *University of Toronto Quarterly* 82, no. 4 (Fall 2013): 842.
24 Louis-Georges Schwartz, *Mechanical Witness: A History of Motion Picture Evidence in US Courts* (Oxford University Press, 2009), 10.
25 *Payne v. Tennessee,* 501 U.S. 808, 822, 827 (1991).
26 *Payne v. Tennessee,* 501 U.S. 808, 822, 827 (1991).

27 Emily Holland, "Moving Pictures Maintaining Justice-Clarifying the Right Role for Victim Impact Videos in the Capital Context," *Berkeley Journal of Criminal Law* 17 (2012): 155.
28 Holland, 156.
29 *Payne v. Tennessee*, 501 U.S. 808, 822, 827 (1991).
30 Regina Austin, "Documentation, Documentary, and the Law: What Should Be Made of Victim Impact Videos?" *University of Pennsylvania Law School: Faculty Scholarship* Paper 313 (2010): 984.
31 Austin, 988.
32 Richard Chalfen, *Snapshot Versions of Life* (Bowling Green: Bowling Green State University Popular Press, 1987), 8.
33 The victim impact video presented in *People v. Kelly* can be viewed at www.youtube.com/watch?v=wcA09wMl6eo.
34 Frye's film is currently available at http://vimeo.com/90760839.
35 Christine M. Kennedy, "Victim Impact Videos: The New-Wave of Evidence in Capital Sentencing Hearings," *Quinnipiac Law Review* 26 (2007): 1092.
36 Schwartz, 84.
37 Schwartz, 50.
38 I have discussed this experience elsewhere as the "archive affect." See Jaimie Baron, *The Archive Effect: Found Footage and the Audiovisual Experience of History* (London: Routledge, 2014), Chapter 4.
39 Lily E. Hirsch, *Music in American Crime Prevention and Punishment* (Ann Arbor: University of Michigan Press, 2012), 137.
40 Carol Vernallis, *Experiencing Music Video : Aesthetics and Cultural Context* (New York: Columbia University Press, 2004), 177.
41 Tobias Ebbrecht-Hartmann, "Trophy, Evidence, Document: Appropriating an Archive Film from Liepaja, 1941," *Historical Journal of Film, Radio and Television* 36, no. 4 (2016): 522.
42 Ebbrecht-Hartmann, 523.

## Chapter 5 Abusing Images

1 Vivian Sobchack, "Inscribing Ethical Space," in *Carnal Thoughts: Embodiment and Moving Image Culture* (Berkeley: University of California Press, 2004), 253.
2 Courtney Baker, *Humane Insight: Looking at Images of African American Suffering and Death* (Champaign, Illinois: University of Illinois Press, 2015), 5.
3 Josephine Livingstone and Lovia Gyarkye, "The Case Against Dana Schutz," *The New Republic*, 22 March 2017. http://newrepublic.com/article/141506/case-dana-schutz.
4 Siddhartha Mitter, "'What Does It Mean to Be Black and Look at This?' A Scholar Reflects on the Dana Schutz Controversy" (interview with Christina Sharpe), *Hyperallergic*, 24 March 2017. https://hyperallergic.com/368012/what-does-it-mean-to-be-black-and-look-at-this-a-scholar-reflects-on-the-dana-schutz-controversy/.
5 Coco Fusco, "Censorship, Not the Painting, Must Go: On Dana Schutz's Image of Emmett Till," *Hyperallergic*, 27 March 2017. https://hyperallergic.com/368290/censorship-not-the-painting-must-go-on-dana-schutzs-image-of-emmett-till/.
6 Livingstone and Gyarkye, "The Case Against Dana Schutz."

7 Roland Barthes, *Camera Lucida: Reflections on Photography*, trans. Richard Howard (New York: Hill and Wang, 1981), 5.
8 See my discussion of the "occluded gaze" in Chapter 1.
9 Mitter, "'What Does It Mean to Be Black and Look at This?'"
10 Fusco, "Censorship, Not the Painting, Must Go."
11 Livingstone and Gyarkye, "The Case Against Dana Schutz."
12 Alicia Eler, "Painting of Philando Castile's death on display in New York's Whitney Museum," *Star Tribune,* 23 June 2017, http://www.startribune.com/painting-of-philando-castile-s-death-on-display-in-new-york-s-whitney-museum/430375453/.
13 See Alex Greenberger, "'The Painting Must Go': Hannah Black Pens Open Letter to the Whitney About Controversial Biennial Work," *ArtNews,* 21 March 2017. www.artnews.com/2017/03/21/the-painting-must-go-hannah-black-pens-open-letter-to-the-whitney-about-controversial-biennial-work/.
14 Fusco, "Censorship, Not the Painting, Must Go."
15 Elizabeth Alexander, "Can you be BLACK and Look at This?": Reading the Rodney King Video(s)," *Public Culture* 7, no.1 (1994): 88.
16 Sobchack, 249.
17 Keesha Beckford, "Dear White Moms," *HuffPost,* 22 August 2014, https://www.huffpost.com/entry/dear-white-moms_b_5698431.
18 Baker, 47.
19 How Farah found the image is unclear. Apparently, due to the controversy surrounding *Open Casket*, Schutz's email accounts may have been hacked, so it is also possible that the image was never published online. See Lizzie Crocker, "The Controversial Painting of Emmett Till Stays on Show at The Whitney," *The Daily Beast,* 23 March 2017. www.thedailybeast.com/the-controversial-painting-of-emmett-till-stays-on-show-at-the-whitney.
20 Silke Hohmann, "Kunst als Rache: Künstler malt Sohn von Dana Schutz," *Monopol,* 15 June 2018. www.monopol-magazin.de/kuenstler-malt-sohn-von-dana-schutz.
21 Olamiju Fajemisin, "'The spectacle of Black trauma': Why Double Standards in Representation Need to End in the Arts," *C&,* 23 July 2018. www.contemporaryand.com/gazines/why-double-standards-in-representation-need-to-end-in-the-arts/.
22 Famjemisin, "'The spectacle of Black trauma.'"
23 Andrew Marantz, "Neo-Nazi No-No's," *The New Yorker,* 15 January 2018.
24 Marantz, "Neo-Nazi No-No's."
25 Alan Dundes and Thomas Hauschild, "Auschwitz Jokes," *Western Folklore* 42, no. 4 (October 1983): 249.
26 Dundes and Hauschild, 250.
27 Sigmund Freud, *Jokes and Their Relation to the Unconscious,* trans. James Strachey (New York: W.W. Norton & Company, 1963), 134.
28 Dundes and Hauschild, 251.
29 Dundes and Hauschild, 254.
30 Dundes and Hauschild, 253.
31 Asaf Nissenbaum and Limor Shifman, "Internet Memes as Contested Cultural Capital: The Case of 4chan's/b/board," *New Media & Society* 19, no. 4 (2017): 484.
32 Ryan M. Milner, "Hacking the Social: Internet Memes, Identity Antagonism, and the Logic of Lulz," *Fibreculture Journal* 22: Trolls and The Negative Space of the Internet (2013): 64.

33 Milner, "Hacking the Social," 66.
34 Milner, "Hacking the Social," 66.
35 Milner, "Hacking the Social," 75.
36 Milner, "Hacking the Social," 74.
37 Milner, "Hacking the Social," 76.
38 There are others I have found that do not fit into any of these categories, but I will not discuss them all here. My aim is not to be comprehensive but simply to outline a few major tendencies among these memes.
39 David Wertheim, "Remediation as a Moral Obligation: Authenticity, Memory, and Morality in Representations of Anne Frank," in *Mediation, Remediation, and the Dynamics of Cultural Memory,* ed. Astrid Erll and Ann Rigney (De Gruyter, 2009): 158.
40 Whitney Phillips, "LOLing at Tragedy: Facebook trolls, memorial pages and resistance to grief online," *First Monday* 16, no. 12 (2011). http://journals.uic.edu/ojs/index.php/fm/rt/printerFriendly/3168/3115.
41 Michael Billig, "Humour and Hatred: The Racist Jokes of the Ku Klux Klan," *Discourse & Society* 12, no. 3 (2001): 279.
42 Billig, 286.
43 Lauren Gambino, "Journalist who profiled Melania Trump hit with barrage of antisemitic abuse," *The Guardian,* 29 April 2016. www.theguardian.com/us-news/2016/apr/28/julia-ioffe-journalist-melania-trump-antisemitic-abuse.
44 Soraya Nadia McDonald, "Gaming vlogger Anita Sarkeesian is forced from home after receiving harrowing death threats," *The Washington Post,* 29 August 2014.
45 "Beat Up Anita Sarkeesian," www.newgrounds.com/portal/view/598591.

# Bibliography

Abrams, M. H. *A Glossary of Literary Terms*. Orlando, FL: Holt, Rinehart and Winston, 1985.

Acland, Charles. "Imaxtechnology and the Tourist Gaze." *Cultural Studies* 12, no. 3 (1998): 429–445.

Alexander, Elizabeth. "Can you be BLACK and Look at This?": Reading the Rodney King Video(s)." *Public Culture* 7, no. 1 (1994): 77–94.

Anderson, Steve. *Technologies of History: Visual Media and the Eccentricity of the Past.* Hanover, NH: Dartmouth College Press, 2011.

Arthur, Paul. "The Status of Found Footage." *Spectator* 20, no. 1 (Fall 1999–Winter 2000): 57–69.

Aufderheide, Patricia, and Peter Jaszi. *Reclaiming Fair Use: How to Put Balance Back in Copyright.* Chicago: University of Chicago Press, 2011.

Austin, Regina, "Documentation, Documentary, and the Law: What Should Be Made of Victim Impact Videos?" *University of Pennsylvania Law School: Faculty Scholarship* Paper 313 (2010): 979–1017.

Babwah, Lorelle A. "Climbing in Our Windows & Snatching Our Likenesses Up: Viral Videos and the Scope of the Right of Publicity on the Internet." *North Carolina Journal of Law & Technology* 12 (2010): 57–76.

Baker, Courtney. *Humane Insight: Looking at Images of African American Suffering and Death.* Champaign, IL: University of Illinois Press, 2015.

Bakhtin, Mikhail. "Forms of Time and Chronotope in the Novel." In *The Dialogic Imagination: Four Essays,* translated by Caryl Emerson and Michael Holquist. Austin, TX: University of Texas Press, 1982.

Barerra, Jorge. "Tanya Tagaq 'Out for Blood' over 'Racist' Experimental Documentary by Quebec Filmmaker." *Aboriginal People's Television Network,* 25 November 2015.

Barker, Jennifer. "Out of Sync, Out of Sight: Synaesthesia and Film Spectacle." *Paragraph* 31, no. 2 (2008): 236–251.

Baron, Jaimie. *The Archive Effect: Found Footage and the Audiovisual Experience of History*. London: Routledge, 2014.

———. "The Art of the (In)appropriate." In *Misdirect Movies*, edited by Andrew Bracey and John Rimmer, 16–19. Manchester: Cornerhouse Publications, 2013.

———. "Christopher Harris' Experimental Audiovisual Historiography." In *History in Images: Towards an (Audio)Visual Historiography,* edited by Peter Aronsson, Andrej Slávik, and Birgitta Svensson, 191–200. Stockholm: Royal Swedish Academy of Letters, History and Antiquities, 2020.

———. "The Ethics of Appropriation: 'Misusing' the Found Document in *Suitcase of Love and Shame* and *A Film Unfinished*." In *Contemporary Documentary*, edited by Selmin Kara and Daniel Marcus, 156–170. London: Routledge, 2015.

———. "(In)appropriation: Productions of Laughter in Contemporary Experimental Found Footage Films." In *Sampling Media,* edited by Laurel Westrup and David Laderman, 168–182. London: Oxford University Press, 2014.

———. "Un « Indien » dans les archives : le document trouvé et l'image composite." *Decadrages: Cinéma, a travers champs: Cinéma de re-montage 34-36* (Fall 2016/Spring 2017): 56–64.

———. "Ventriloquizing Obama, or, the Ethics of Archival Ventriloquism." In *Media Ventriloquism,* edited by Jaimie Baron, Jennifer Fleeger, and Shannon Wong Lerner, forthcoming from Oxford University Press.

———. "Translating the Document Across Time and Space: William E. Jones' Tearoom." *Spectator* 30, no. 1 (Spring 2010): 51–54.

Barthes, Roland. *Camera Lucida: Reflections on Photography*, trans. Richard Howard. New York: Hill and Wang, 1981.

BBC. "BBQ Becky: Woman Photoshopped into black history after barbecue complaint." *BBC News*. www.bbc.com/news/newsbeat-44167760.

Bean, Jennifer. "Technologies of Early Stardom and the Extraordinary Body." *Camera Obscura* 16, no. 3 (2001): 9–56.

Beckford, Keesha. "Dear White Moms." *HuffPost,* 22 August 2014. https://www.huffpost.com/entry/dear-white-moms_b_5698431.

Bell, Jacqueline. *Vloggers, Celebrities, Gods and Kings: The Politics of Publicness in Natalie Bookchin's* Now he's out in public and everyone can see. Master's thesis, University of Southern California, 2013.

Bennett, Colin J. "In Defense of Privacy: The Concept and the Regime." *Surveillance & Society* 8, no. 4 (2011): 485–496.

Bergson, Henri. *Laughter: An Essay on the Meaning of the Comic.* New York: Macmillan, 1911.

Bershad, Jon. "Creepy/Funny Video Edits Down Palin's Speech To Just The Exasperated Breaths." *Mediaite.com.* 13 January 2011. http://www.mediaite.com/online/creepyfunny-video-edits-down-palins-speech-to-just-the-exasperated-breaths/.

Biber, Katherine, and Derek Dalton. "Making Art from Evidence: Secret Sex and Police Surveillance in the Tearoom." *Crime, Media, Culture* 5, no. 3 (2009): 243–267.

Billig, Michael. "Humour and Hatred: The Racist Jokes of the Ku Klux Klan." *Discourse & Society* 12, no. 3 (2001): 267–289.

Bogle, Donald. *Toms, Coons, Mulattoes, Mammies, and Bucks: An Interpretive History of Blacks in American Films*. London and New York: Continuum, 1994.

Bok, Sissela. *Secrecy: On the Ethics of Concealment and Revelation*. New York: Vintage Books, 1989.

Böser, Ursula. "*A Film Unfinished*: Yael Hersonski's Re-representation of Archival Footage from the Warsaw Ghetto." *Film Criticism* 37, no. 2 (2013): 38–56.

Bradshaw, Peter. "*Four Days Inside Guantánamo*—Review." *The Guardian*, 6 October 2011. www.theguardian.com/film/2011/oct/06/four-days-inside-guantanamo-review.

Brooks, Daphne A. "'Sister, Can You Line It Out?': Zora Neale Hurston and the Sound of Angular Black Womanhood." *Amerikastudien / American Studies* 55, no. 4: African American Literary Studies: New Texts, New Approaches, New Challenges (2010): 617–627.

Butler, Todd. "Victim Impact Statements, New Media Technologies, and the Classical Rhetoric of Sincerity." *University of Toronto Quarterly* 82, no. 4 (Fall 2013): 841–863.

*Campbell v. Acuff-Rose Music* (92-1292), 510 U.S. 569 (1994).

Canadian Broadcasting Corporation (CBC). "Tanya Tagaq Threatens Legal Action Against 'Racist' Quebec Film 'Of The North.'" *Huffington Post Canada*, 25 November 2015.

Carlsson, Mats. "The Strange Object of the Voice: A Bad Lip Reading." *Senses of Cinema* 67 (July 2013). http://sensesofcinema.com/2013/feature-articles/the-strange-object-of-the-voice-a-bad-lip-reading/.

Chalfen, Richard. *Snapshot Versions of Life*. Bowling Green, OH: Bowling Green State University Popular Press, 1987.

Chion, Michel. *Audio-Vision: Sound on Screen*. Translated by Claudia Gorbman. New York: Columbia University Press, 1994.

Cocker, Emma. "Ethical Possession: Borrowing from the Archives." In *Cultural Borrowings: Appropriation, Reworking, Transformation*, edited by Iain Robert Smith, 92–110 (Scope, 2009): 100.

Colletta, Lisa. "Political Satire and Postmodern Irony in the Age of Stephen Colbert and Jon Stewart." *The Journal of Popular Culture* 42, no. 5 (2009): 856–874.

Connor, Steven. *Dumbstruck: A Cultural History of Ventriloquism.* Oxford: Oxford University Press, 2003.

Cooper, Sarah. "Looking Back, Looking Onwards: Selflessness, Ethics, and French Documentary." *Studies in French Cinema* 10, no. 1 (2010): 57–68.

———. *Selfless Cinema?: Ethics and French Documentary*. London: Legenda, 2006.

Cornellier, Bruno. "Extracting Inuit: The *of the North* Controversy and the White Possessive." *American Indian Culture and Research Journal* 40, no. 4 (2016): 23–48.

Cothran, George. "Shut Up, Little Man: The squalor and acrimony of the lives of a couple of hard-drinking retirees are dwarfed by the avarice that their celebrity has inspired in others." *The San Francisco Weekly*, 2 August 1995. www.sfweekly.com/sanfrancisco/shut-up-little-man/Content?oid=2132286.

Crocker, Lizzie. "The Controversial Painting of Emmett Till Stays on Show at The Whitney." *The Daily Beast*, 23 March 2017. www.thedailybeast.com/the-controversial-painting-of-emmett-till-stays-on-show-at-the-whitney.

Cuevas, Efrén. "Change of Scale: Home Movies as Microhistory in Documentary Films," In *Amateur Filmmaking: The Home Movie, the Archive, the Web*, Laura Rascaroli, Gwenda Young, and Barry Monahan, eds. 139–151. New York: Bloomsbury Publishing USA, 2014.

———. "Home Movies as Personal Archives in Autobiographical Documentaries." *Studies in Documentary Film* 17, no. 1 (2013): 17–29.

Culp, Jonathan. "Trashing Culture: Dominic Gagnon's Art of Appropriation." *Now*, 6 January 2016.

Debord, Guy, and Gil Wolman. "A User's Guide to Détournement (Debord and Wolman, 1956)." In *The Situationist International Anthology,* edited by Ken Knabb, 14–20. Berkeley, CA: Bureau of Public Secrets, 2006.

DeLaure, Marilyn, and Moritz Fink. "Introduction." In *Culture Jamming: Activism and the Art of Cultural Resistance,* edited by Marilyn DeLaure and Moritz Fink, 12–24. New York: New York University Press, 2017.

Denbeaux, Mark, Joshua W. Denbeaux, David Gratz, Jennifer Ellick, Michael Ricciardelli, and Matthew Darby. "Captured on Tape: Interrogation and Videotaping of Detainees in Guantánamo," *Seton Hall Law Review* 41 (2011): 1307–1317.

Dery, Mark. "Foreword." In *Culture Jamming: Activism and the Art of Cultural Resistance,* edited by Marilyn DeLaure and Moritz Fink, xi–xvi. New York: New York University Press, 2017.

Dundes, Alan, and Thomas Hauschild. "Auschwitz Jokes." *Western Folklore* 42, no. 4 (October 1983): 249–260.

Durant, Mark Alice. "Jane Gillooly." *Saint Lucy*. http://saint-lucy.com/conversations/jane-gillooly/.

Ebbrecht-Hartmann, Tobias. "Trophy, Evidence, Document: Appropriating an Archive Film from Liepaja, 1941." *Historical Journal of Film, Radio and Television* 36, no. 4 (2016): 509–528.

Eler, Alicia. "Painting of Philando Castile's death on display in New York's Whitney Museum." *Star Tribune,* 23 June 2017. http://www.startribune.com/painting-of-philando-castile-s-death-on-display-in-new-york-s-whitney-museum/430375453/?refresh=true.

Elsaesser, Thomas. "The Ethics of Appropriation: Found Footage between Archive and Internet." *Found Footage Magazine* 1 (October 2016): 30–37.

Everett-Green, Robert. "Debate Rages on over Dominic Gagnon and Consent in the Age of YouTube." *The Globe and Mail,* 25 March 2016.

Fajemisin, Olamiju. "'The spectacle of Black trauma': Why Double Standards in Representation Need to End in the Arts." *C&,* 23 July 2018. www.contemporaryand.com/magazines/why-double-standards-in-representation-need-to-end-in-the-arts/.

Fernandez, Maria and Faith Wilding. "Situating Cyberfeminisms." In *Domain Errors!: Cyberfeminist Practices,* edited by Maria Fernandez, Faith Wilding, and Michelle M. Wright, 17–28. Brooklyn, NY: Autonomedia, 2002.

Finkelstein, David. *Film Threat,* 2 November 2008. http://filmthreat.com/uncategorized/speechless/.

Found Footage Festival, The. www.foundfootagefest.com/2013/01/jazzercise/.

Freud, Sigmund. *Jokes and Their Relation to the Unconscious.* Translated by James Strachey. New York: W.W. Norton & Company, 1963.

Fusco, Coco. "Censorship, Not the Painting, Must Go: On Dana Schutz's Image of Emmett Till." *Hyperallergic,* 27 March 2017. https://hyperallergic.com/368290/censorship-not-the-painting-must-go-on-dana-schutzs-image-of-emmett-till/.

Gambino, Lauren. "Journalist who profiled Melanía Trump hit with barrage of antisemitic abuse." *The Guardian,* 29 April 2016. www.theguardian.com/us-news/2016/apr/28/julia-ioffe-journalist-melania-trump-antisemitic-abuse.

*Gardner v. Florida* 430 U.S. 349 (1977).

Ginsburg, Faye. "Isuma TV, Visual Sovereignty and the Arctic Media World." In *Arctic Cinemas and the Documentary Ethos,* edited by Lilya Kaganovsky, Scott MacKenzie, and Anna Westerstahl Stenport, 254–274. Bloomington, IN: Indiana University Press, 2017.

Goffman, Erving. *Notes on the Management of Spoiled Identity*. New York: Simon and Schuster, 2009.

Greenberger, Alex. "'The Painting Must Go': Hannah Black Pens Open Letter to the Whitney About Controversial Biennial Work." *ArtNews,* 21 March 2017. www.artnews.com/2017/03/21/the-painting-must-go-hannah-black-pens-open-letter-to-the-whitney-about-controversial-biennial-work/.

Guerin, Frances. "Introduction." In *On Not Looking: The Paradox of Contemporary Visual Culture*, edited by Frances Guerin, 1–40. NY: Routledge, 2015.

———. "The Energy of Disappearing: Problems of Recycling Nazi Amateur Film Footage." *Screening the Past* 17 (2004), http://tlweb.latrobe.edu.au/humanities/screeningthepast/firstrelease/fr_17/FGfr17.html.

Hall, Rachel. "Missing Dolly, Mourning Slavery: the Slave Notice as Keepsake." *Camera Obscura* 21, no. 1 (2006): 71–103.

Hansen, Mark. "The Time of Affect, or Bearing Witness to Life." *Critical Inquiry* 30, no. 3 (2004): 584–626.

Henriquez, Patricio. "Some Images of the Unseen: On the Making of the Film *You Don't Like the Truth: 4 Days Inside Guantánamo.*" Translated by Mark Abley. In *Omar Khadr, O Canada,* edited by Janice Williamson. Montreal: McGill-Queen's University Press, 2012. 113–117.

Hirsch, Lily E. *Music in American Crime Prevention and Punishment.* Ann Arbor: University of Michigan Press, 2012.

Hirsch, Marianne. "Surviving Images: Holocaust Photographs and the Work of Postmemory." *The Yale Journal of Criticism* 14, no. 1 (2001): 5–37.

Hohmann, Silke. "Kunst als Rache: Künstler malt Sohn von Dana Schutz." *Monopol,* 15 June 2018. www.monopol-magazin.de/kuenstler-malt-sohn-von-dana-schutz.

Holland, Emily. "Moving Pictures Maintaining Justice-Clarifying the Right Role for Victim Impact Videos in the Capital Context." *Berkeley Journal of Criminal Law* 17 (2012): 147–194.

Huizinga, Johan. *Homo Ludens*. London: Routledge, 1998 [original pub. 1938].

*Katz v. United States*, 389 U.S. at 361 (Harlan, J., concurring) (1967).

Katz, John Stuart, and Judith Milstein Katz. "Ethics and the Perception of Ethics in Autobiographical Film." In *Image Ethics: The Moral Rights of Subjects in Photographs, Film, and Television*, edited by Larry Gross, John Stuart Katz, and Jay Ruby, 119–134. London: Oxford University Press, 1988.

Kennedy, Christine M. "Victim Impact Videos: The New-Wave of Evidence in Capital Sentencing Hearings." *Quinnipiac Law Review* 26 (2007): 1069–1105.

Lancioni, Judith. "The Rhetoric of the Frame: Revisioning Archival Photographs in *The Civil War*." *Western Journal of Communication* 60, no. 4 (1996): 397–414.

Lessig, Lawrence. *Remix: Making Art and Commerce Thrive in the Hybrid Economy*. New York: Penguin, 2008.

Levin, Erica. "Toward a Social Cinema Revisited." *Millennium Film Journal* 58 (2013): 30–36.

Liebman, Stuart. "The Never-Ending Story: Yael Hersonski's *A Film Unfinished*." *Cineaste* 36, no. 3 (2011): 15–19.

Livingstone, Josephine, and Lovia Gyarkye. "The Case Against Dana Schutz." *The New Republic,* 22 March 2017. http://newrepublic.com/article/141506/case-dana-schutz.

MacDonald, Scott. "Cine-Surveillance: 3 Avant-Docs Interviews with Amie Siegel, Sharon Lockhart, Jane Gillooly." *Film Quarterly* 66, no. 4 (2013): 28–40.

Manovich, Lev. "Remix Strategies in Social Media." In *The Routledge Companion to Remix Studies,* edited by Eduardo Navas, Owen Gallagher, and xtine burrough, 135–153. London: Routledge, 2015.

Marantz, Andrew. "Neo-Nazi No-No's." *The New Yorker,* 15 January 2018.

McCarthy, J. Thomas. *The Rights of Publicity and Privacy*, 2nd ed. Eagan, MN: Thomas Reuters, 2009.

McCormack, Tom. "Compilation Nation: The History and the Rise of the Supercut." *Moving Image Source,* 25 April 2011. www.movingimagesource.us/articles/compilation-nation-20110425.

McDonald, Soraya Nadia. "Gaming vlogger Anita Sarkeesian is forced from home after receiving harrowing death threats," *The Washington Post,* 29 August 2014.

McLeod, Kembrew, and Peter DiCola. *Creative License: The Law and Culture of Digital Sampling*. Durham, NC: Duke University Press, 2011.

Merleau-Ponty, Marcel. *The Phenomenology of Perception.* Translated by Colin Smith. London and New York: Routledge, 2002 [originally published in French, 1945].

Milner, Ryan M. "FCJ-156 Hacking the Social: Internet Memes, Identity Antagonism, and the Logic of Lulz." *The Fibreculture Journal* 22: Trolls and The Negative Space of the Internet (2013): 62–92.

Miranda, Carolina A. "Bravo's *Work of Art* Riles Up the Art World." *Time,* 4 August 2010.

Mitter, Siddhartha. "'What Does It Mean to Be Black and Look at This?' A Scholar Reflects on the Dana Schutz Controversy." *Hyperallergic,* 24 March 2017. https://hyperallergic.com/368012/what-does-it-mean-to-be-black-and-look-at-this-a-scholar-reflects-on-the-dana-schutz-controversy/.

Mulvey, Laura. "Rear-Projection and the Paradoxes of Hollywood Realism." In *Theorizing World Cinema,* edited by Lúcia Nagib, Rajinder Dudrah, and Chris Perriam, 207–220. IB Tauris, 2011.

———. "Visual Pleasure in Narrative Cinema." *Screen* 16, no. 3 (Autumn 1975): 6–18.

National Film Board of Canada. *Sisters and Brothers.* www.nfb.ca/film/sisters_brothers/.

Neal, Mark Anthony. *Looking for Leroy: Illegible Black Masculinities.* New York: New York University Press, 2013.

Nichols, Bill. *Representing Reality: Issues and Concepts in Documentary*. Bloomington: Indiana University Press, 1991.

Nissenbaum, Asaf, and Limor Shifman. "Internet memes as contested cultural capital: The case of 4chan's /b/ board." *New Media & Society* 19, no. 4 (2017): 483–501.

Nunnally, Shayla C. *Trust in Black America: Race, Discrimination, and Politics*. New York: New York University Press, 2012.

Nussbaum, Martha. *Love's Knowledge: Essays on Philosophy and Literature.* New York: Oxford University Press, 1992.

"of The North: Un groupe de cinéastes dénonce un cas apparenté à la censure," *Voir,* 25 February 2016. https://voir.ca/cinema/2016/02/25/of-the-north-un-groupe-de-cineastes-denonce-un-cas-apparente-a-la-censure/ [Original in French].

O'Meara, Jennifer. "Identity Politics and Vocal 'Whitewashing' in Celebrity Lip Syncs." In *Media Ventriloquism,* edited by Jaimie Baron, Jennifer Fleeger, and Shannon Wong Lerner, forthcoming from Oxford University Press.

*Payne v. Tennessee*, 501 U.S. 808, 822, 827 (1991).

Phillips, Whitney. "LOLing at tragedy: Facebook trolls, memorial pages and resistance to grief online." *First Monday* 16, no. 12 (2011). http://journals.uic.edu/ojs/index.php/fm/rt/printerFriendly/3168/3115.

Pinchevski, Amit. "The Ethics of Interruption: Toward a Levinasian Philosophy of Communication." *Social Semiotics* 15, no. 2 (2005): 211–234.

Polchin, James. "The Men in the Bathroom: Reflections on William E. Jones' *Tearoom.*" In *On Not Looking*, edited by Frances Guerin, 77–101. New York: Routledge, 2015.

Prager, Brad. "On the Liberation of Perpetrator Photographs in Holocaust Narratives." In *Visualizing the Holocaust: Documents, Aesthetics, Memory*, edited by David Bathrick, Brad Prager, and Michael D. Richardson, 19–37. Rochester, NY: Camden House, 2008.

Pryluck, Calvin. "Ultimately We Are All Outsiders: The Ethics of Documentary Filmmaking." In *New Challenges for Documentary*, edited by Alan Rosenthal and John Corner, 194–208. Manchester: Manchester University Press, 2005.

Pugliese, Joseph. "Apostrophe of Empire: Guantánamo Bay, Disneyland." *Borderlands E-Journal: New Spaces in the Humanities* 8, no. 3 (December 2009): 1–26.

Ratcliffe, Krista. "Eavesdropping as Rhetorical Tactic: History, Whiteness, and Rhetoric." *JAC: A Journal of Rhetoric, Culture, and Politics* 20, no. 1 (2000): 87–119.

Roe, Annabelle Honess. *Animated Documentary*. New York: Palgrave Macmillan, 2013.

Russell, Byron. "Appropriation is Activism." In *The Routledge Companion to Remix Studies*, edited by Eduardo Navas, Owen Gallagher, and xtine burrough, 217–223. New York: Routledge, 2014.

Sánchez-Biosca, Vicente. "Perpetrator Images, Perpetrator Artifacts: The Nomad Archives of Tuol Sleng (S-21)." *Cinema & Cie International Film Studies Journal* 15, no. 24 (2015): 103–116.

Schaeffer, Neil. *The Art of Laughter.* New York: Columbia University Press, 1981.

Schwartz, Louis-Georges. *Mechanical Witness: A History of Motion Picture Evidence in US Courts.* Oxford: Oxford University Press, 2009.

Skoller, Jeffrey. *Shadows, Specters, Shards: Making History in Avant-Garde Film.* Minneapolis: University of Minnesota Press, 2005.

Sobania, Neal. "But Where Are the Cattle? Popular Images of Maasai and Zulu across the Twentieth Century." *Visual Anthropology* 15, no. 3/4 (July 2002): 313–346.

Sobchack, Vivian. "Inscribing Ethical Space: Ten Propositions on Death, Representation, and Documentary." In *Carnal Thoughts: Embodiment and Moving Image Culture*, 226–257. Berkeley: University of California Press, 2004 [1984].

Sontag, Susan. "Notes on Camp." In *Camp: Queer Aesthetics and the Performing Subject: A Reader*, edited by Fabio Cleto, 53–65. Ann Arbor: University of Michigan Press, 1999 [original 1964].

Sonvilla-Weiss, Stefan. "Good Artists Copy; Great Artists Steal: Reflections on Cut-Copy-Paste Culture." In *The Routledge Companion to Remix Studies*, edited by Eduardo Navas, Owen Gallagher, and xtine burrough, 54–67. London: Routledge, 2015.

Spratt, Michael. "Dislike of Khadr settlement does not entitle critics to disregard law or facts." *Canadian Lawyer*, 24 July 2017. www.canadianlawyermag.com/author

/michael-spratt/dislike-of-khadr-settlement-does-not-entitle-critics-to-disregard-law-or-facts-3695/.

Stadler, Jane. *Pulling Focus: Intersubjective Experience, Narrative Film, and Ethics*. New York: Continuum, 2012.

Stevens, Rachel. "Our Nixon." *Millennium Film Journal* (Spring 2014): 12–17.

Stewart, Michelle. "Of Digital Selves and Digital Sovereignty: *of the North*." *Film Quarterly* 70, no. 4 (2017): 23–38.

Stob, Jennifer. "Détournement as Optic: Debord, Derisory Documents and the Aerial View." *Philosophy of Photography* 5, no. 1 (2014): 19–34.

Streible, Dan. "The Role of Orphan Films in the 21st Century Archive." *Cinema Journal* 46, no. 3 (Spring 2007): 124–28.

Suwajanakorn, Supasorn, Steven M. Seitz, and Ira Kemelmacher-Shlizerman. "Synthesizing Obama: Learning Lip Sync from Audio." *ACM Transactions on Graphics (TOG)* 36, no. 4 (2017): Article 95.

Truth and Reconciliation Commission of Canada, The. *Canada's Residential Schools: Missing Children and Unmarked Burials, The Final Report of the Truth and Reconciliation Commission of Canada, Volume 4*. The Truth and Reconciliation Commission of Canada. Montreal & Kingston: McGill-Queen's University Press, 2015.

Vernallis, Carol. *Experiencing Music Video : Aesthetics and Cultural Context*. New York: Columbia University Press, 2004.

Vincent, James. "Lyrebird claims it can recreate any voice using just one minute of sample audio." *The Verge*, 24 April 2017.

VNS Matrix. "Cyberfeminist Manifesto for the 21st Century." www.sterneck.net/cyber/vns-matrix/index.php.

Wees, William C. "The Ambiguous Aura of Hollywood Stars in Avant-Garde Found-Footage Films." *Cinema Journal* 41, no. 2 (2002): 3–18.

Wertheim, David. "Remediation as a Moral Obligation: Authenticity, Memory, and Morality in Representations of Anne Frank." In *Mediation, Remediation, and the Dynamics of Cultural Memory*, edited Astrid Erll and Ann Rigney, 157–172. Berlin: De Gruyter, 2009.

White House, The. "Remarks by the President at a Campaign Event in Roanoke, Virginia." www.whitehouse.gov/the-press-office/2012/07/13/remarks-president-campaign-event-roanoke-virginia.

Whyte, Kyle Powys, Evan Selinger, and Kevin Outterson. "Poverty Tourism and the Problem of Consent." *Journal of Global Ethics* 7, no. 3 (2011): 337–348.

Winton, Ezra. "Curating the North: Documentary Screening Ethics and Inuit Representation in (Festival) Cinema." *Art Threat*, 17 December 2015.

Young, Miriama. *Singing the Body Electric: The Human Voice and Sound Technology*. London: Routledge, 2016.

Zhao, Christina. "'BBQ Becky,' White Woman Who Called Cops on Black BBQ, 911 Audio Released: 'I'm Really Scared! Come Quick!'" *Newsweek*, 4 September 2018. www.newsweek.com/bbq-becky-white-woman-who-called-cops-black-bbq-911-audio-released-im-really-1103057.

# Index

## About the Author

**JAIMIE BARON** is an associate professor of film studies at the University of Alberta. She is the author of *The Archive Effect: Found Footage and the Audiovisual Experience of History* as well as numerous other book chapters and articles. She is the founder, director, and co-curator of the Festival of (In)appropriation, a yearly international festival of short experimental found footage films and videos. She is also a coeditor of the Docalogue website and book series.